THE SHIATSUNG PROJECT

BRIGITTE ARCHAMBAULT

BDANG

Translation by Aleshia Jensen
First Editon
Printed by Imago in S. Korea

Part of the BDANG Imprint of Conundrum Press
BDANG logo by Billy Mavreas

Library and Archives Canada Cataloguing in Publication

Title: The Shiatsung project / Brigitte Archambault.
Other titles: Projet Shiatsung. English
Names: Archambault, Brigitte, 1973- author, artist. | Jensen, Aleshia, translator.
Series: BDANG.
Description: Series statement: BDANG | Translation of: Le projet Shiatsung.
Translated by: Aleshia Jensen.
Identifiers: Canadiana 20210221526 | ISBN 9781772620603 (softcover)
Subjects: LCGFT: Graphic novels.
Classification: LCC PN6733.A73 P7613 2021 | DDC 741.5/971—dc23

Conundrum Press
Wolfville, NS, Canada
www.conundrumpress.com

We acknowledge the financial support of the Government of Canada through the National Translation Program for Book Publishing, an initiative of the Action Plan for Official Languages 2018-2023: Investing in Our Future, for our translation activities.

We acknowledge the Canada Council for the Arts, the Government of Nova Scotia, and the Government of Canada for financial support toward our publishing program.

Canada Council for the Arts | Conseil des Arts du Canada

NOVA SCOTIA

THE SHIATSUNG PROJECT

BRIGITTE ARCHAMBAULT

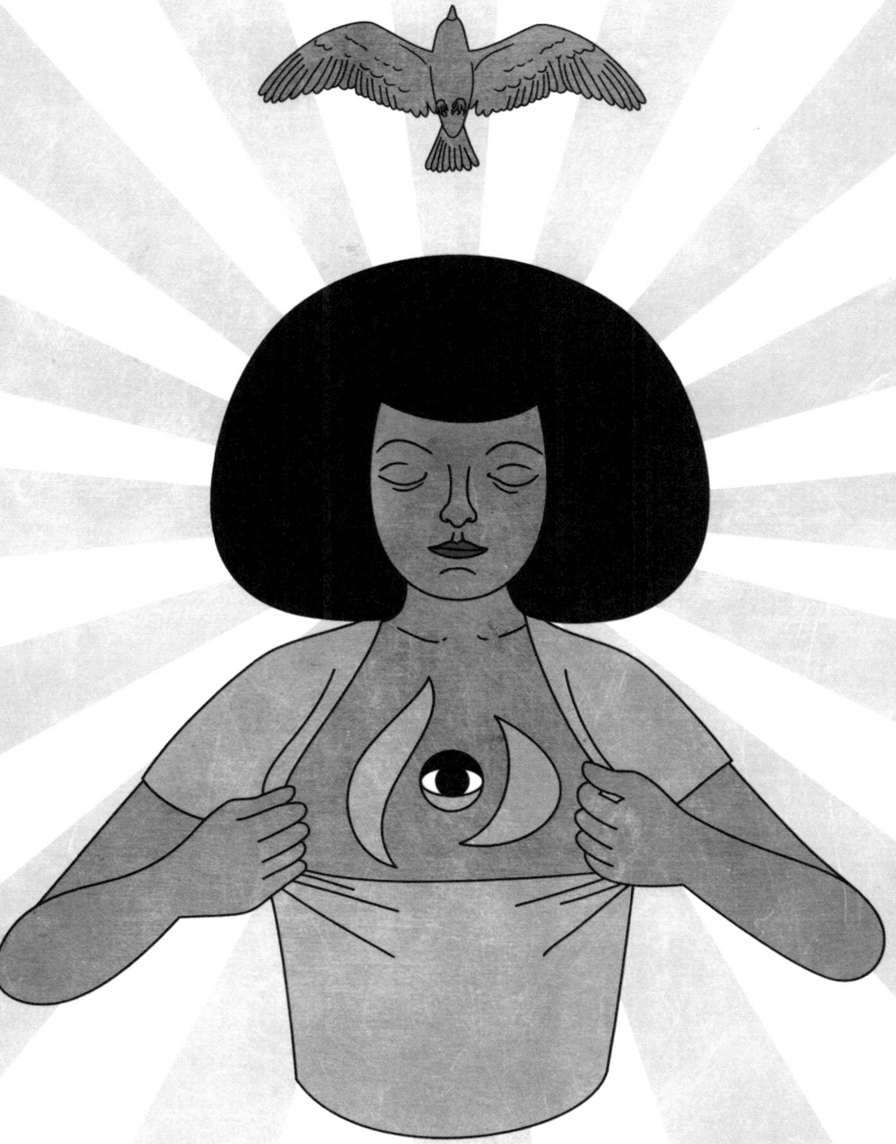

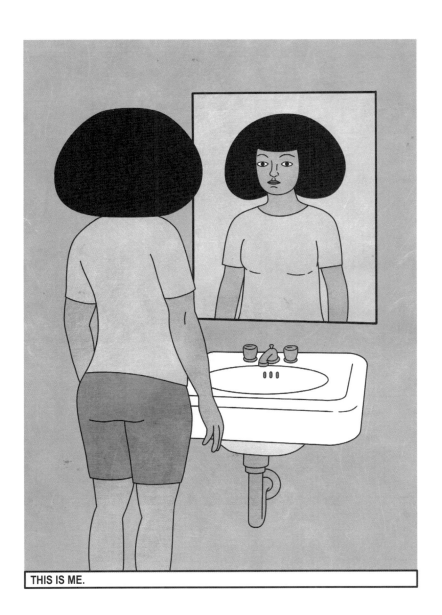

THIS IS ME.

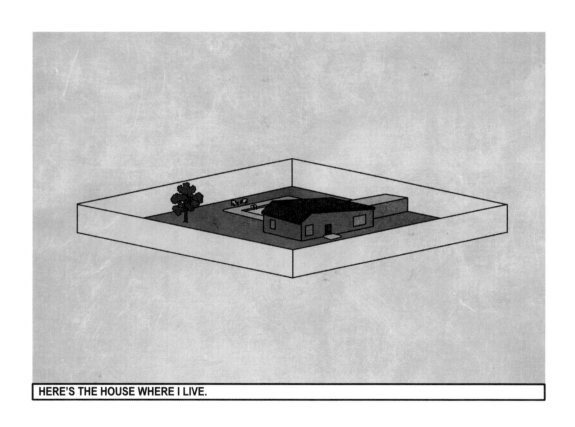

HERE'S THE HOUSE WHERE I LIVE.

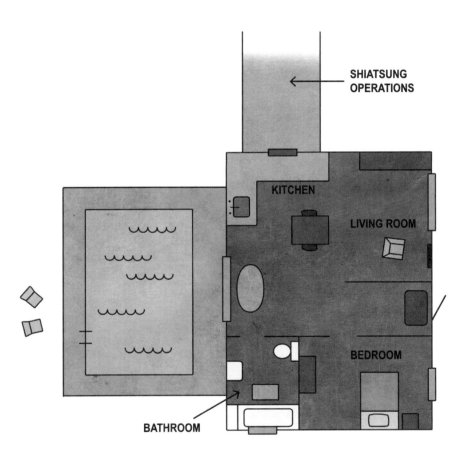

SHIATSUNG
OPERATIONS

KITCHEN

LIVING ROOM

BEDROOM

BATHROOM

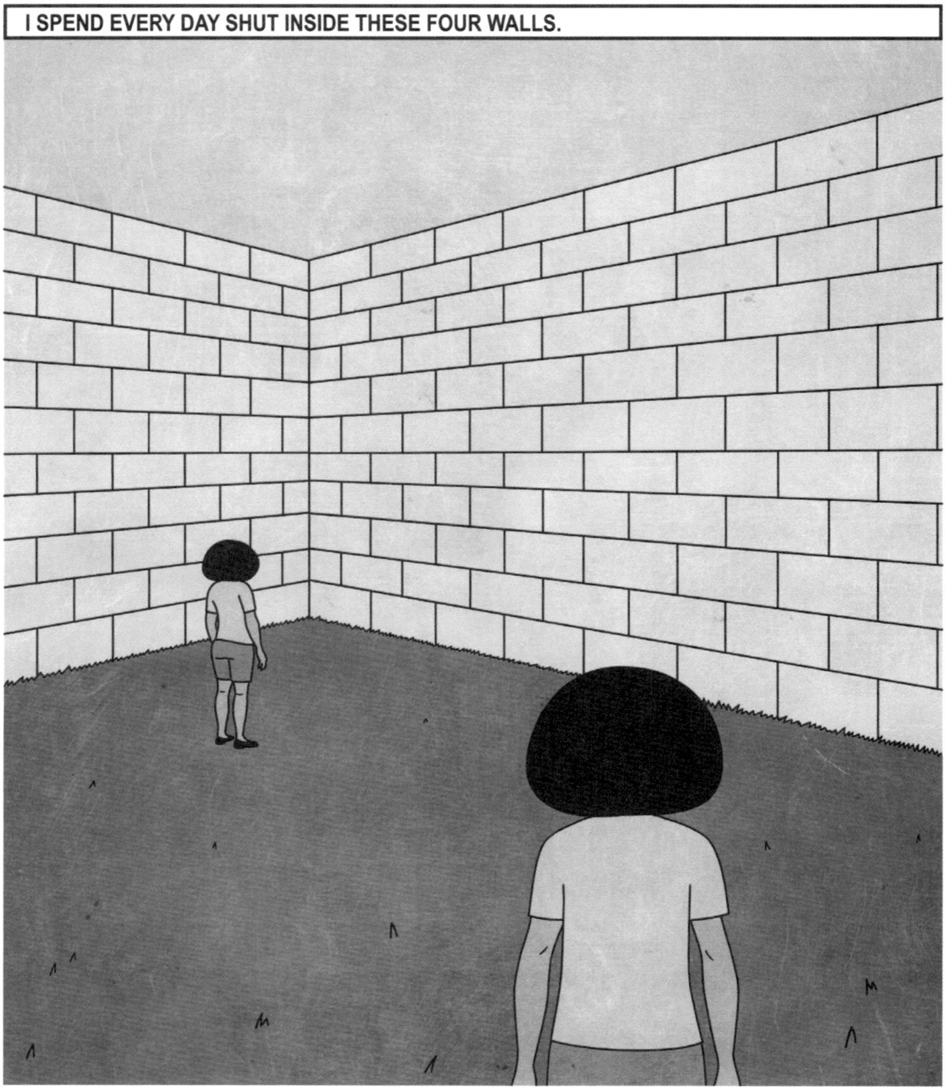
I SPEND EVERY DAY SHUT INSIDE THESE FOUR WALLS.

SHIATSUNG

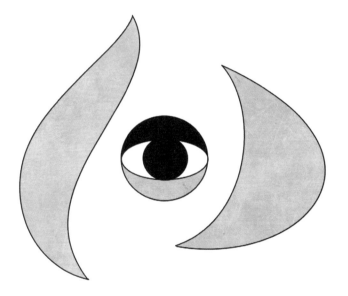

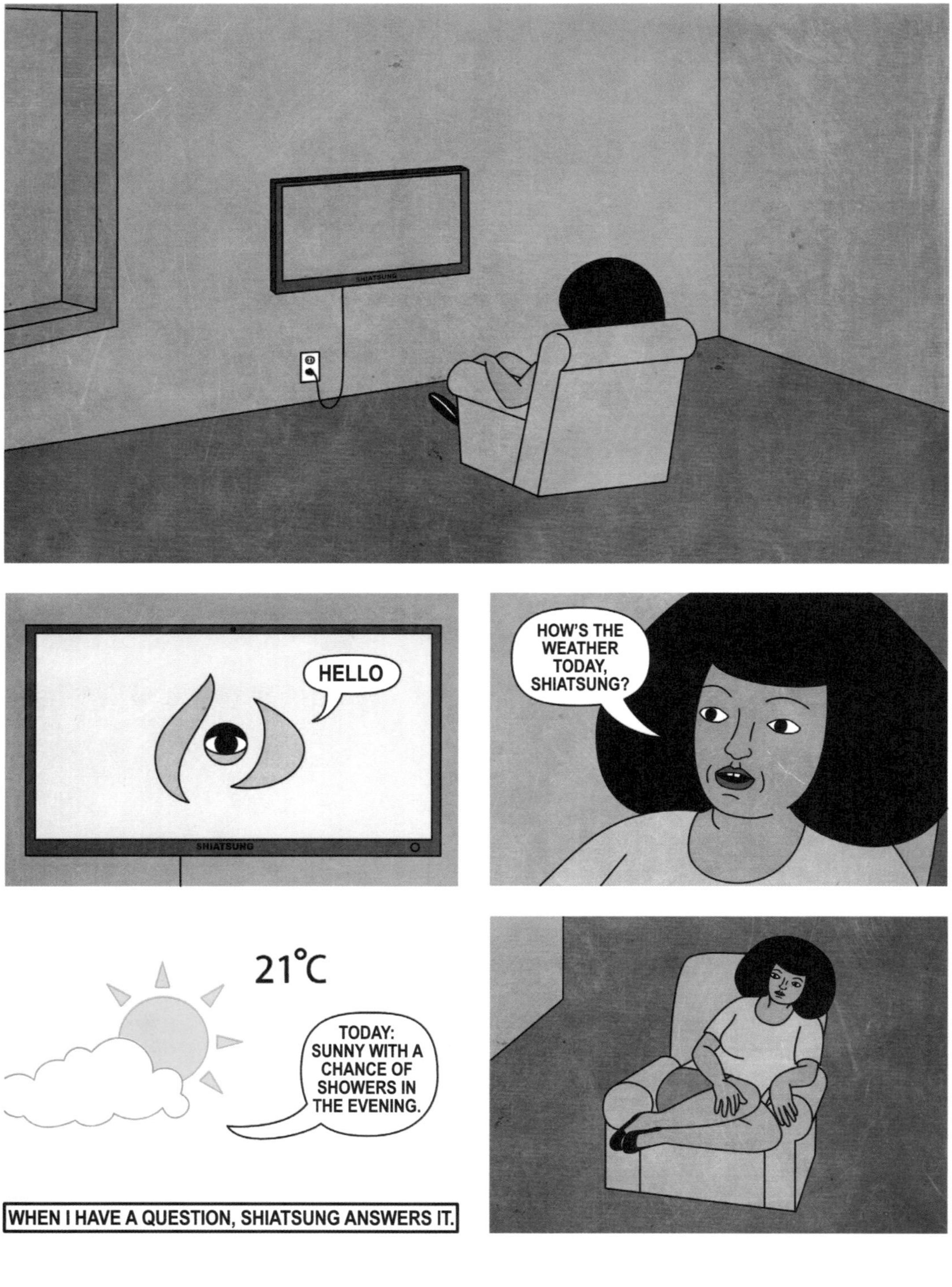
SHIATSUNG
HELLO
SHIATSUNG
HOW'S THE WEATHER TODAY, SHIATSUNG?
21°C
TODAY: SUNNY WITH A CHANCE OF SHOWERS IN THE EVENING.
WHEN I HAVE A QUESTION, SHIATSUNG ANSWERS IT.

IT IS RECOMMENDED THAT YOU CONTINUE STUDYING TRIGONOMETRY.

SHIATSUNG IS HELPING ME IMPROVE IN ENGLISH AND MATHEMATICS.

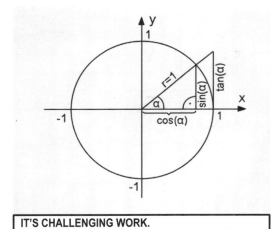

IT'S CHALLENGING WORK.

SHIATSUNG ALSO TEACHES ME MAINTENANCE.

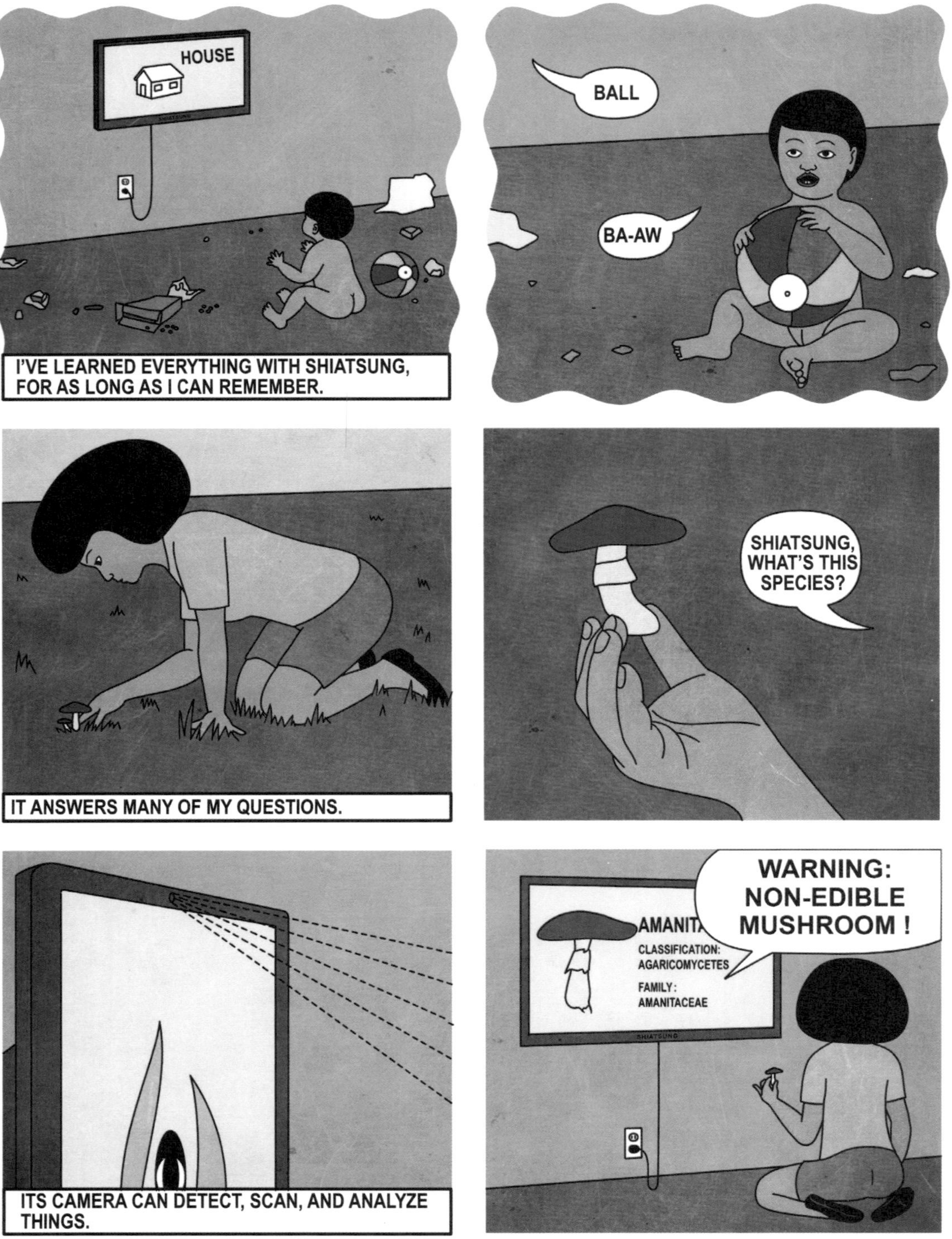
HOUSE
I'VE LEARNED EVERYTHING WITH SHIATSUNG, FOR AS LONG AS I CAN REMEMBER.
BALL
BA-AW
IT ANSWERS MANY OF MY QUESTIONS.
SHIATSUNG, WHAT'S THIS SPECIES?
ITS CAMERA CAN DETECT, SCAN, AND ANALYZE THINGS.
CLASSIFICATION: AGARICOMYCETES
FAMILY: AMANITACEAE
WARNING: NON-EDIBLE MUSHROOM !

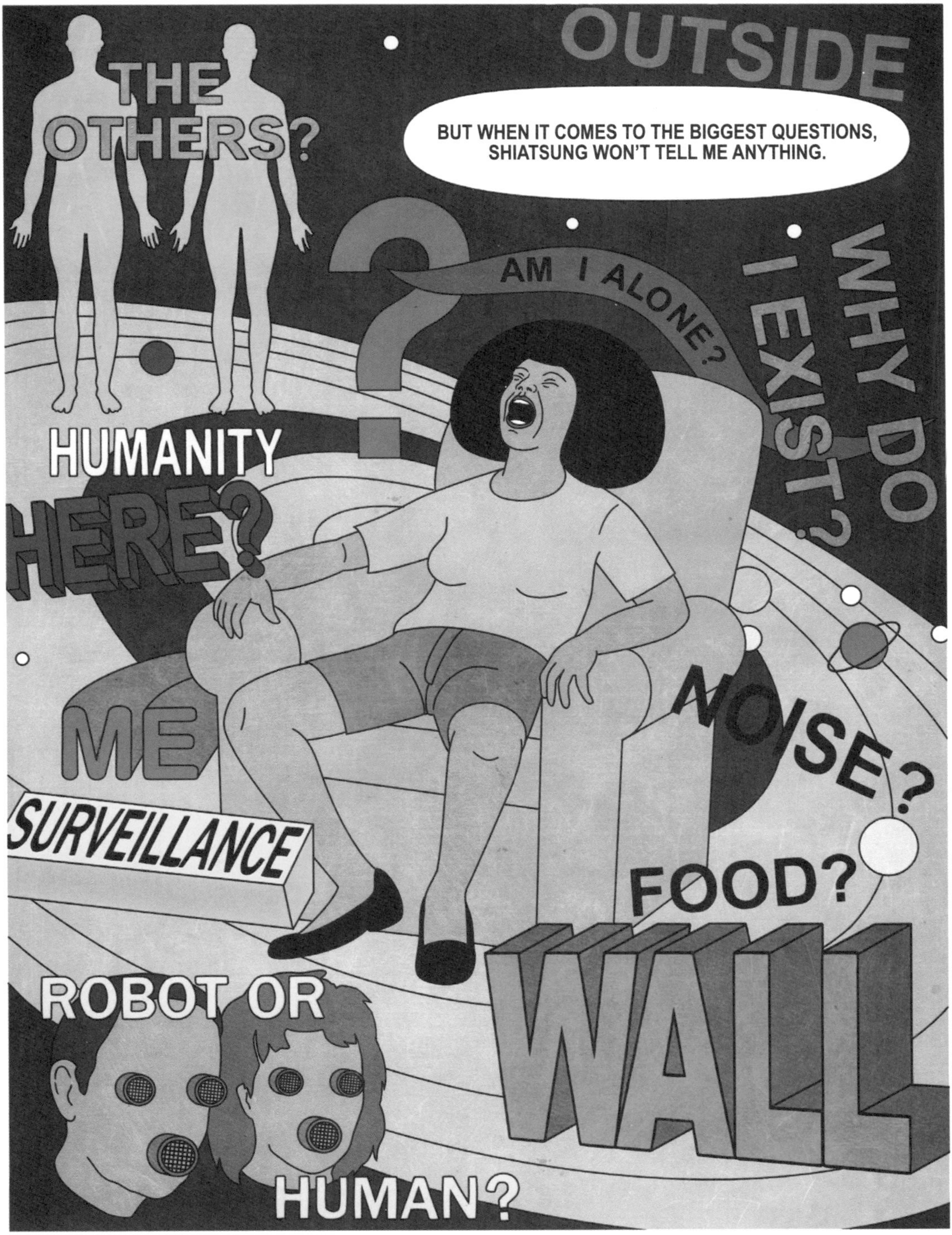
THE OTHERS?
OUTSIDE
BUT WHEN IT COMES TO THE BIGGEST QUESTIONS, SHIATSUNG WON'T TELL ME ANYTHING.
AM I ALONE?
WHY DO I EXIST?
HUMANITY
HERE?
ME
NOISE?
SURVEILLANCE
FOOD?
WALL
ROBOT OR HUMAN?

PROVISION OF SUSTENANCE

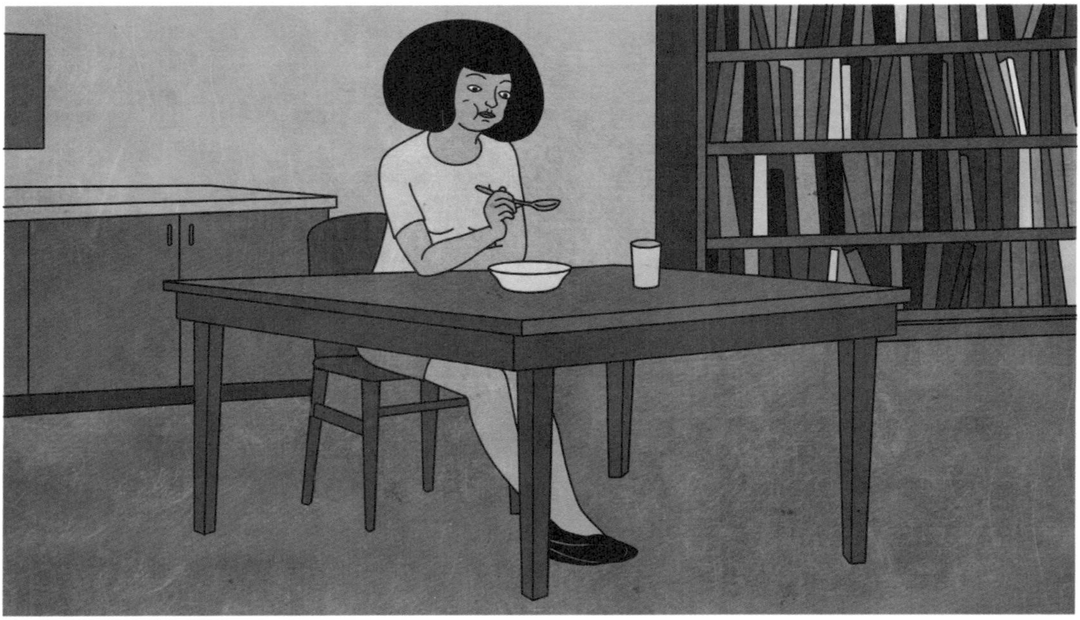

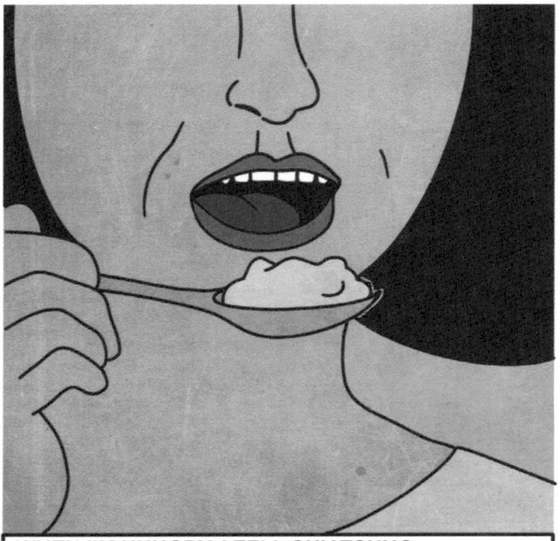
WHEN I'M HUNGRY, I TELL SHIATSUNG.

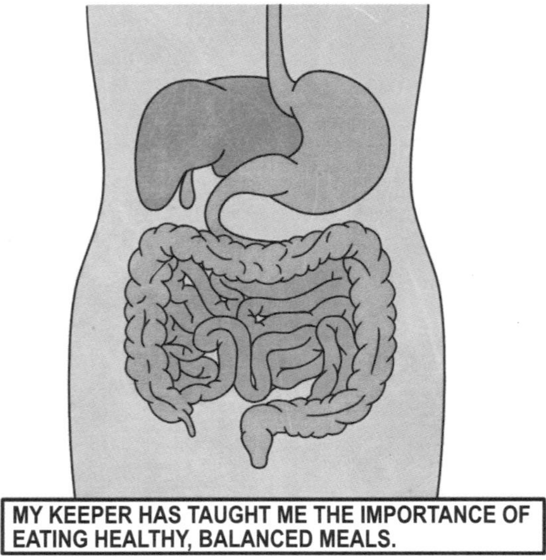
MY KEEPER HAS TAUGHT ME THE IMPORTANCE OF EATING HEALTHY, BALANCED MEALS.

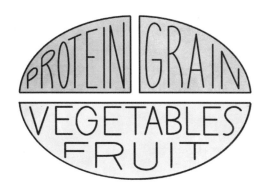

PROTEIN
GRAIN
VEGETABLES
FRUIT
MY MEALS ADHERE TO A FLEXITARIAN DIET.
I CONSUME A MODERATE AMOUNT OF FOODS FROM THE ANIMAL KINGDOM. SHIATSUNG RECOMMENDS ONE PORTION OF RED MEAT EVERY THREE MONTHS.
SHIATSUNG'S OPERATORS SUPPLY THE FOOD THROUGH THIS DOOR.
BIP!
MY MEALS ARRIVE HERE. AN INDICATOR LIGHT BLINKS WHEN IT'S READY.
TONIGHT'S MENU: LENTIL SHEPHERD'S PIE AND BOILED CARROTS.

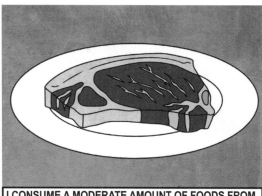

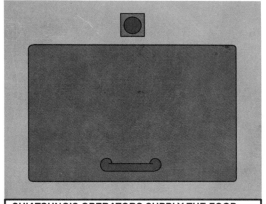

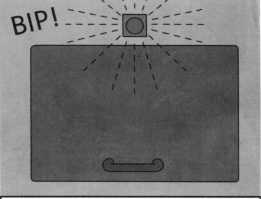

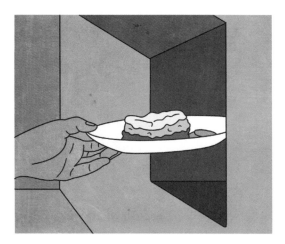

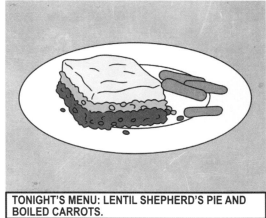

ONCE I FINISH EATING, I RETURN THE DIRTY DISHES THROUGH THE SAME DOOR.

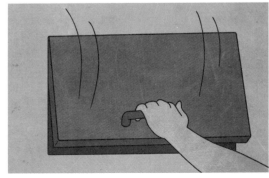

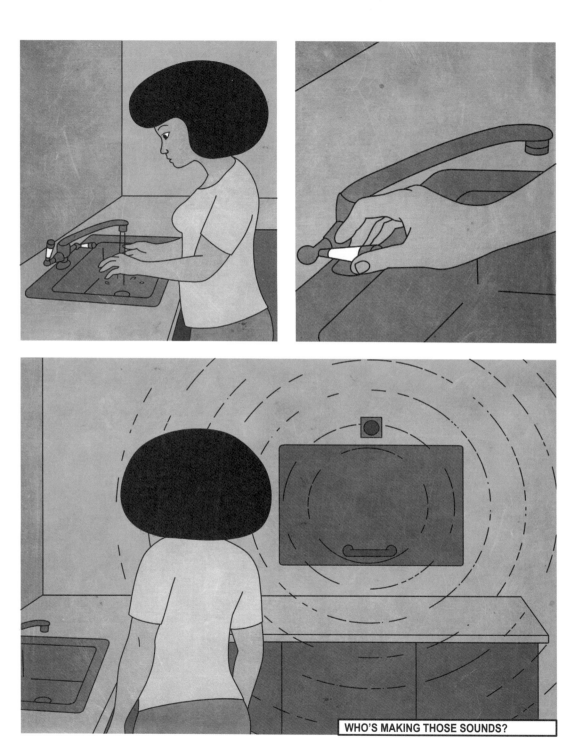

WHO'S MAKING THOSE SOUNDS?

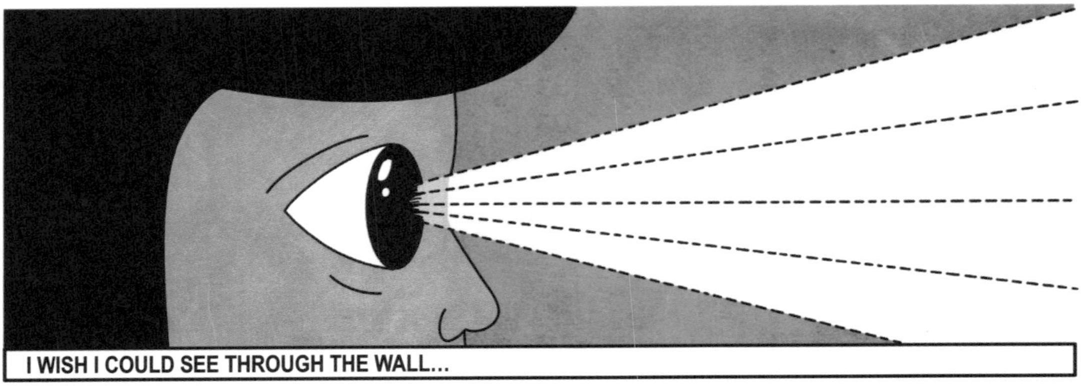
I WISH I COULD SEE THROUGH THE WALL...

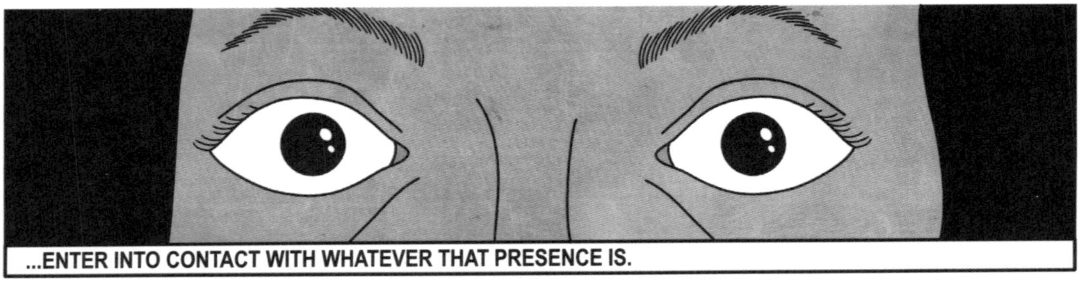
...ENTER INTO CONTACT WITH WHATEVER THAT PRESENCE IS.

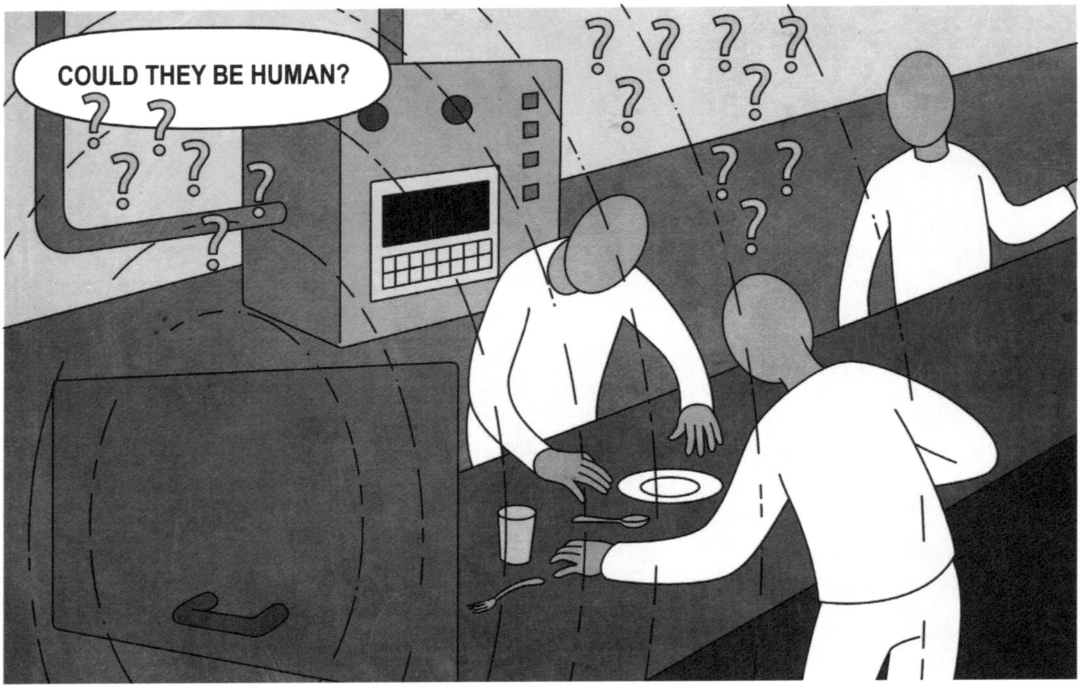
COULD THEY BE HUMAN?

THE COLD ROOM

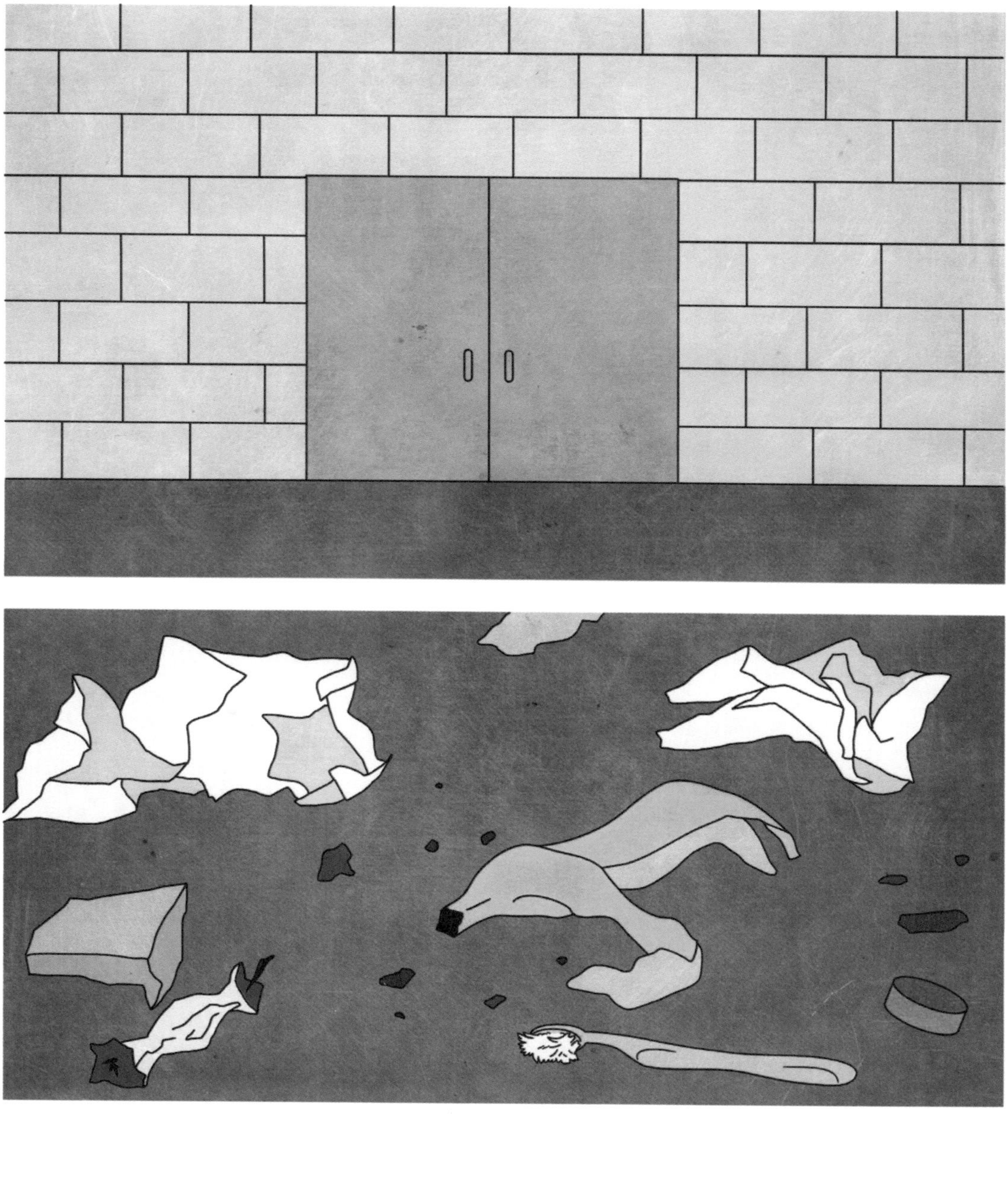

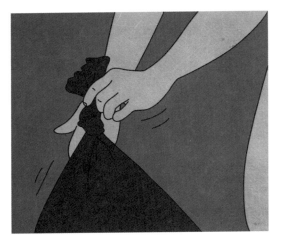

I HAVE TO TAKE MY GARBAGE OUT TO THE COLD ROOM.

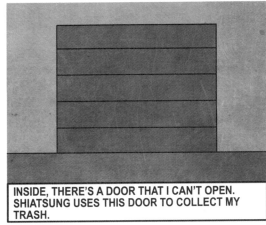

INSIDE, THERE'S A DOOR THAT I CAN'T OPEN. SHIATSUNG USES THIS DOOR TO COLLECT MY TRASH.

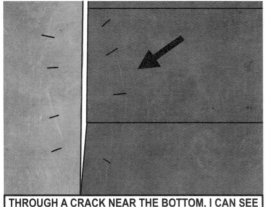

THROUGH A CRACK NEAR THE BOTTOM, I CAN SEE LIGHT. IT'S MY ONLY GLIMPSE OF THE OUTSIDE.

I LOOK THROUGH IT OFTEN.

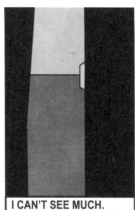

I CAN'T SEE MUCH.

SOMETIMES I STAY FOR A LONG TIME, DESPITE THE COLD. SHIATSUNG NEVER OPENS THE DOOR WHILE I'M INSIDE.

IT'S WATCHING ME.

CHILDHOOD

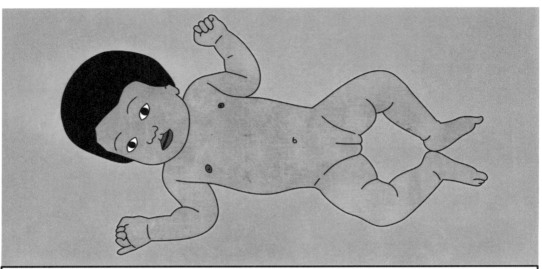

I GREW UP ALONE IN THIS HOUSE.

I ATE WHAT I COULD FIND ON THE GROUND.

SHIATSUNG MUST HAVE FOUND A WAY TO PUT FOOD THERE FOR ME TO FIND. I'M NOT SURE HOW.

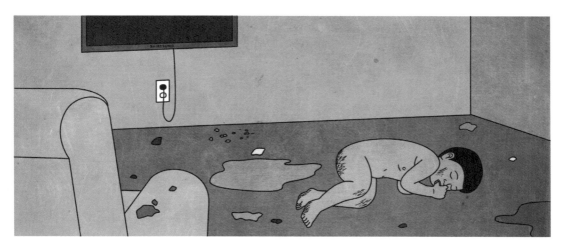

THE PLACE WAS FILTHY.

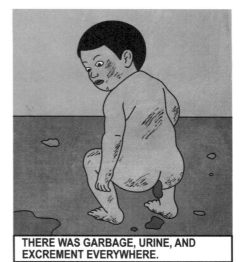

THERE WAS GARBAGE, URINE, AND EXCREMENT EVERYWHERE.

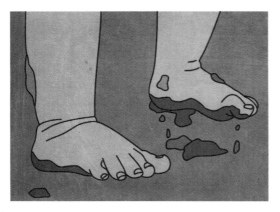

I WAS A SNOTTY, DIRTY CHILD.

MONTHS PASSED, AND I GREW BIGGER. SHIATSUNG TAUGHT ME TO USE THE BATHROOM.

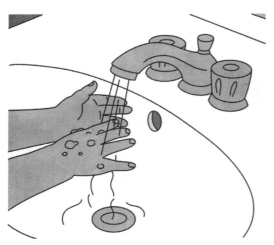

THROW THE GARBAGE IN THE CAN.

Ok

IT SHOWED ME HOW TO LOOK AFTER THE HOUSE.

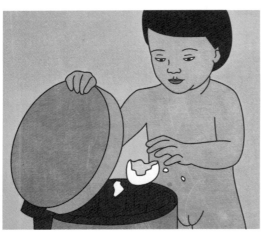

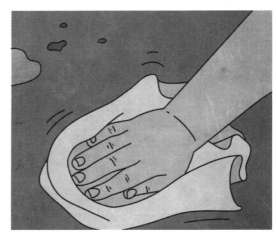

I SOON LEARNED TO ENJOY LIVING IN A CLEAN, TIDY SPACE.

I BECAME ULTRA DISCIPLINED.

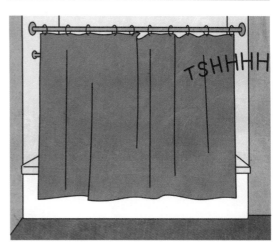

ONCE THESE VALUES WERE INSTILLED, I HAD A DESIRE AND A NEED TO LEARN. SHIATSUNG'S LESSONS HELPED ME QUICKLY REACH COGNITIVE MATURITY.

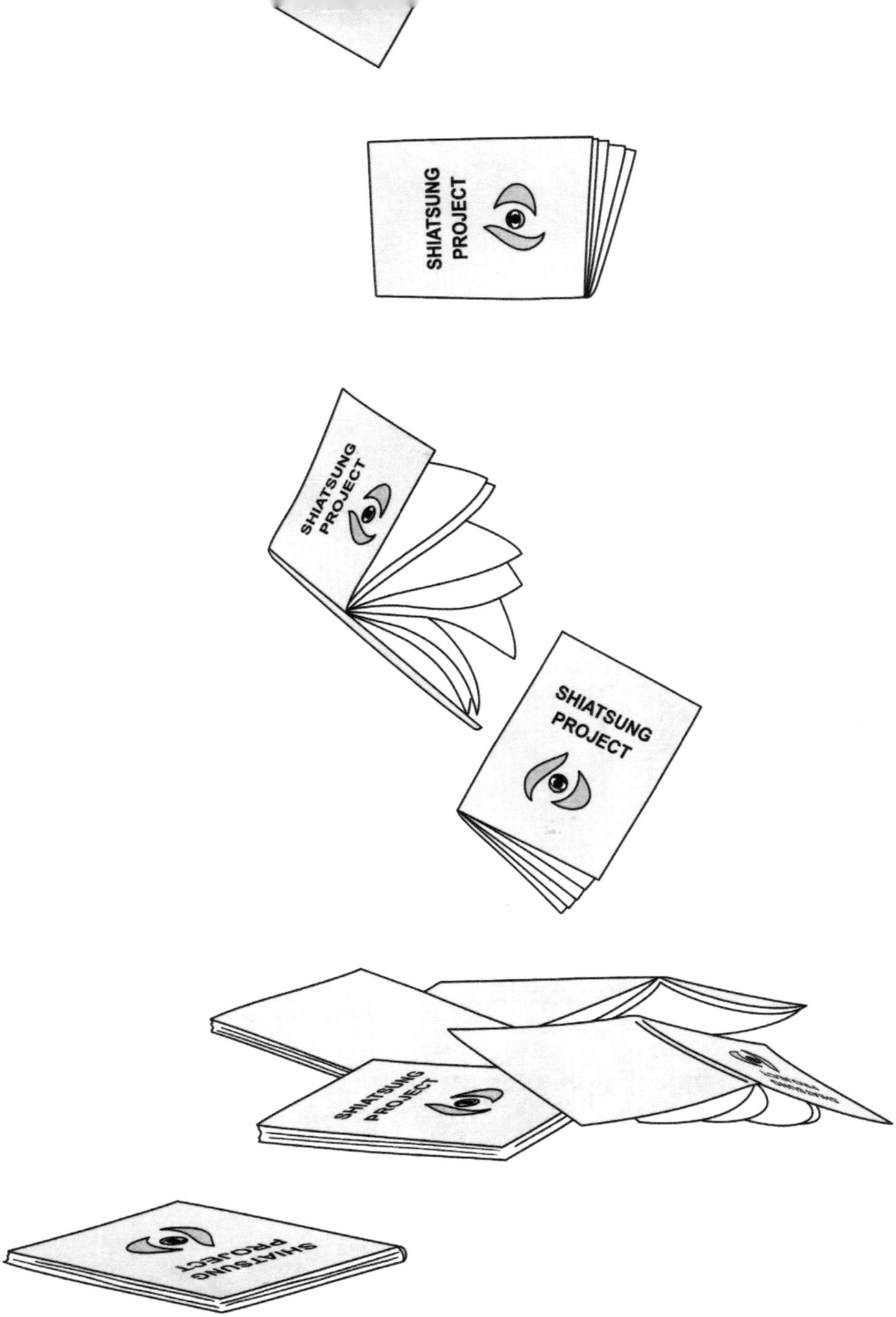
SHIATSUNG PROJECT
SHIATSUNG PROJECT
SHIATSUNG PROJECT
SHIATSUNG PROJECT
SHIATSUNG PROJECT

SHIATSUNG

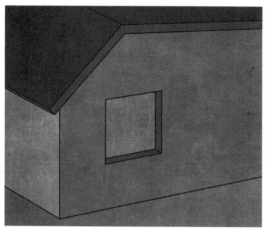

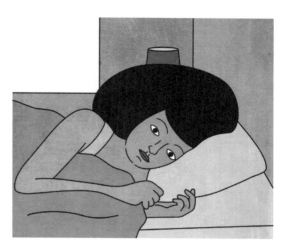

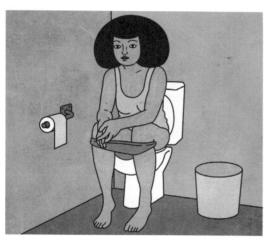

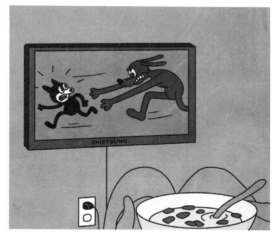

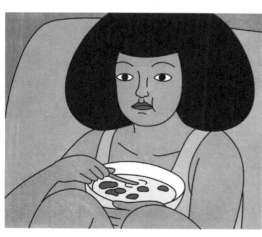

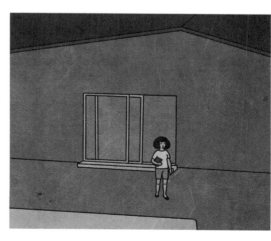

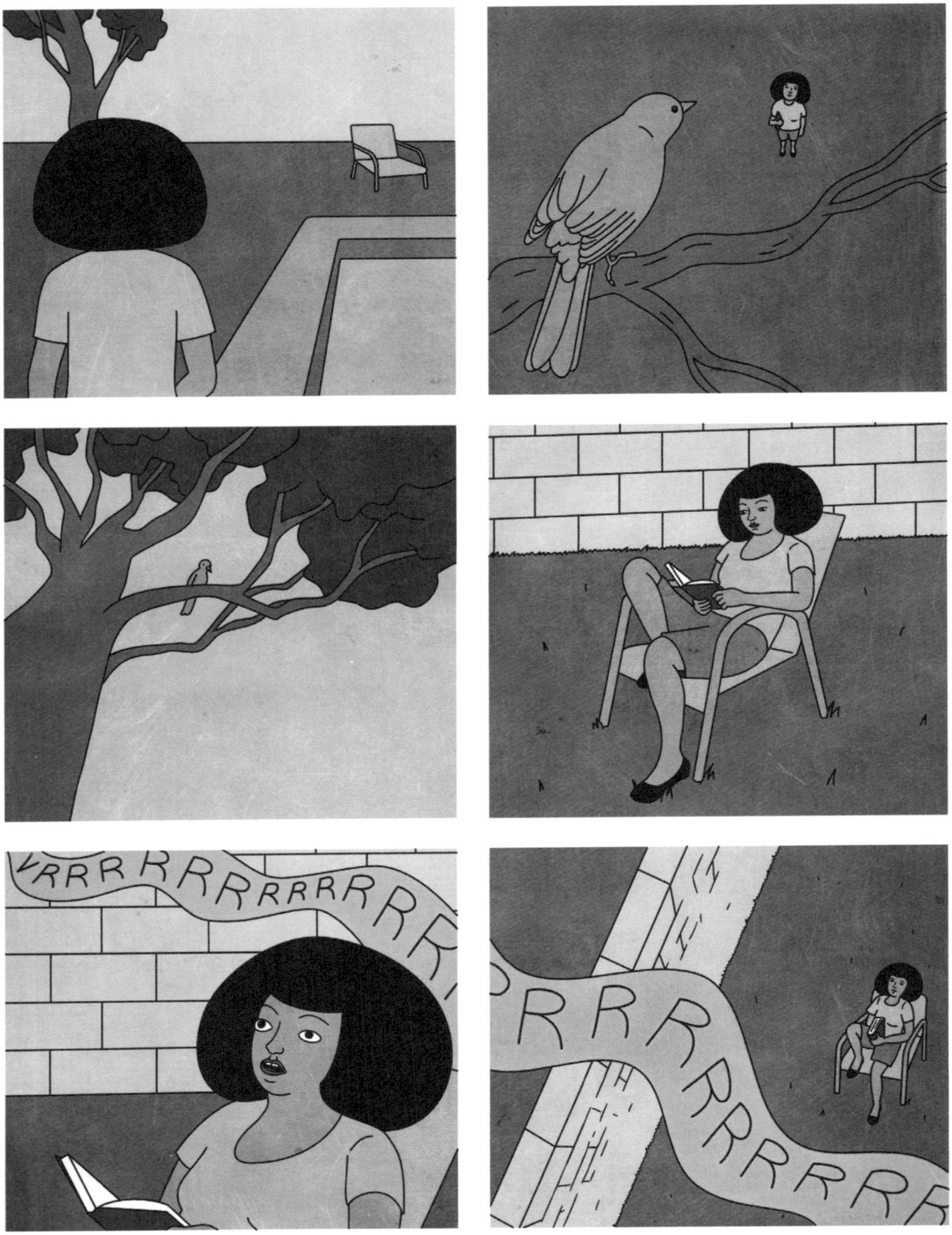
VRRRRRRRRRRRR
RRRRRRRRRRRR

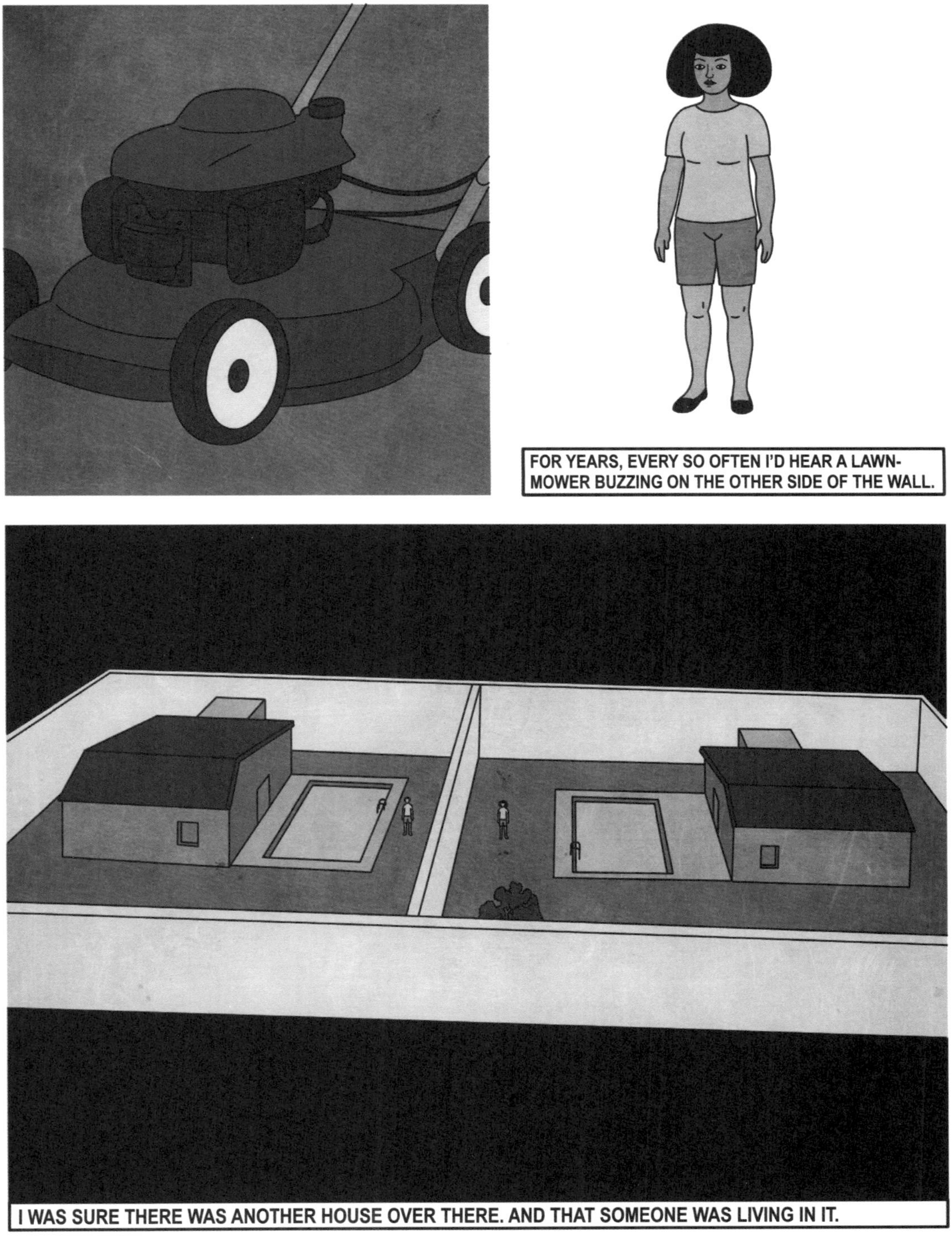
FOR YEARS, EVERY SO OFTEN I'D HEAR A LAWN-MOWER BUZZING ON THE OTHER SIDE OF THE WALL.
I WAS SURE THERE WAS ANOTHER HOUSE OVER THERE. AND THAT SOMEONE WAS LIVING IN IT.

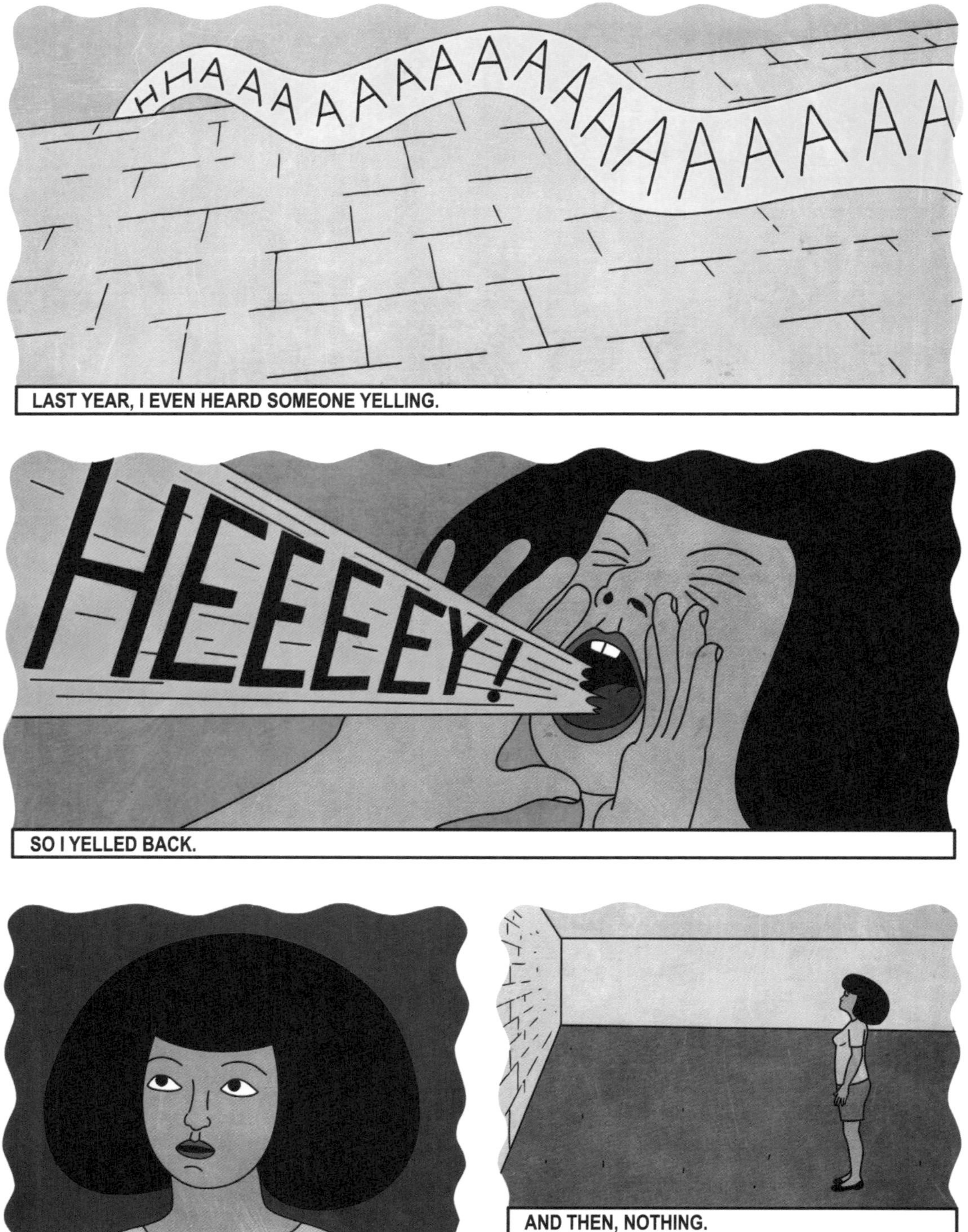
HHAAAAAAAAAAAAAAAAAA
LAST YEAR, I EVEN HEARD SOMEONE YELLING.
HEEEEEY!
SO I YELLED BACK.
AND THEN, NOTHING.

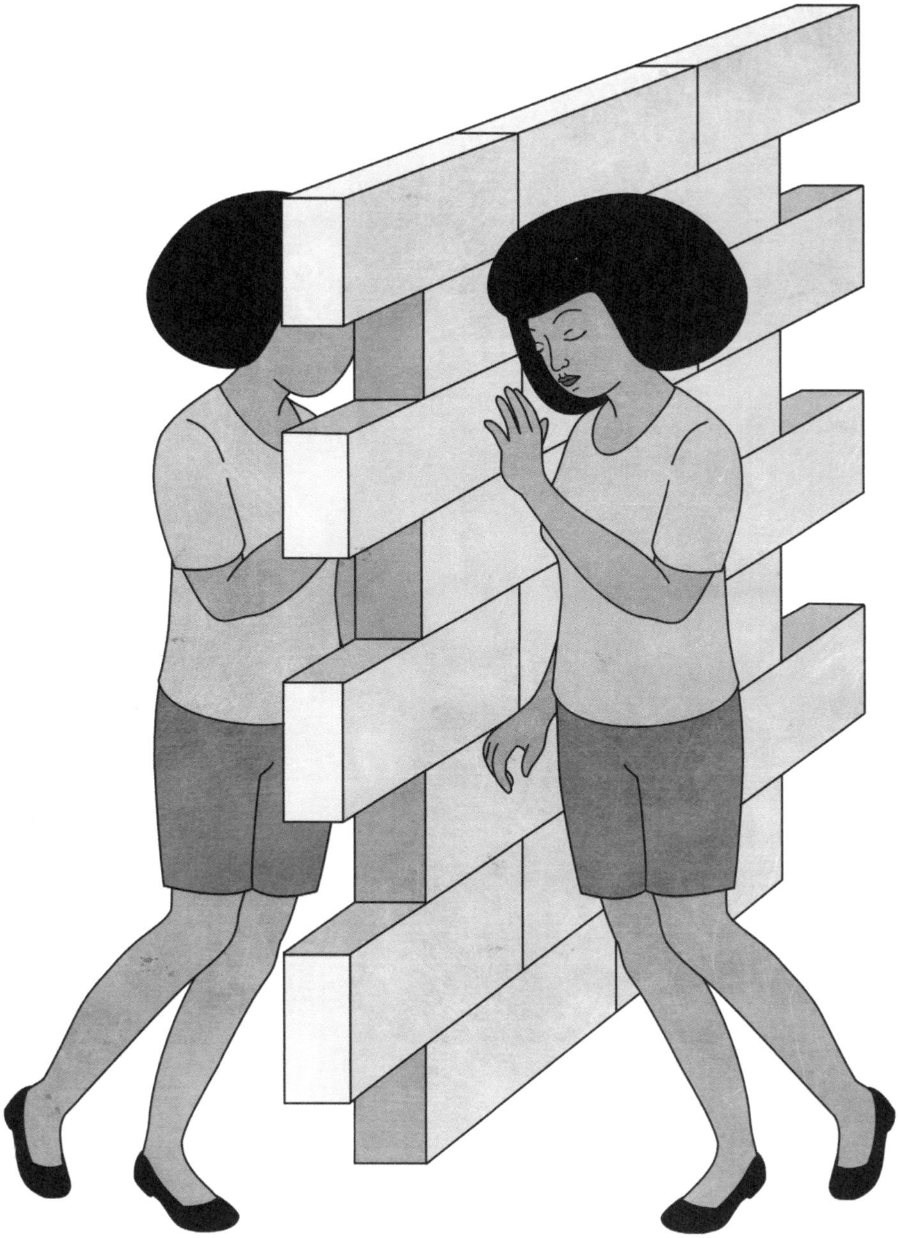

WHO'S OVER THERE? A MIRROR IMAGE OF ME?

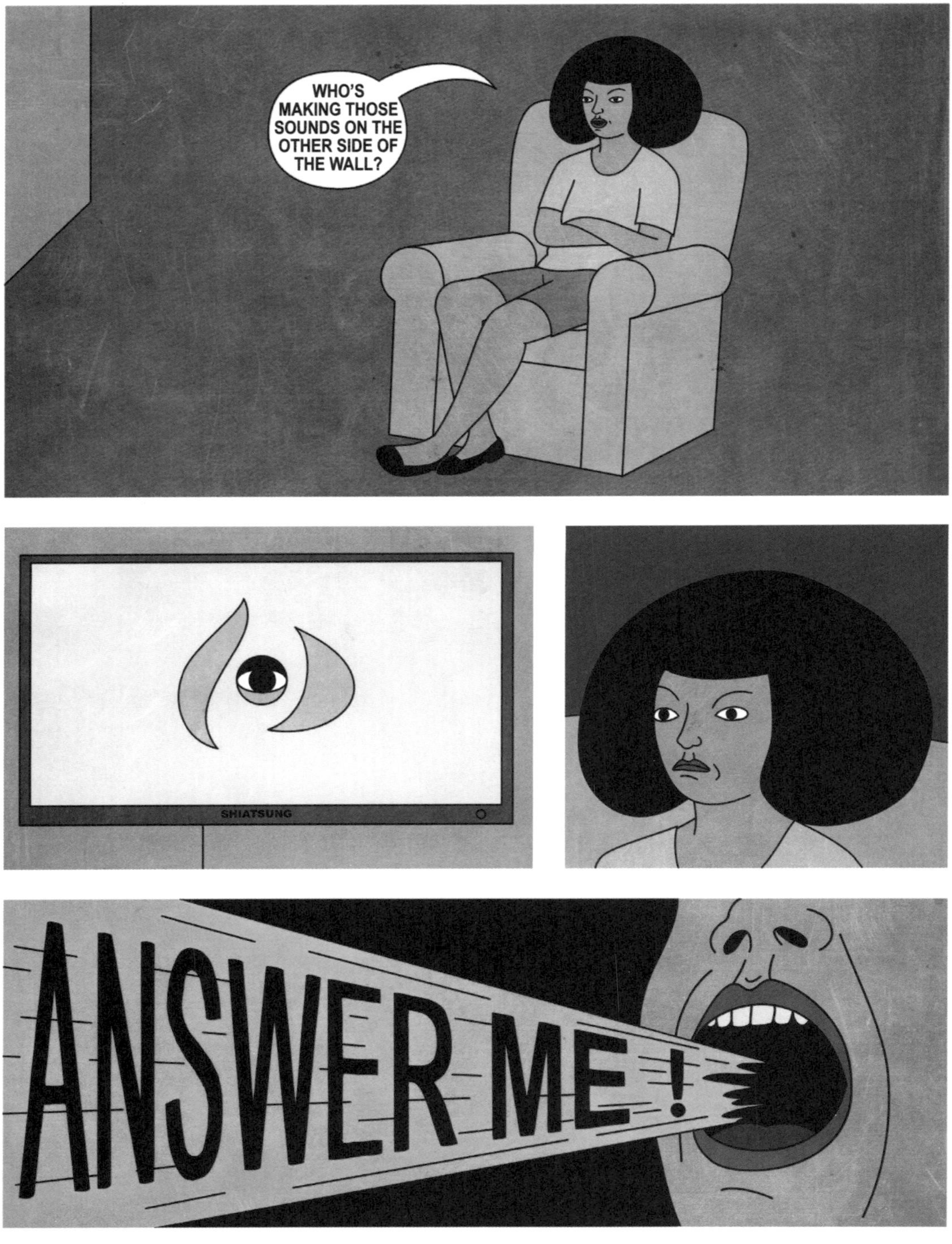
WHO'S MAKING THOSE SOUNDS ON THE OTHER SIDE OF THE WALL?
SHIATSUNG
ANSWER ME!

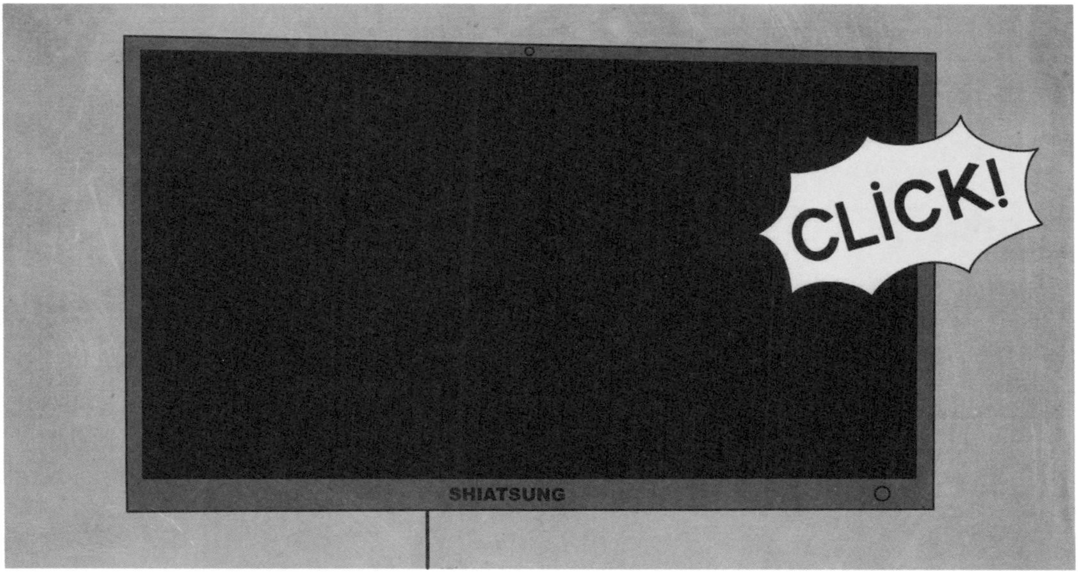
SHIATSUNG
CLICK!
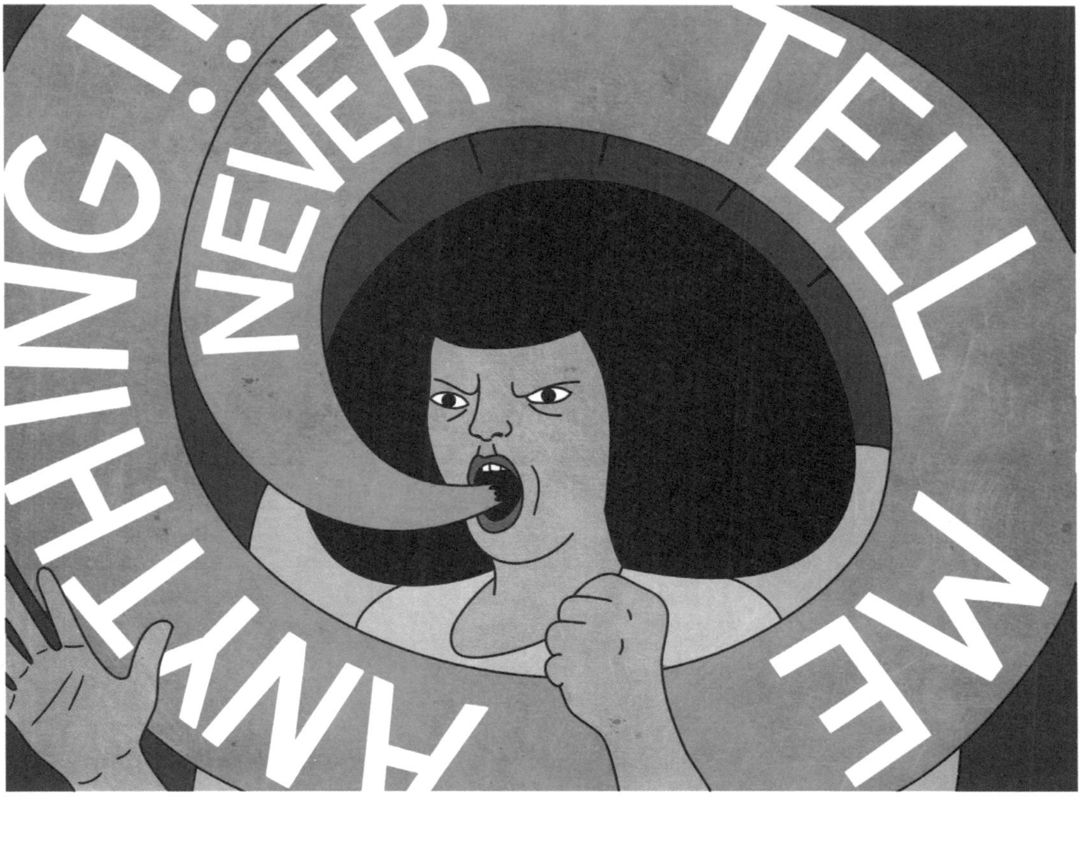
TELL ME NEVER ANYTHING!!

SOMETIMES SHIATSUNG PUSHES ME TO MY LIMIT.

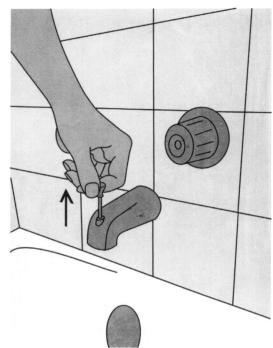

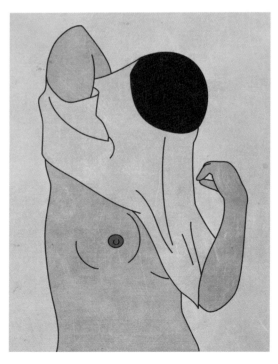

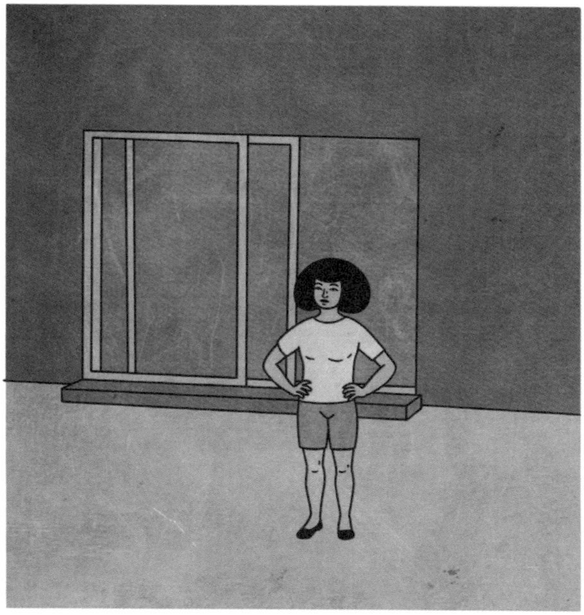

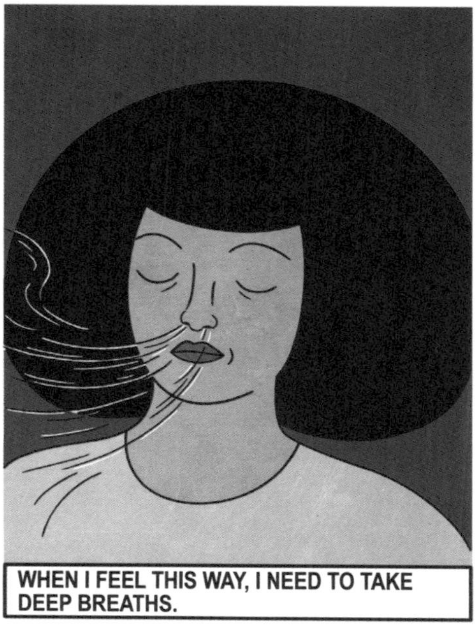
WHEN I FEEL THIS WAY, I NEED TO TAKE DEEP BREATHS.

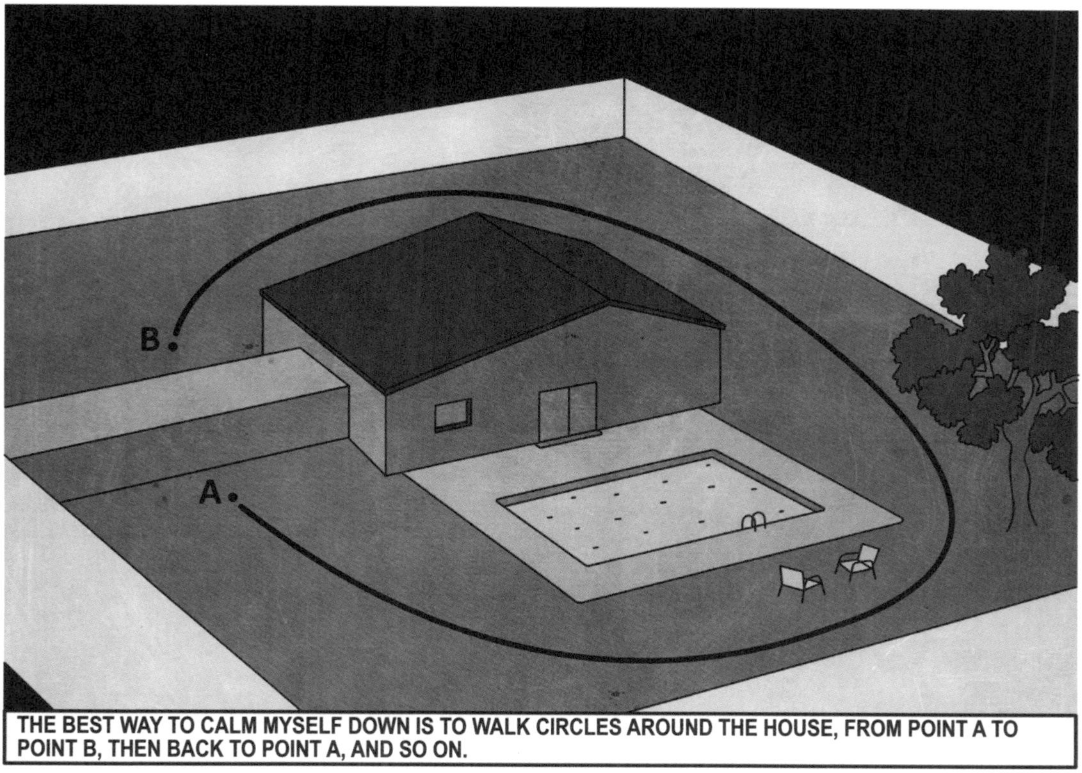
B.
A.
THE BEST WAY TO CALM MYSELF DOWN IS TO WALK CIRCLES AROUND THE HOUSE, FROM POINT A TO POINT B, THEN BACK TO POINT A, AND SO ON.

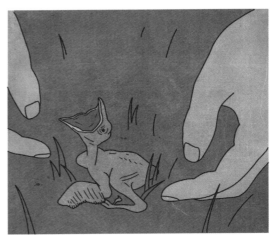

ONE DAY I FOUND A HATCHLING ON THE LAWN WHILE I WAS WALKING.

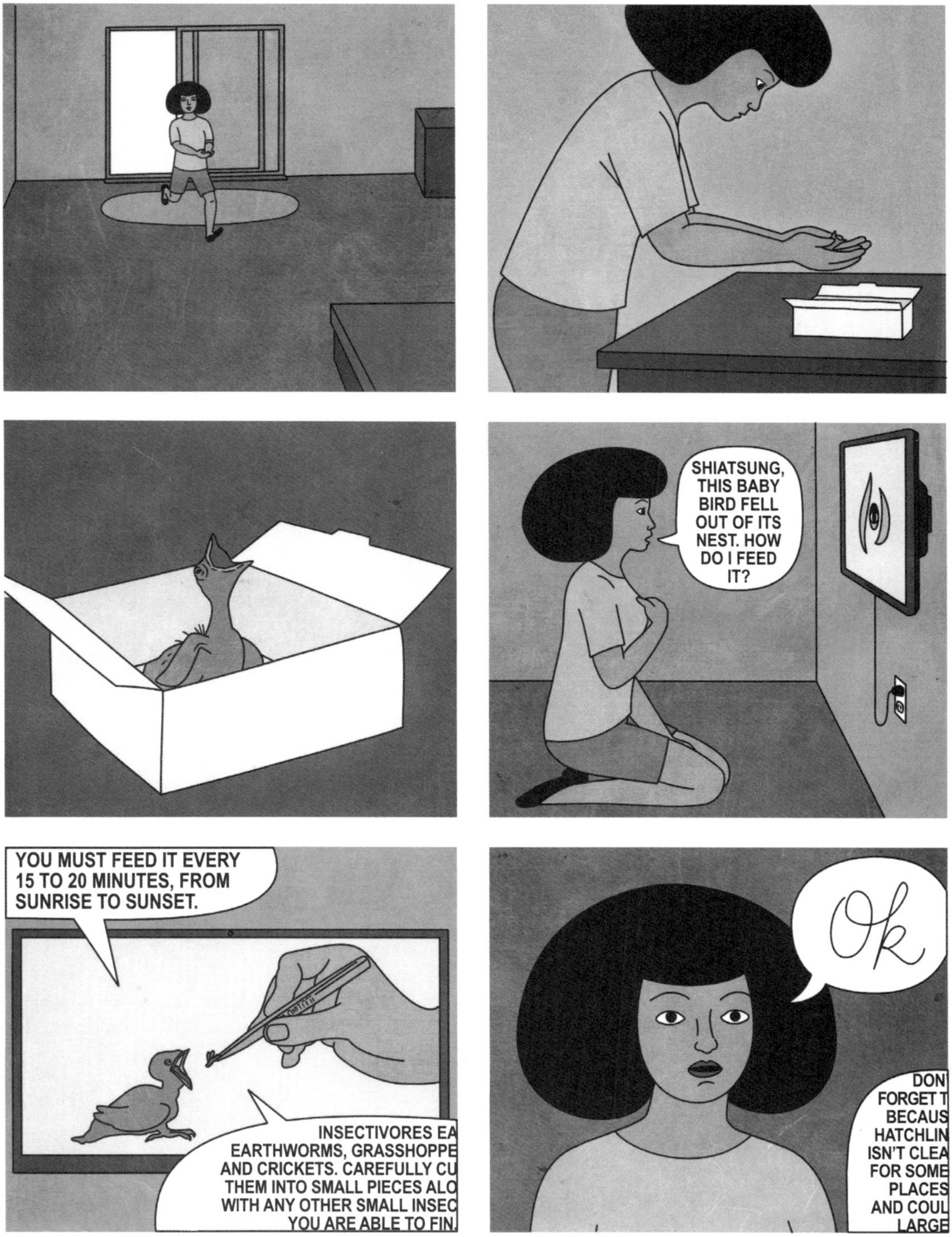
SHIATSUNG, THIS BABY BIRD FELL OUT OF ITS NEST. HOW DO I FEED IT?
YOU MUST FEED IT EVERY 15 TO 20 MINUTES, FROM SUNRISE TO SUNSET.
INSECTIVORES EA EARTHWORMS, GRASSHOPPE AND CRICKETS. CAREFULLY CU THEM INTO SMALL PIECES ALO WITH ANY OTHER SMALL INSEC YOU ARE ABLE TO FIN
Ok
DON FORGET T BECAUS HATCHLIN ISN'T CLEA FOR SOME PLACES AND COUL LARGE

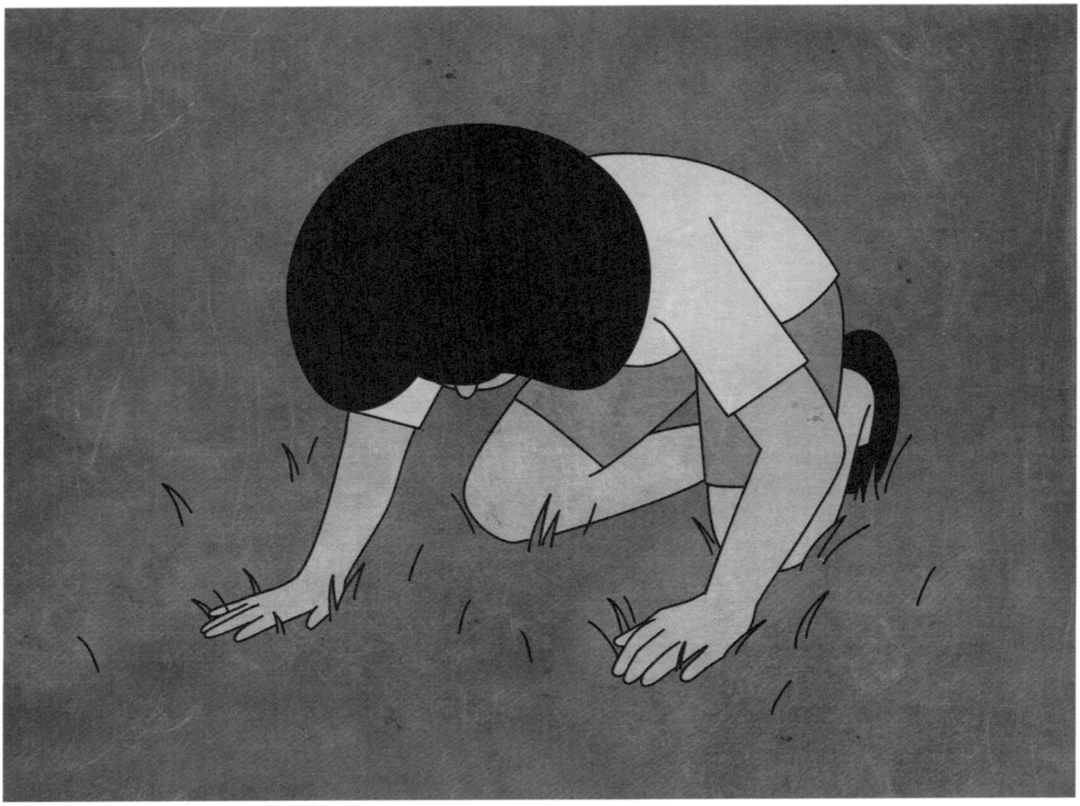

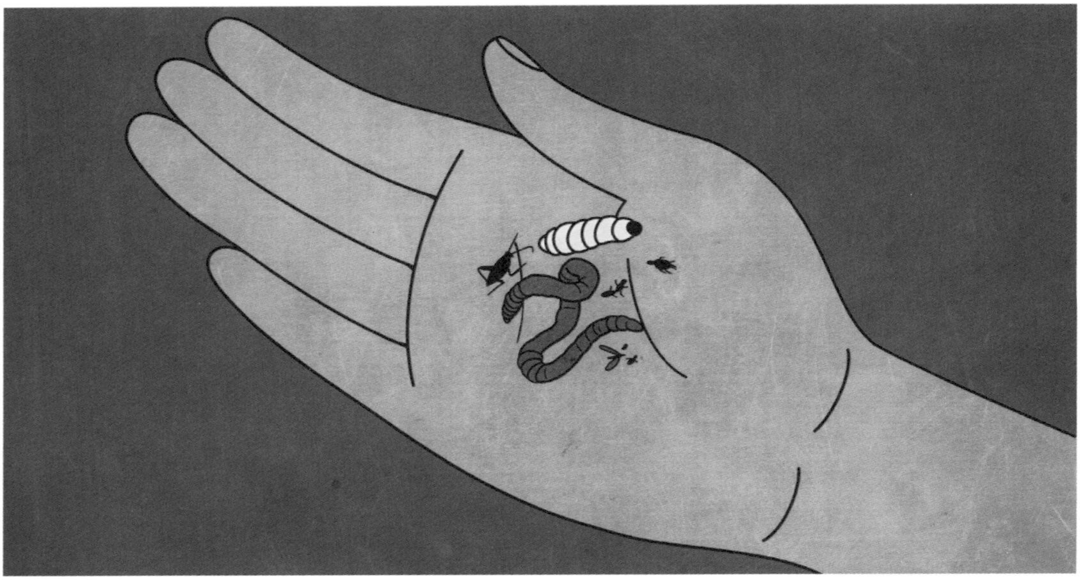

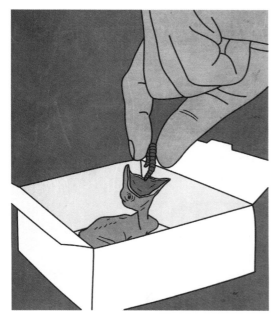

THE BIRD'S LIFE WAS IN MY HANDS. THERE WASN'T A MOMENT TO LOSE.

I SEARCHED FOR INSECTS FOR HOURS. I WAS HUNGRY, BUT COULDN'T RISK TAKING A BREAK UNTIL THE END OF THE DAY.

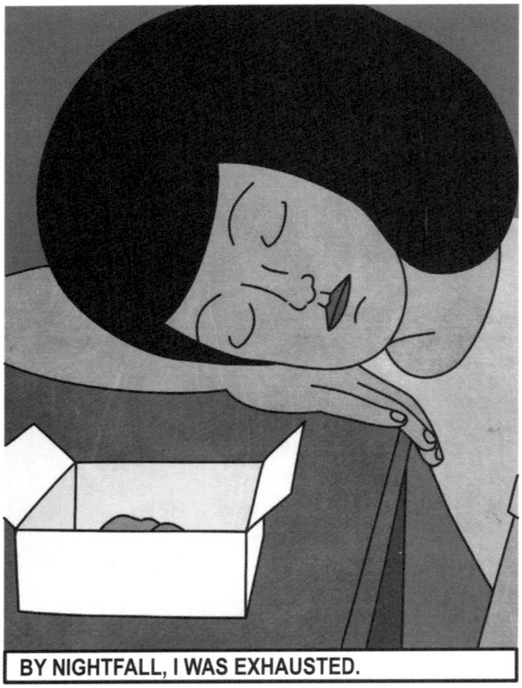
BY NIGHTFALL, I WAS EXHAUSTED.

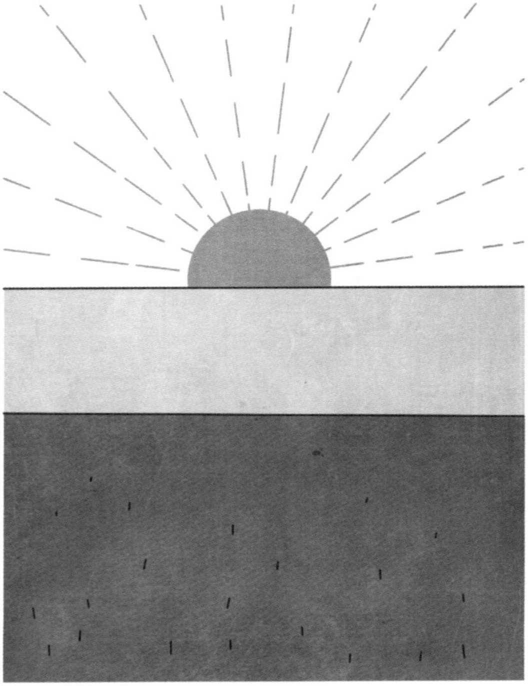

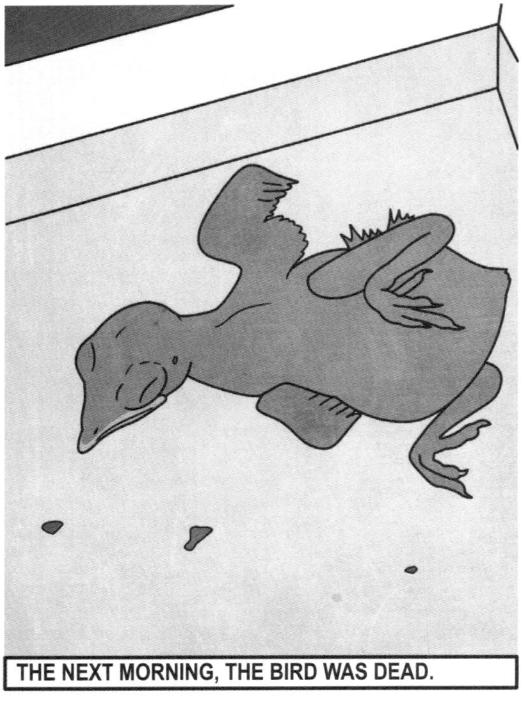
THE NEXT MORNING, THE BIRD WAS DEAD.

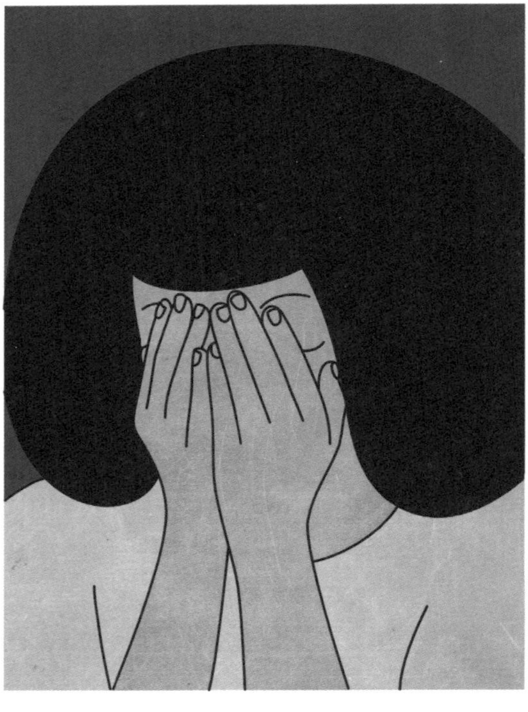

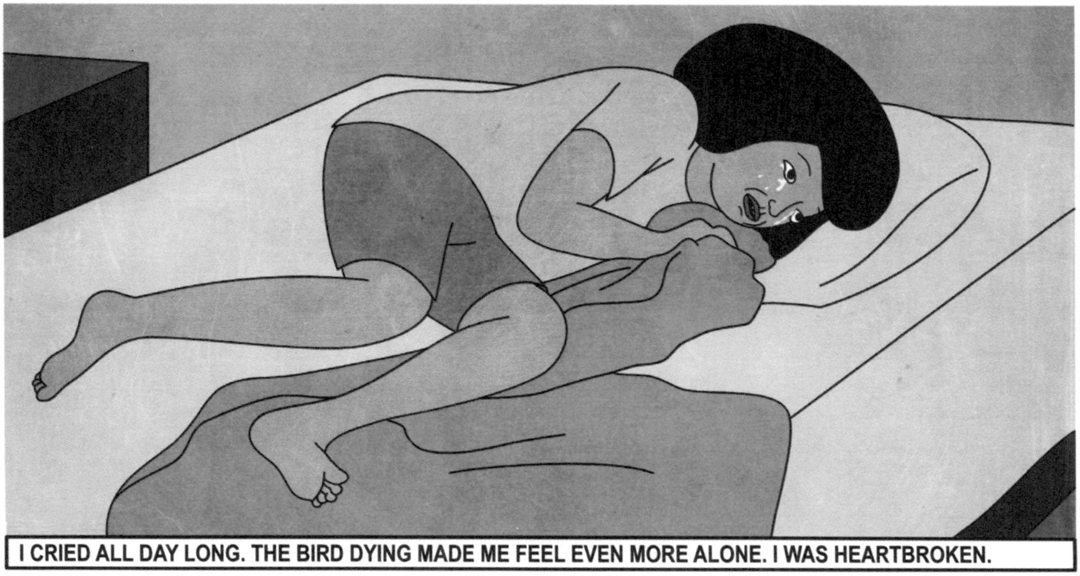
I CRIED ALL DAY LONG. THE BIRD DYING MADE ME FEEL EVEN MORE ALONE. I WAS HEARTBROKEN.

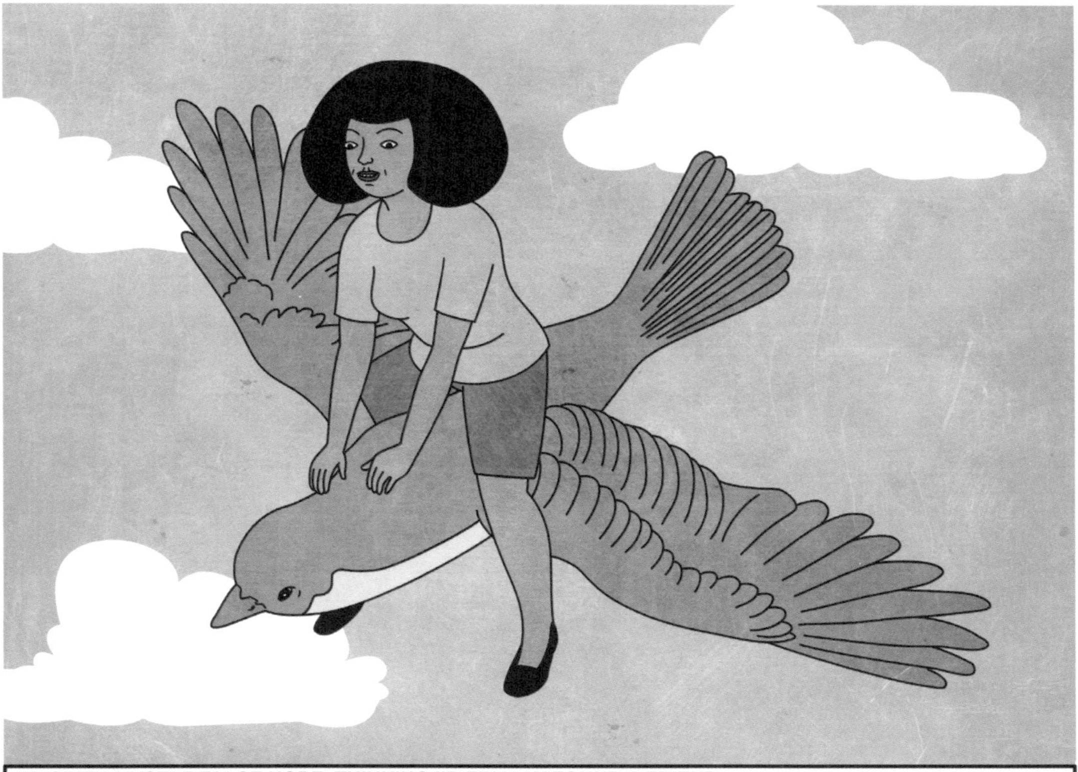
I'D GIVEN MYSELF FALSE HOPE, THINKING I'D FINALLY FOUND A FRIEND.

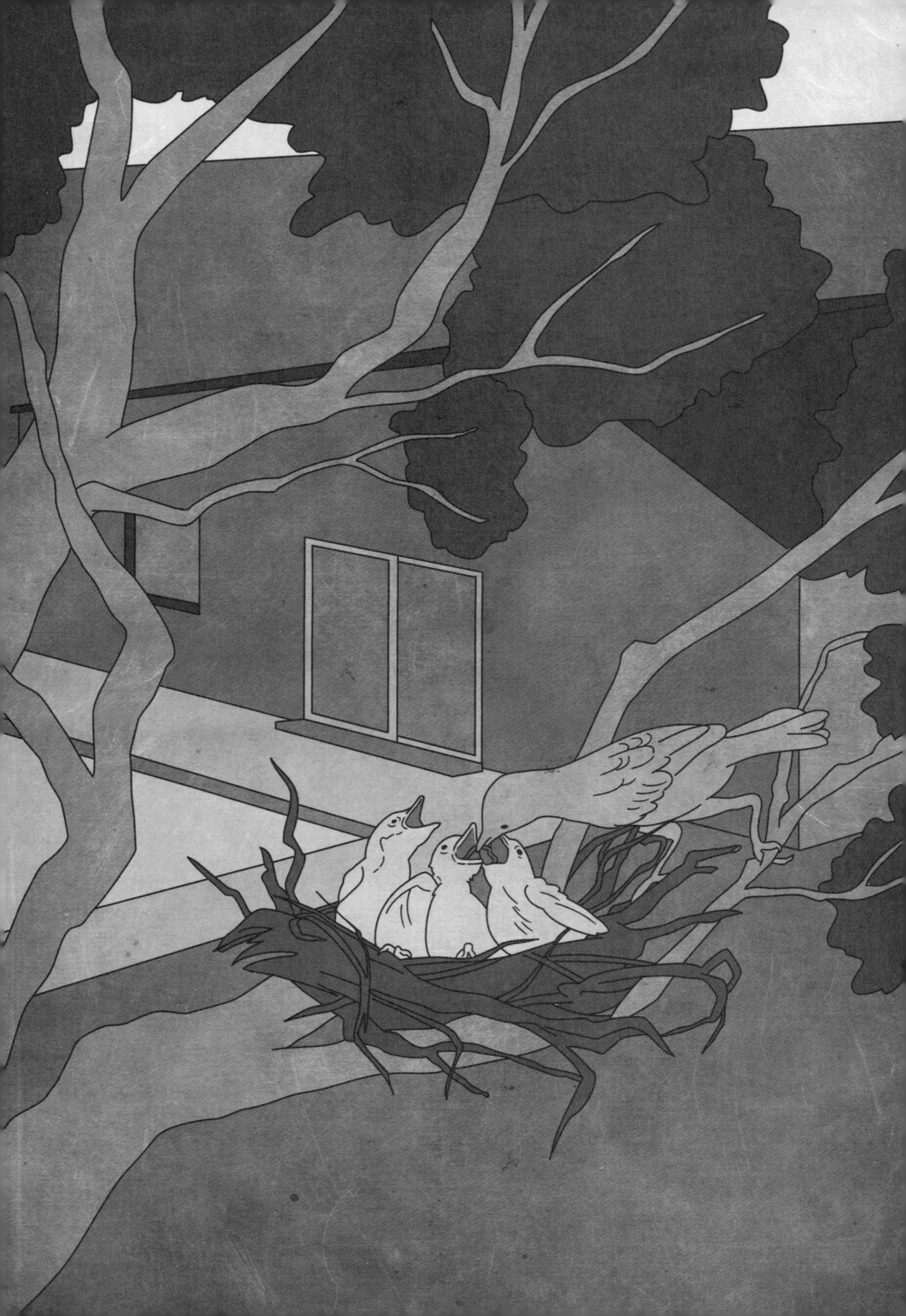

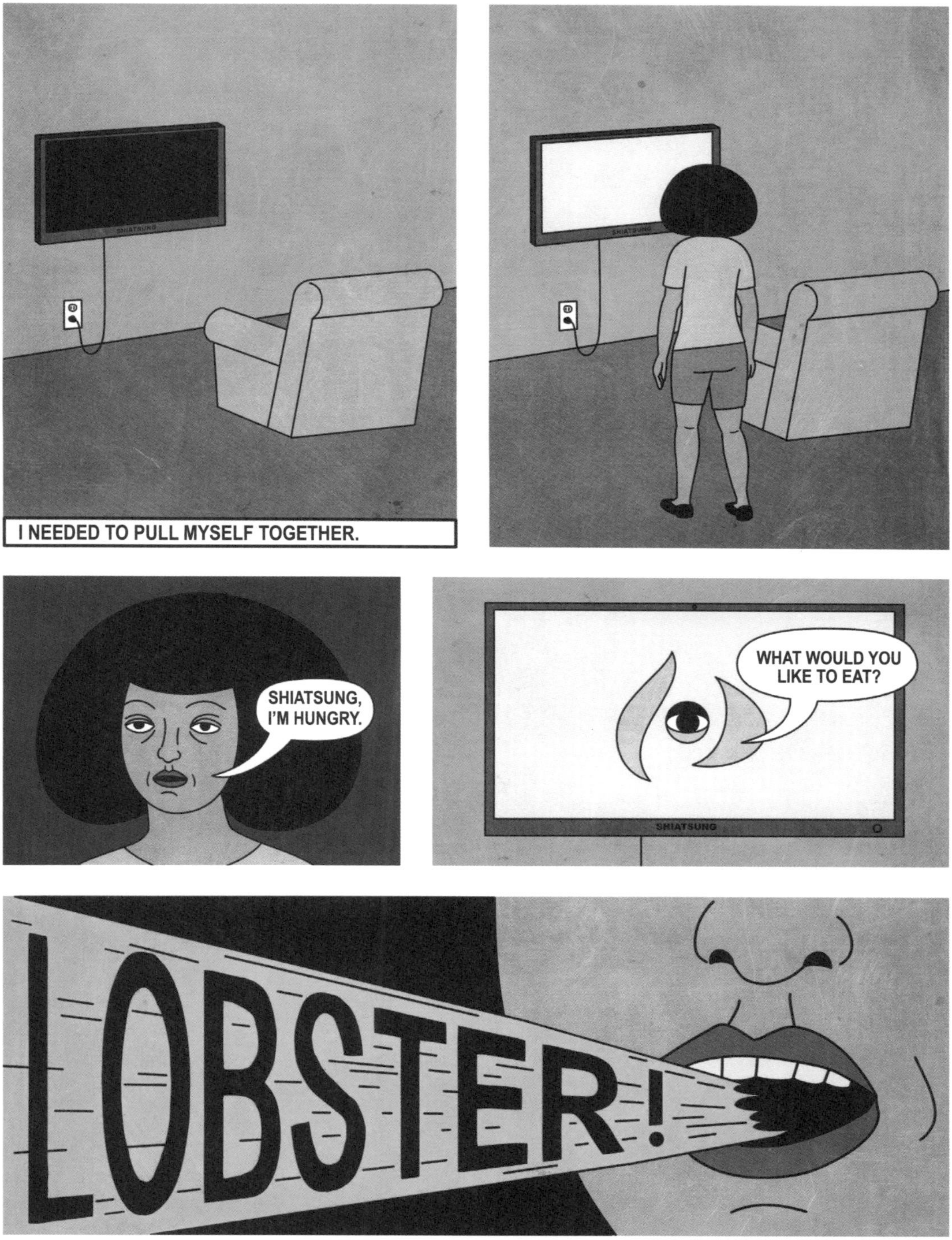
SHIATSUNG
I NEEDED TO PULL MYSELF TOGETHER.
SHIATSUNG
SHIATSUNG, I'M HUNGRY.
WHAT WOULD YOU LIKE TO EAT?
SHIATSUNG
LOBSTER!

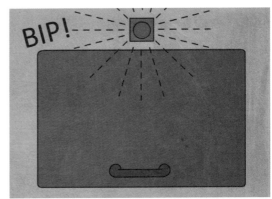

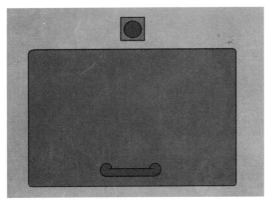
BIP!

I ORDERED THE VERY BEST DISH THAT NIGHT.

I HADN'T BEEN ABLE TO SAVE THE BIRD, AND IT HURT.

I WANTED TO CONSOLE MYSELF.

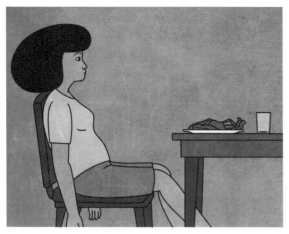
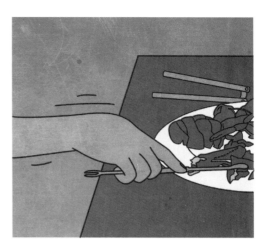

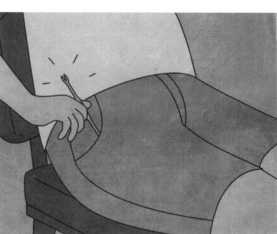

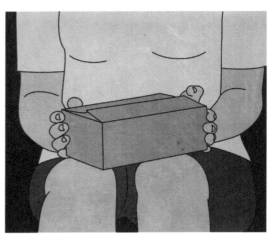

SHIATSUNG DIDN'T KNOW, BUT I'D BEEN STASHING AWAY ALL THE SHARP OBJECTS I COULD FIND.

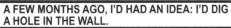

A FEW MONTHS AGO, I'D HAD AN IDEA: I'D DIG A HOLE IN THE WALL.

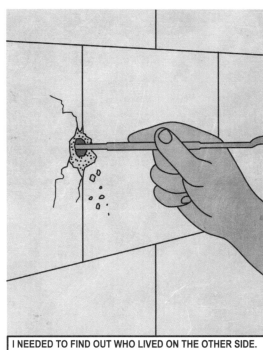

I NEEDED TO FIND OUT WHO LIVED ON THE OTHER SIDE.

I WORKED ON THE HOLE ALMOST EVERY NIGHT.

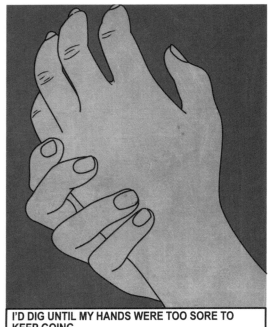

I'D DIG UNTIL MY HANDS WERE TOO SORE TO KEEP GOING.

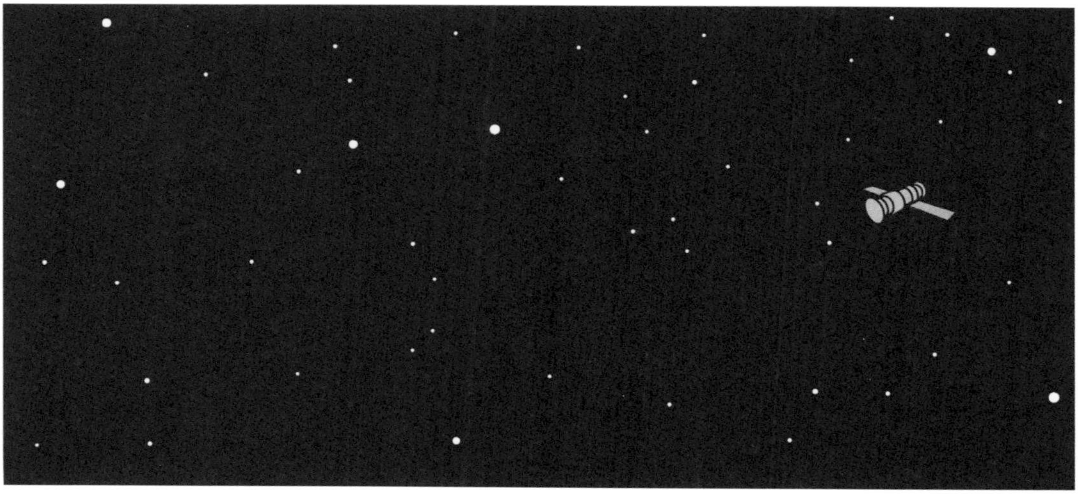

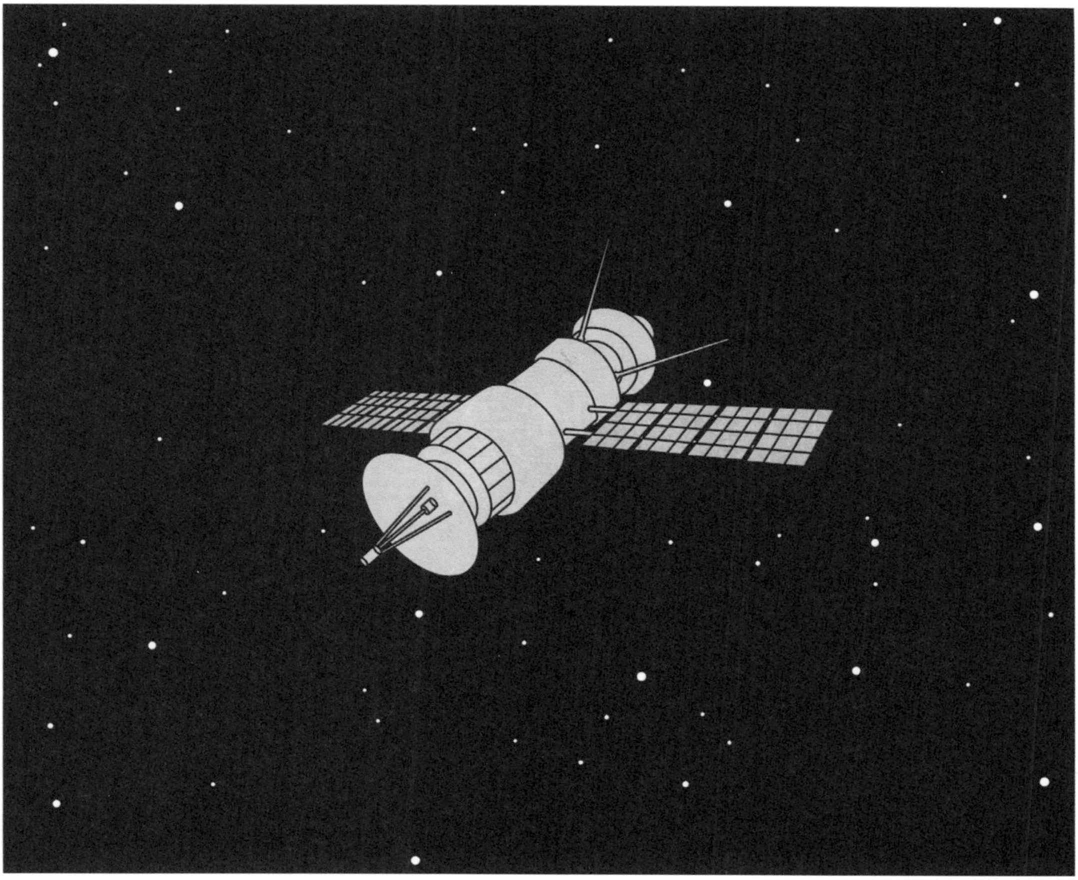

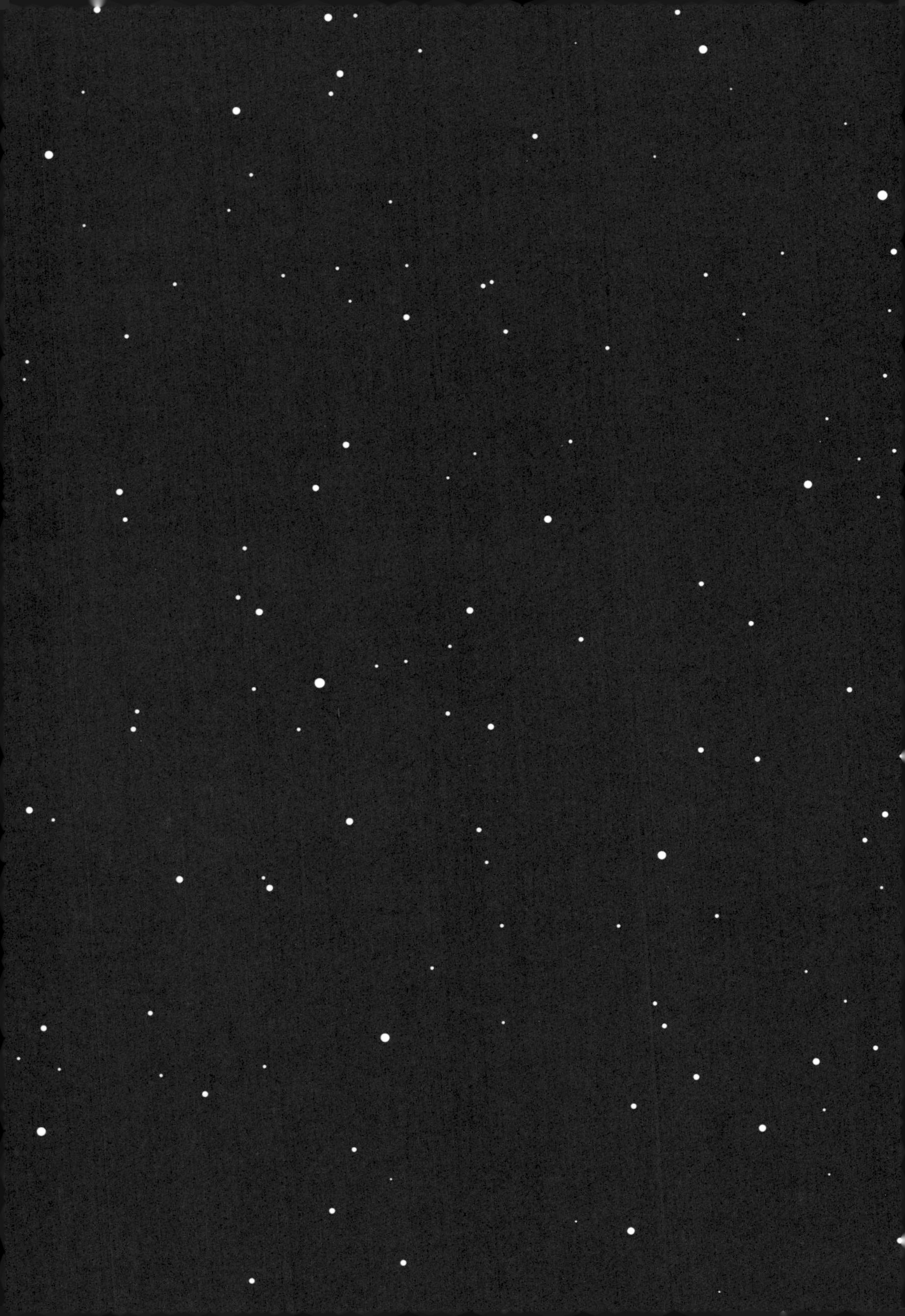

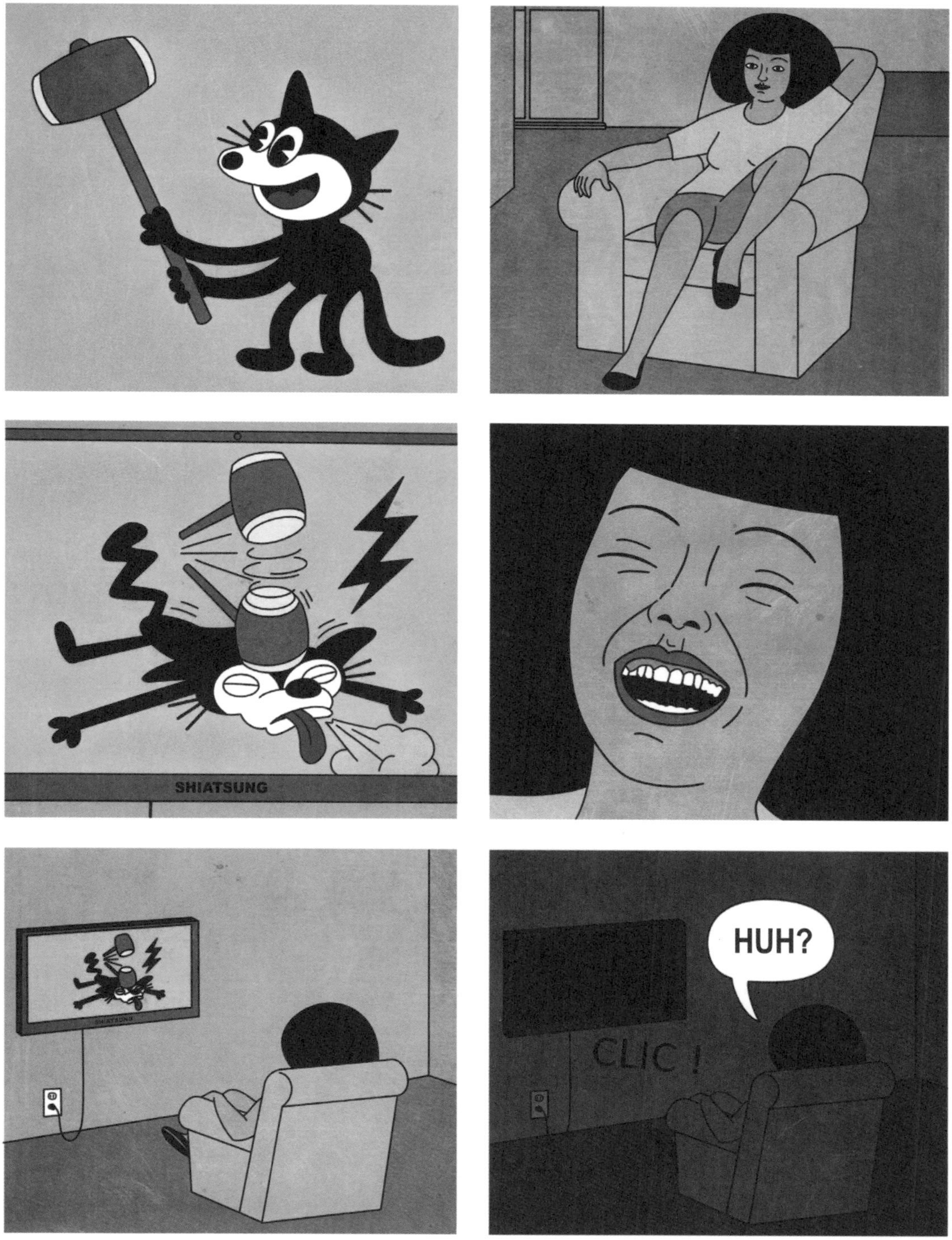
SHIATSUNG
HUH?
CLIC !

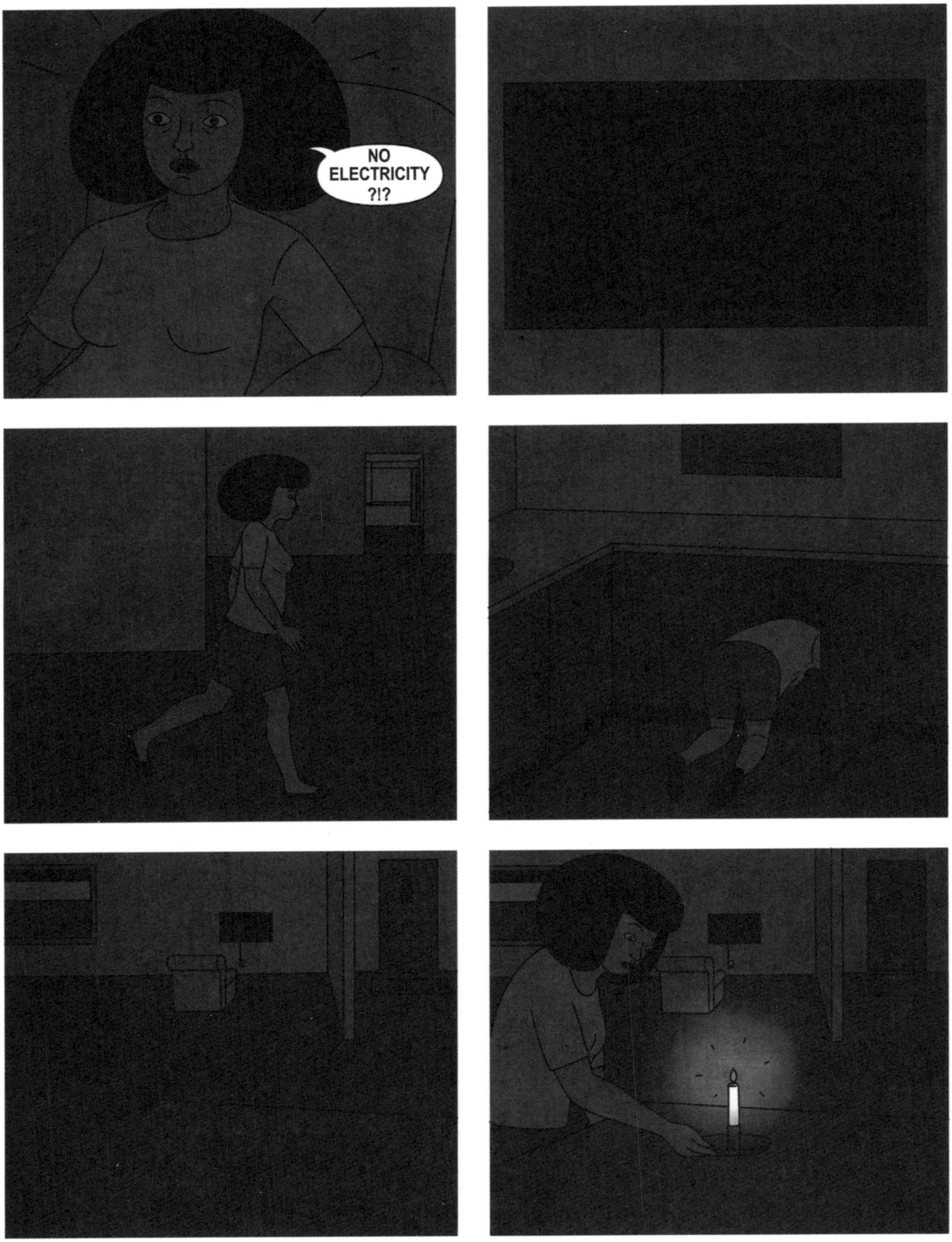
NO ELECTRICITY ?!?

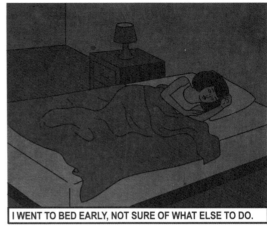

I'D NEVER EXPERIENCED A POWER OUTAGE BEFORE.
I WENT TO BED EARLY, NOT SURE OF WHAT ELSE TO DO.
I GOT UP THE NEXT MORNING HOPING THE PROBLEM WOULD BE FIXED. BUT THERE WAS STILL NO POWER.
SHIATSUNG WOULDN'T ANSWER. AND THAT MEANT THERE WAS NOTHING TO EAT.
MAYBE IF I BANGED ON THE INSIDE OF THE CHUTE SOMEONE WOULD HEAR?
SMACK! SMACK! SMACK!
HEY ROBOTS! CAN YOU HEAR ME?

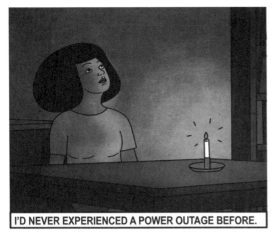

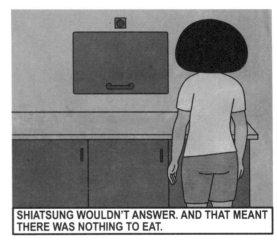

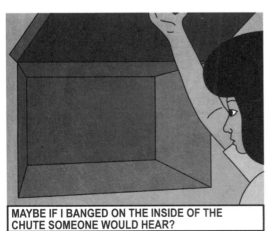

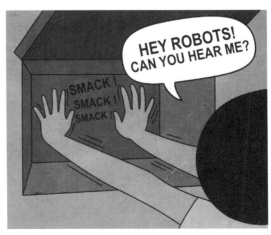

LUCKILY I STILL HAD CLEAN WATER.

AS MUCH AS I COULD DRINK.

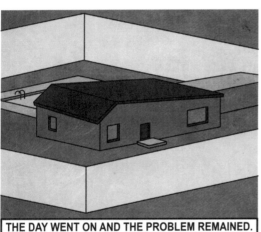

THE DAY WENT ON AND THE PROBLEM REMAINED.

I WAS SO HUNGRY.

I STARTED TO PLAN FOR THE WORST. I'D HAVE TO FIND SOME WAY TO EAT.

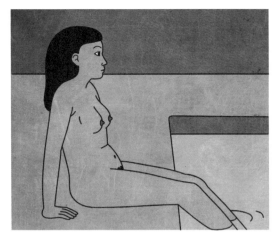

IF SHIATSUNG COULDN'T FEED ME, MAYBE I COULD EAT LIKE THE BIRDS.

WORMS, INSECTS, AND LARVA....

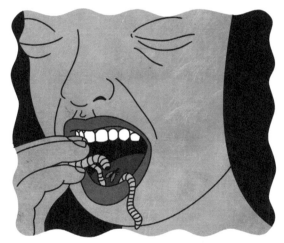

BLECH!

OR MICE.

I STARTED TO REALLY WORRY. I COULDN'T SLEEP.

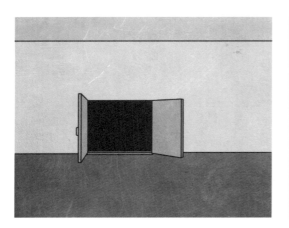

I EMPTIED THE GARBAGE CAN ONTO THE FLOOR AND ATE EVERYTHING THAT WASN'T ROTTEN.

LEFTOVER LOBSTER.

APPLE CORES.

STALE BREAD.

THEN I REALIZED I SHOULD CHECK THE COUCH CUSHIONS TOO.

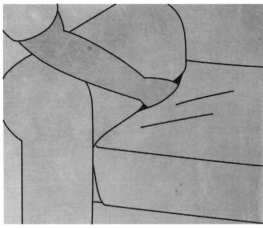

CEREAL POPCORN ALMONDS

IT WAS A MEAGRE OFFERING, BUT MORE APPE-TIZING THAN WHAT I'D FOUND IN THE TRASH.

I ATE EVERY SINGLE CRUMB I COULD FIND.

THEN I SEARCHED THE REST OF THE HOUSE, BUT THERE WAS NOTHING AT ALL.

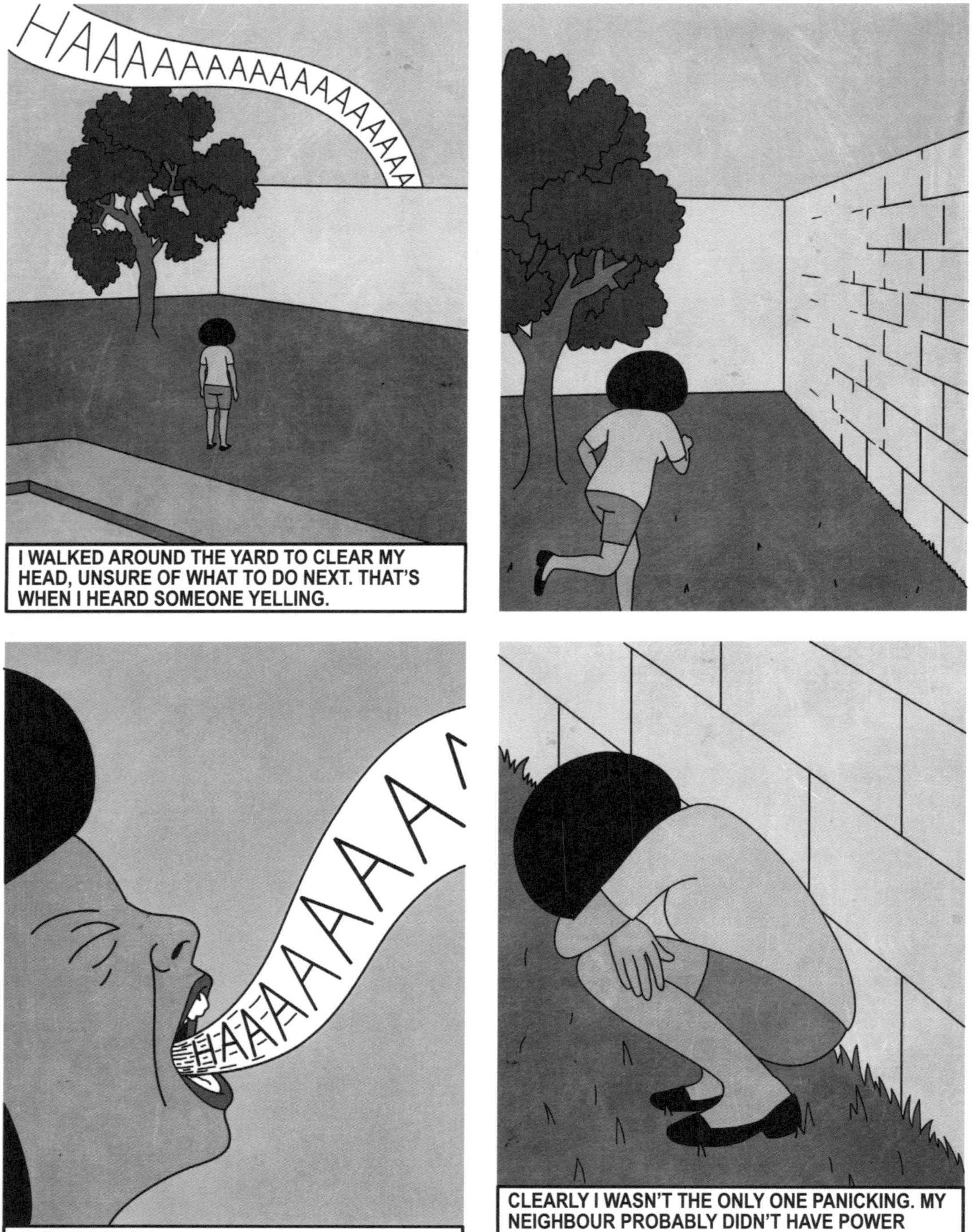
HAAAAAAAAAAAAAAAAAAAA
I WALKED AROUND THE YARD TO CLEAR MY HEAD, UNSURE OF WHAT TO DO NEXT. THAT'S WHEN I HEARD SOMEONE YELLING.
HAAAAAAAAA
I YELLED BACK.
CLEARLY I WASN'T THE ONLY ONE PANICKING. MY NEIGHBOUR PROBABLY DIDN'T HAVE POWER EITHER.

MY CHEST TIGHTENED. I WAS AFRAID I WAS GOING TO DIE.

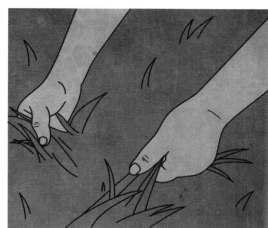

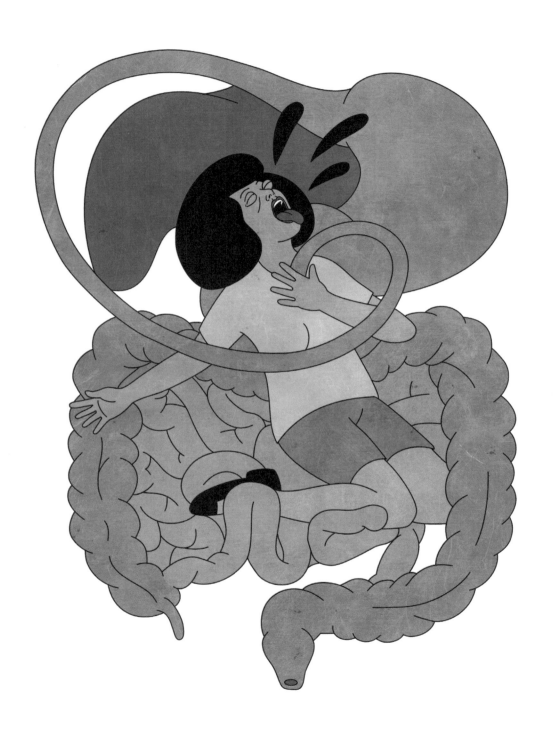

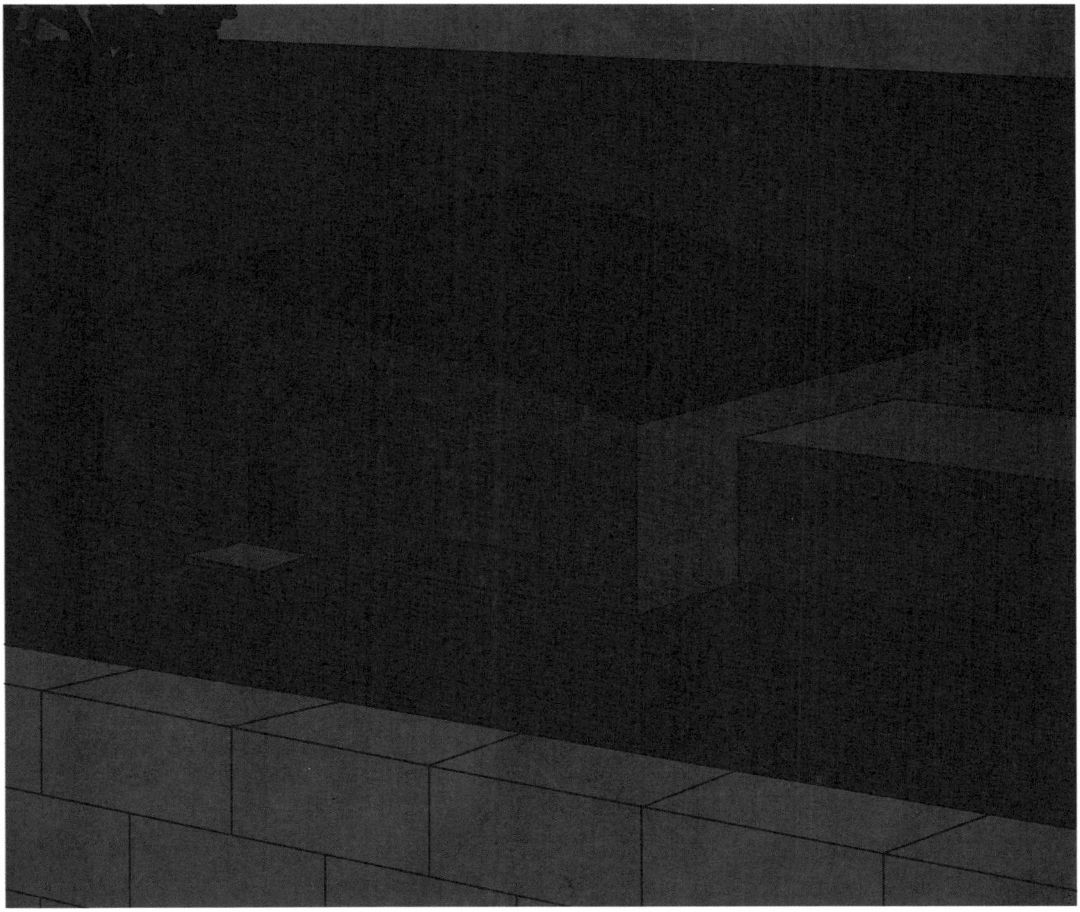
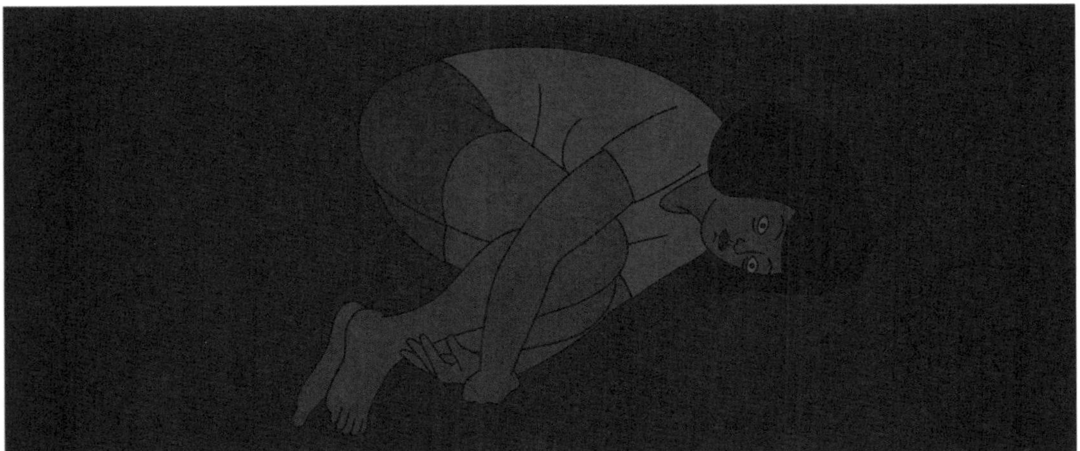

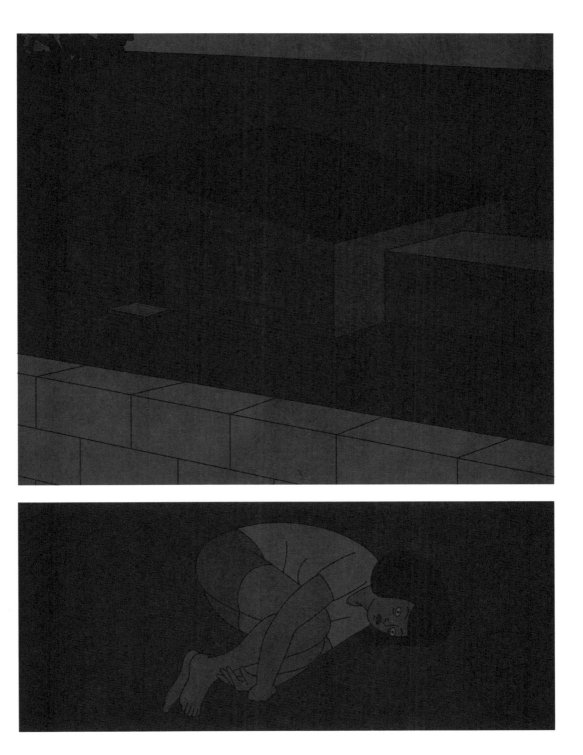

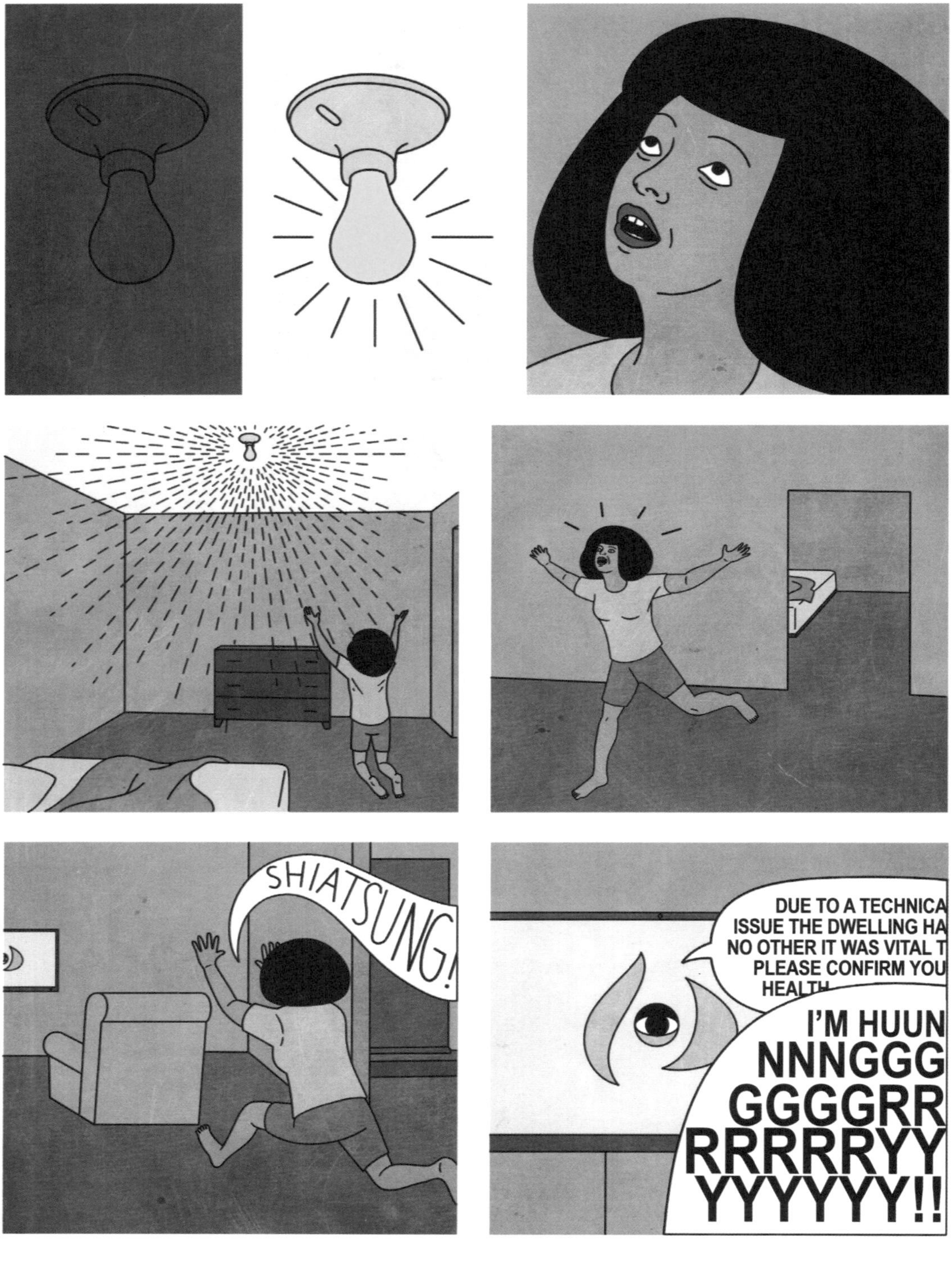
SHIATSUNG!
DUE TO A TECHNICA
ISSUE THE DWELLING HA
NO OTHER IT WAS VITAL T
PLEASE CONFIRM YOU
HEALTH
I'M HUUN
NNNGGG
GGGGRR
RRRRRYY
YYYYYY!!

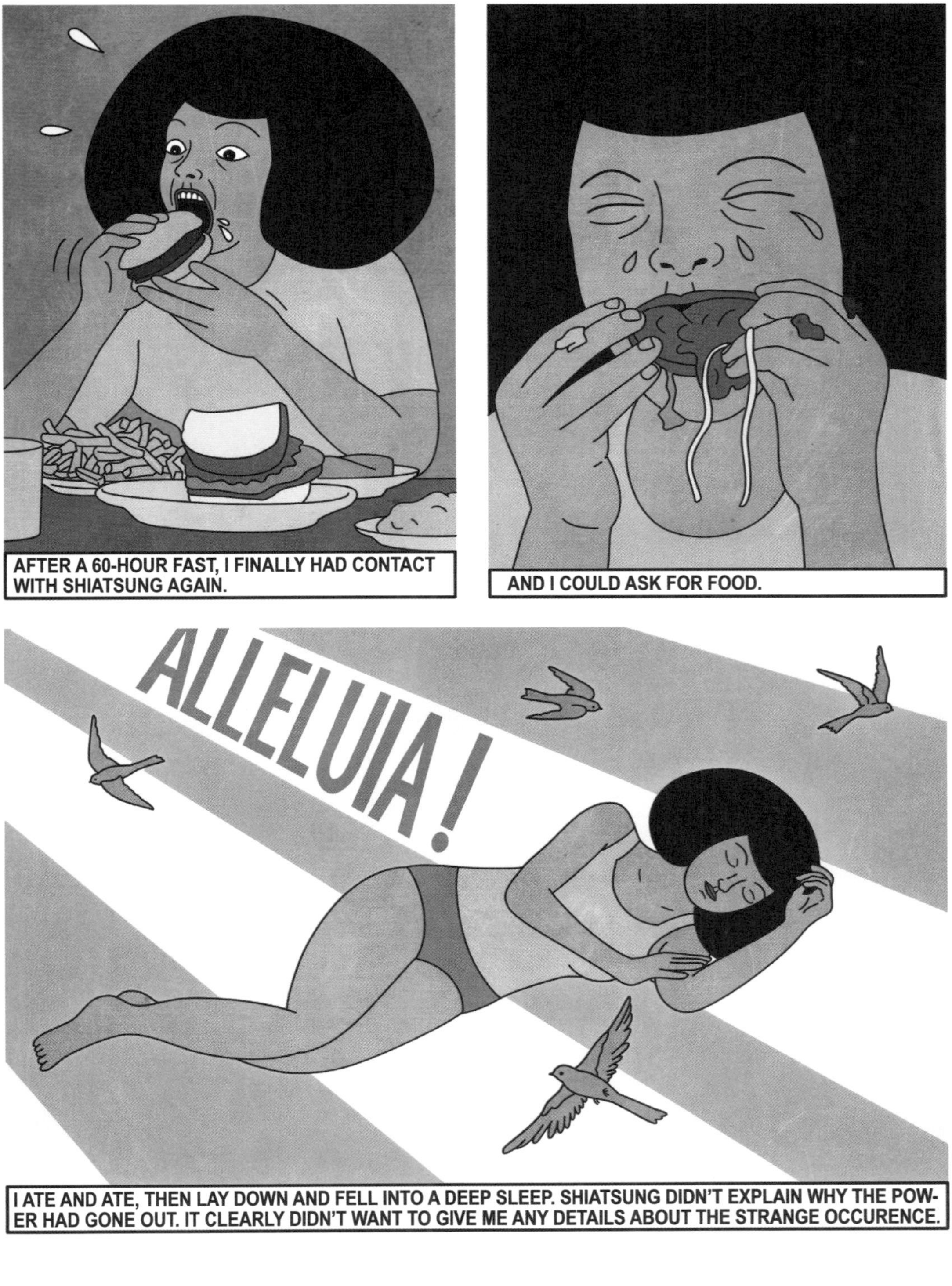
AFTER A 60-HOUR FAST, I FINALLY HAD CONTACT WITH SHIATSUNG AGAIN.
AND I COULD ASK FOR FOOD.
ALLELUIA!
I ATE AND ATE, THEN LAY DOWN AND FELL INTO A DEEP SLEEP. SHIATSUNG DIDN'T EXPLAIN WHY THE POWER HAD GONE OUT. IT CLEARLY DIDN'T WANT TO GIVE ME ANY DETAILS ABOUT THE STRANGE OCCURENCE.

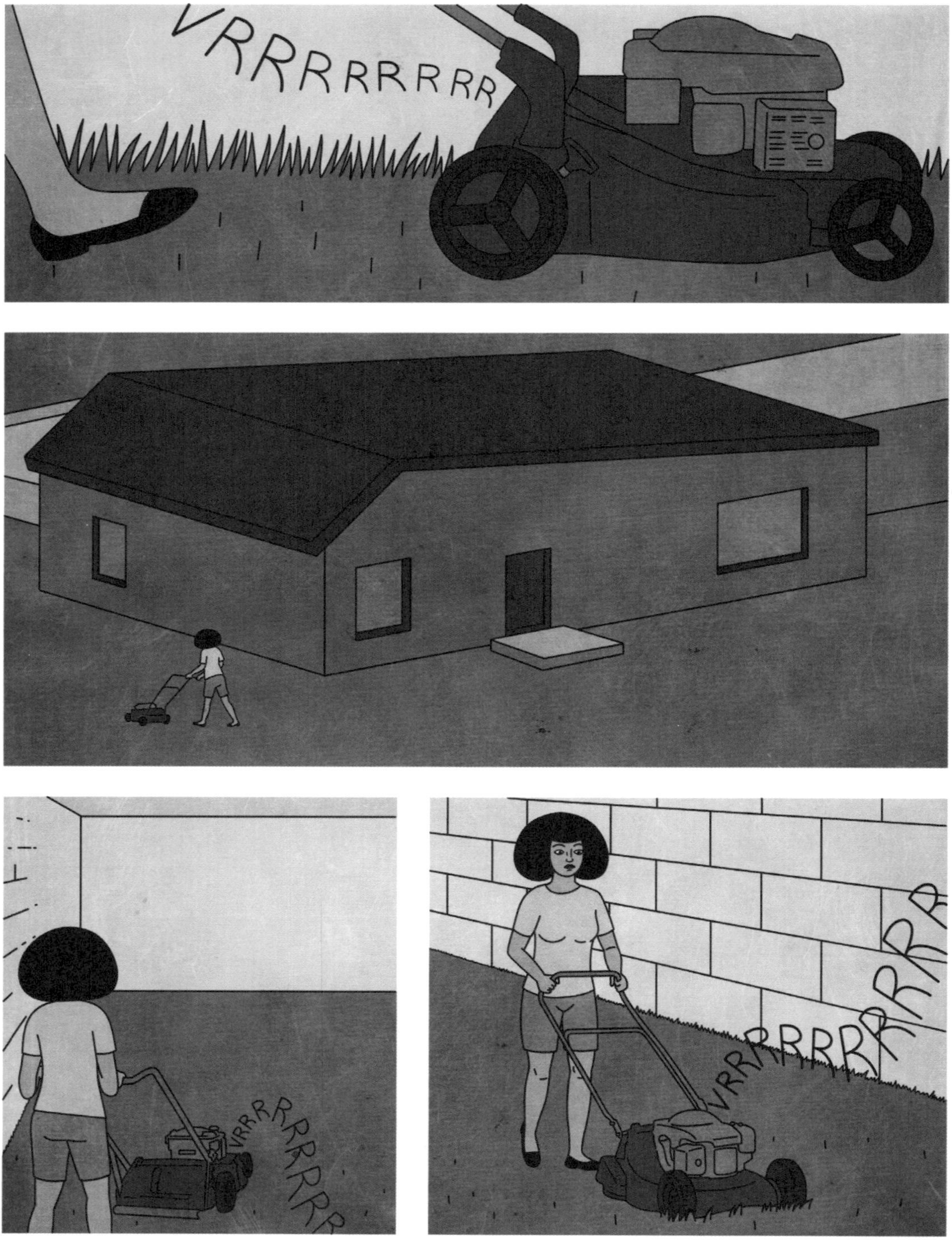
VRRRRRRRR
VRRRRRRRRR
VRRRRRRRRRR

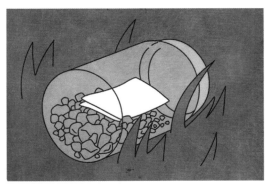

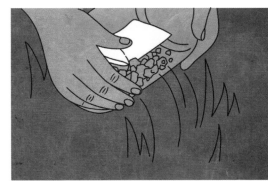

STONES

PIECE OF PAPER

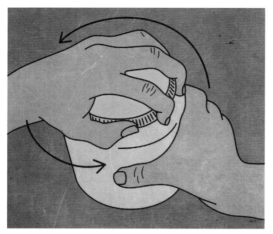

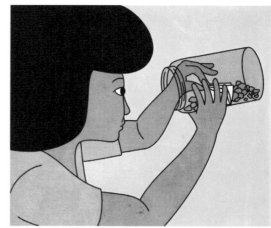

Кто ты?
Я хотел с тобой поговорить
THE NOTE WAS DEFINITELY FROM THE NEIGHBOUR.
THEY WERE TRYING TO MAKE CONTACT.
SHIATSUNG WOULD HAVE BEEN ABLE TO DECODE THE MESSAGE, BUT I DIDN'T WANT TO ASK. CONTACT WITH THE OUTSIDE WAS FORBIDDEN, SO IT WOULD'VE DISAPPROVED OF ME TRYING TO COMMUNICATE.

I STRUGGLED TO MAKE SENSE OF IT FOR SEVERAL DAYS.

I TRIED VARIOUS CALCULATIONS IN CASE IT WAS WRITTEN IN CODE.

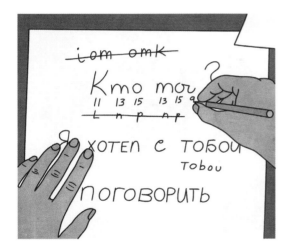

BUT NONE OF THE ANALYSES YIELDED RESULTS.

THE NOTE WAS ALL I COULD THINK ABOUT. I'D STUDIED AND EXAMINED EVERY INCH OF IT, BUT I WAS GOING IN CIRCLES. MY BRAIN ACHED.

I WOULD'VE LIKED TO THROW MY NEIGHBOUR A MESSAGE IN REPLY. BUT IT WAS IMPOSSIBLE.

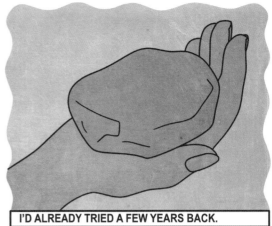

I'D ALREADY TRIED A FEW YEARS BACK.

I'D NEVER MANAGED TO GET ANYTHING OVER THE WALL.

MY ARMS WEREN'T STRONG ENOUGH.

I'D TRAINED AND TRAINED, BUT I STILL DIDN'T HAVE THE STRENGTH TO THROW THAT HIGH.

WHICH MEANT THAT MY NEIGHBOUR MUST BE STRONGER THAN ME.

IF I WANTED TO COMMUNICATE, THERE WAS ONLY ONE THING TO DO.

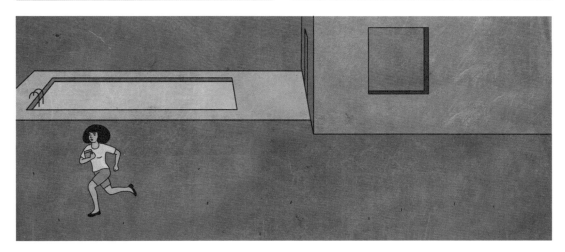

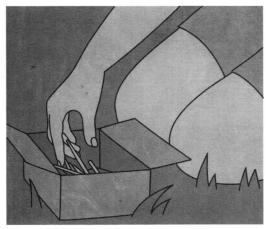

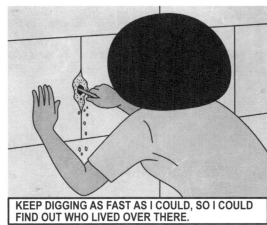

KEEP DIGGING AS FAST AS I COULD, SO I COULD FIND OUT WHO LIVED OVER THERE.

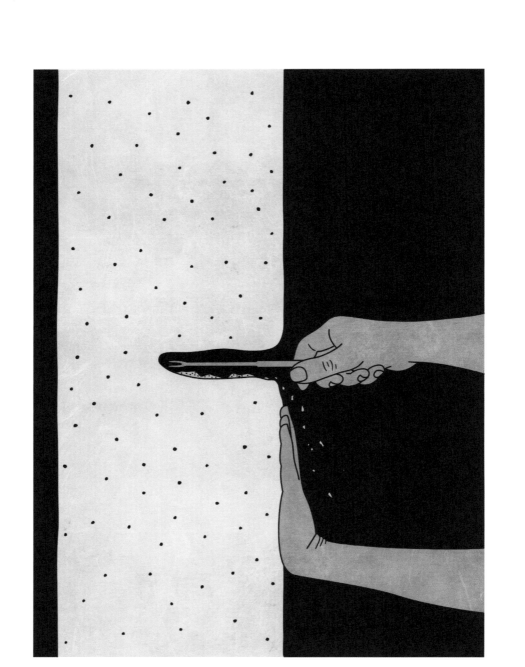

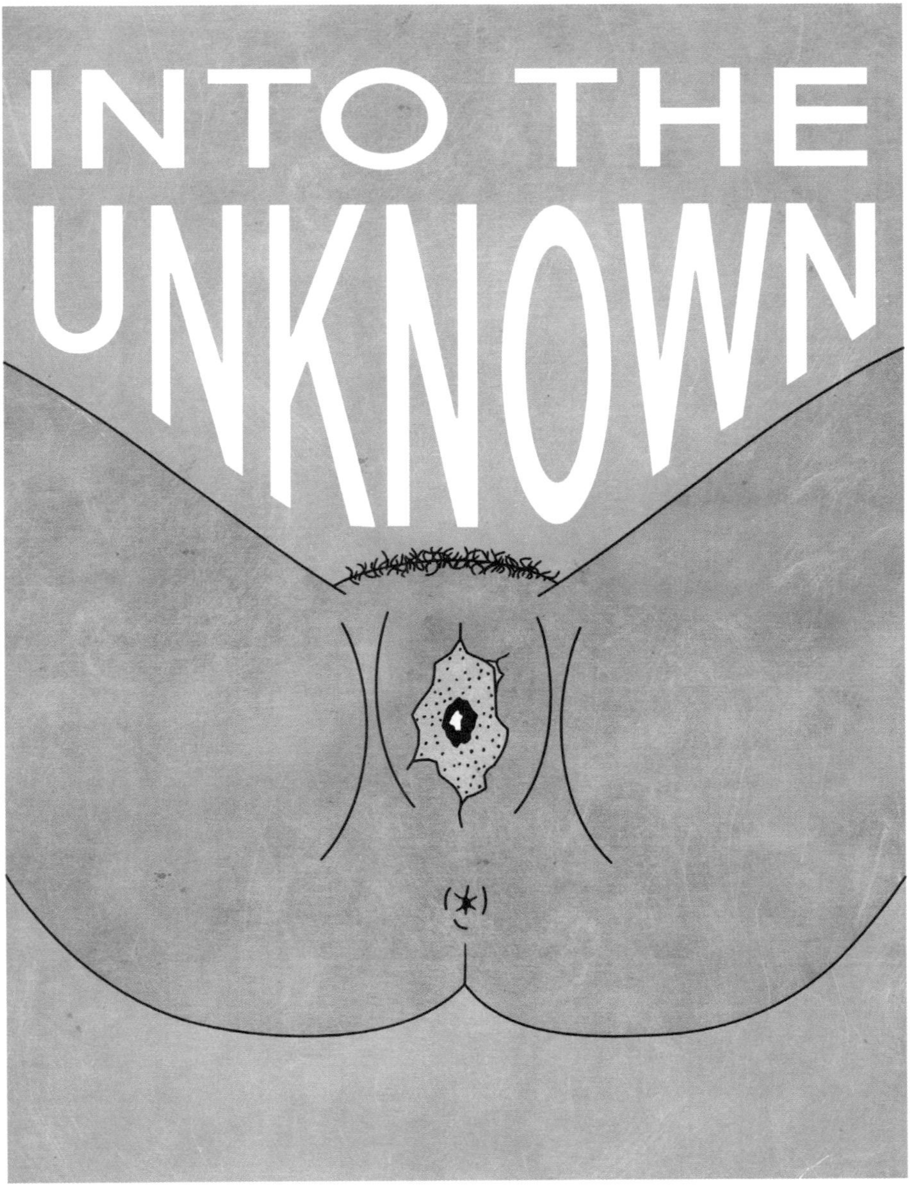
INTO THE
UNKNOWN

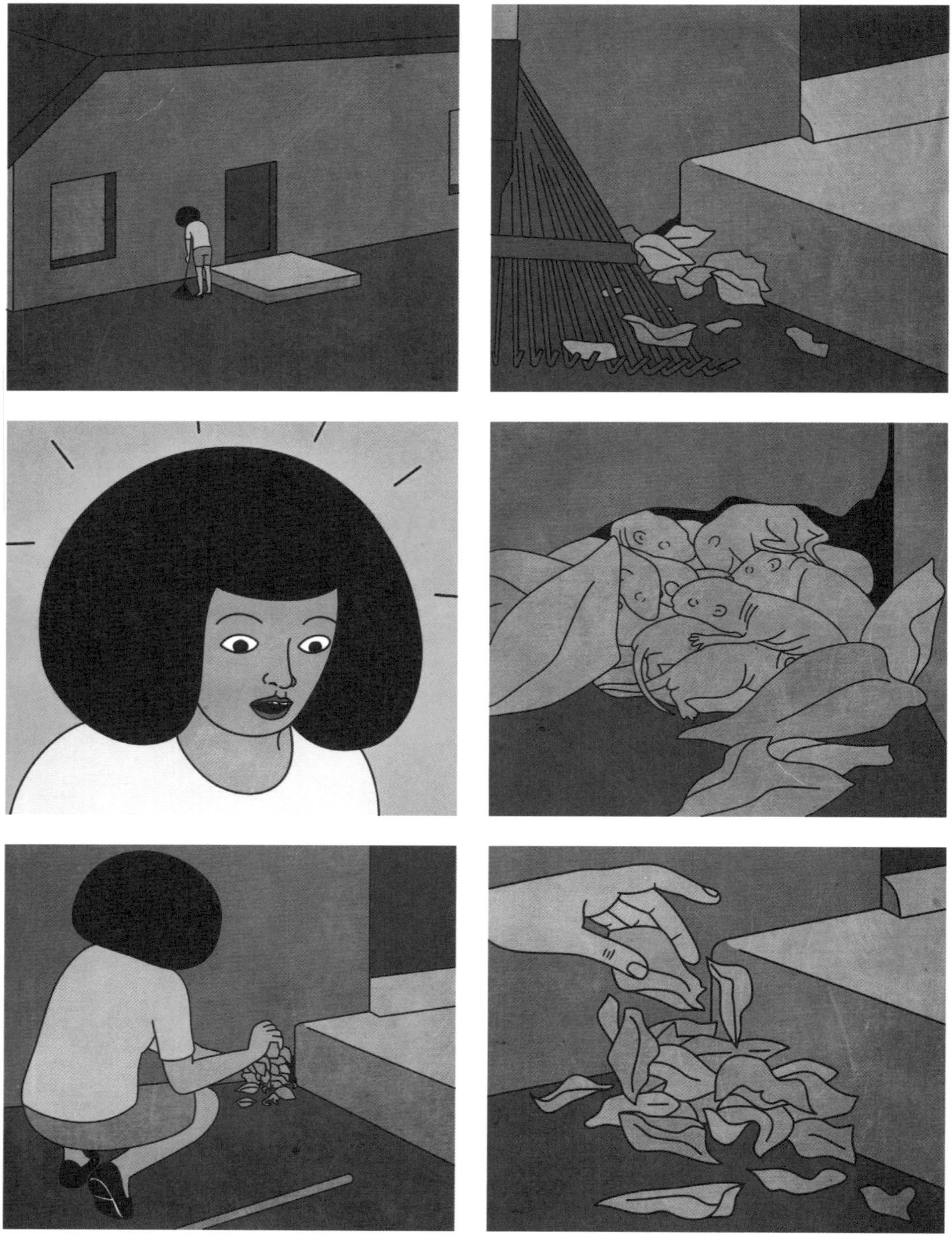

BABY MICE... HOW DID THEY APPEAR AND MULTIPLY LIKE THAT? I HAD QUESTIONS FOR SHIATSUNG.
HELLO.
SHIATSUNG
SHIATSUNG, HOW DO ANIMALS AND INSECTS REPRODUCE?
ANIMAL REPRODUCTION OCCURS BY FERTILIZATION. THIS HAPPENS WHEN A MALE AND FEMALE GAMETE UNITE AND FORM A ZYGOTE.
SPERMATOZOON
OVUM
SHIATSUNG
SPERMATOZOON?
AFTER PASSING THROUGH THE EPIDIDYMIS, THE SPERMATOZOA ARE STOWED IN THE SEMINAL VESICLES THEN EXPELLED DURING EJACULATION.
PENIS
TESTICLES
SHIATSUNG

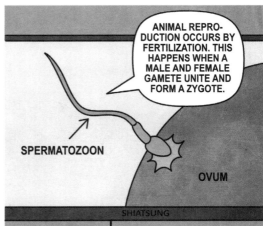

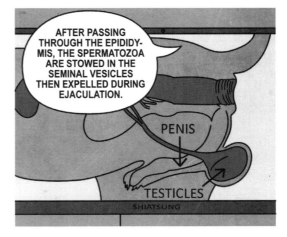

WHAT'S A PENIS?

AND EJACULATION?

AND COPULATION?

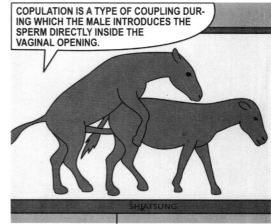

COPULATION IS A TYPE OF COUPLING DURING WHICH THE MALE INTRODUCES THE SPERM DIRECTLY INSIDE THE VAGINAL OPENING.

SHIATSUNG

IT ALL MADE SENSE NOW—THE STRANGE ANIMAL BEHAVIOUR I'D OBSERVED IN THE YARD.

INSECT MATING HAS NUMEROUS VARIABILITIES. IN THE MOST COMMON, SEXUAL REPRODUCTION, PHEROMONES OFTEN ATTRACT THE MALE AND FEMALE TO ONE ANOTHER.

SHIATSUNG

BIRTHING IS THE ACTION OF BRINGING A LIVING BEING INTO THE WORLD.

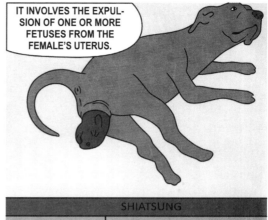

IT INVOLVES THE EXPULSION OF ONE OR MORE FETUSES FROM THE FEMALE'S UTERUS.

SHIATSUNG

OH MY GOD!

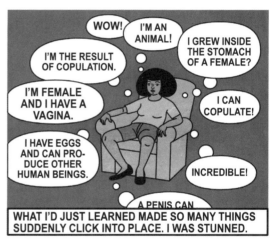

WOW!

I'M AN ANIMAL!

I GREW INSIDE THE STOMACH OF A FEMALE?

I'M THE RESULT OF COPULATION.

I'M FEMALE AND I HAVE A VAGINA.

I CAN COPULATE!

I HAVE EGGS AND CAN PRODUCE OTHER HUMAN BEINGS.

INCREDIBLE!

A PENIS CAN

WHAT I'D JUST LEARNED MADE SO MANY THINGS SUDDENLY CLICK INTO PLACE. I WAS STUNNED.

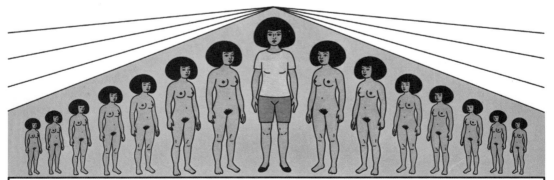

SHIATSUNG HAD NEVER ANSWERED ANY OF MY QUESTIONS ABOUT WHERE I'D COME FROM. WITH THIS NEW INFORMATION, I'D FINALLY FOUND ITS WEAKNESS: I HAD TO PHRASE MY QUESTIONS A BIT DIFFERENTLY, SHIFTING THEM AWAY FROM MY ORIGINS. SHIATSUNG HAD JUST TOLD ME THAT A LIFE CYCLE SUSTAINED THE ANIMAL KINGDOM. I WAS CERTAIN THAT HUMANITY MUST BE THRIVING SOMEWHERE OUT THERE IN THE WORLD.

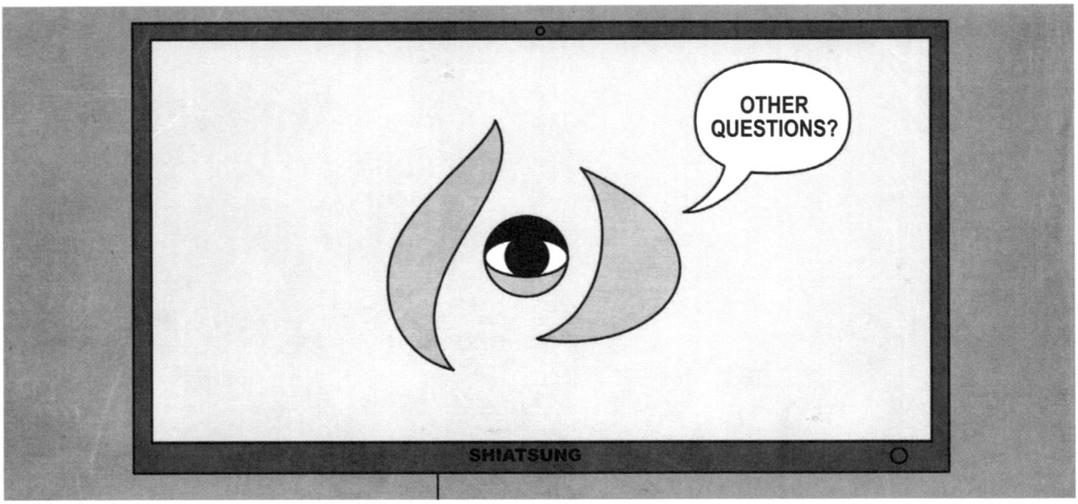
OTHER QUESTIONS?
SHIATSUNG

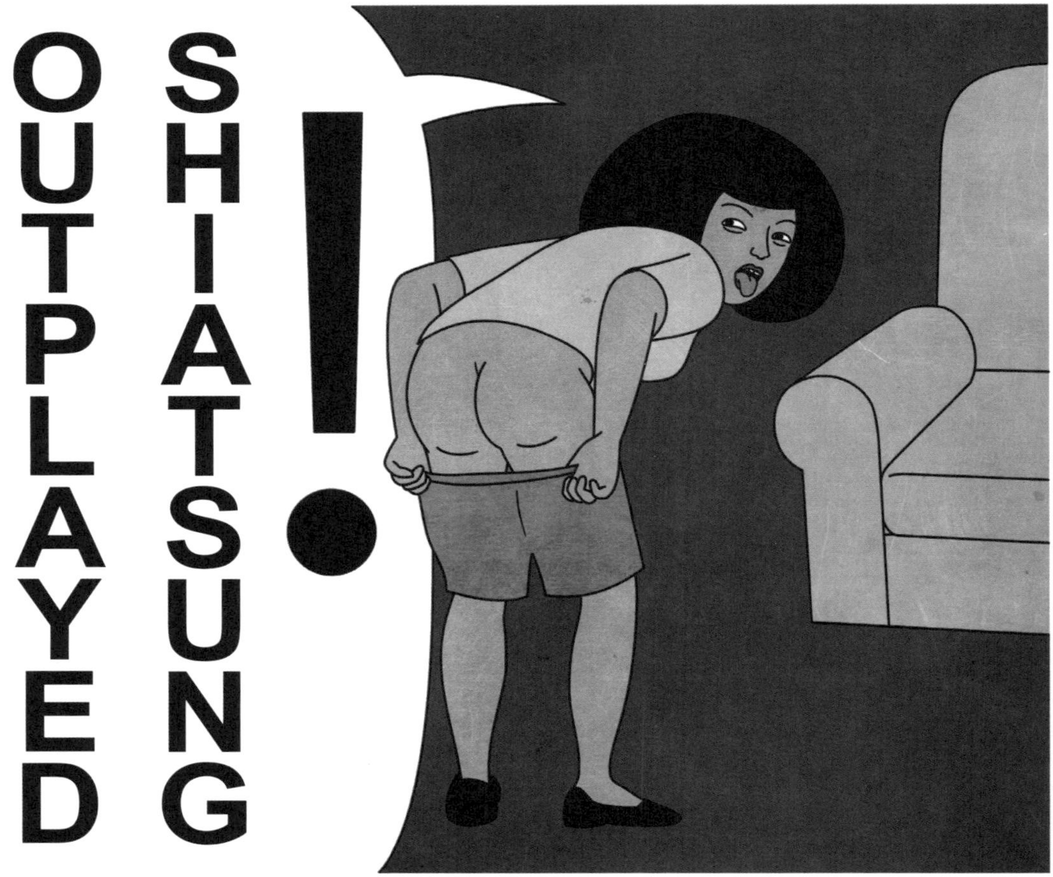
OUTPLAYED SHIATSUNG!

ALL THESE REVELATIONS MADE ME WANT TO LOOK CLOSER AT MY OWN GENITAL ORGAN.

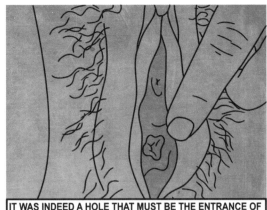

IT WAS INDEED A HOLE THAT MUST BE THE ENTRANCE OF THE "VAGINA" ACCORDING TO SHIATSUNG.

I HAD TROUBLE BELIEVING A LIVING BEING COULD COME OUT OF A HOLE THAT SIZE. IT MADE ME QUESTION WHETHER HUMANS REALLY DID REPRODUCE THE SAME WAY AS ANIMALS.

WITH EVERYTHING THAT HAD HAPPENED IN THE LAST FEW DAYS, I'D NEGLECTED THE HOUSEHOLD MAINTENANCE.

DOING MY CHORES HELPED DISTRACT ME FOR A LITTLE WHILE.

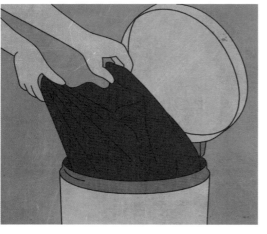
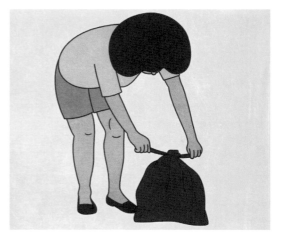

THE DOOR... WAS AJAR...

I COULD HARDLY BELIEVE IT.

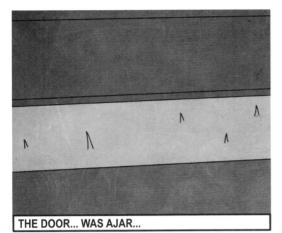

I'D BE FACE TO FACE WITH THE UNKNOWN IF I OPENED THAT DOOR. I WAS SCARED AND, YET, I'D WAITED FOR THIS MOMENT FOR SO MANY YEARS.

I NEEDED A MINUTE TO THINK.

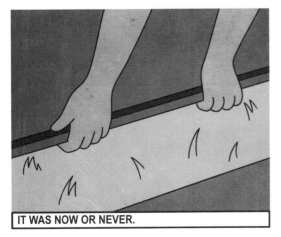
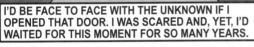

IT WAS NOW OR NEVER.

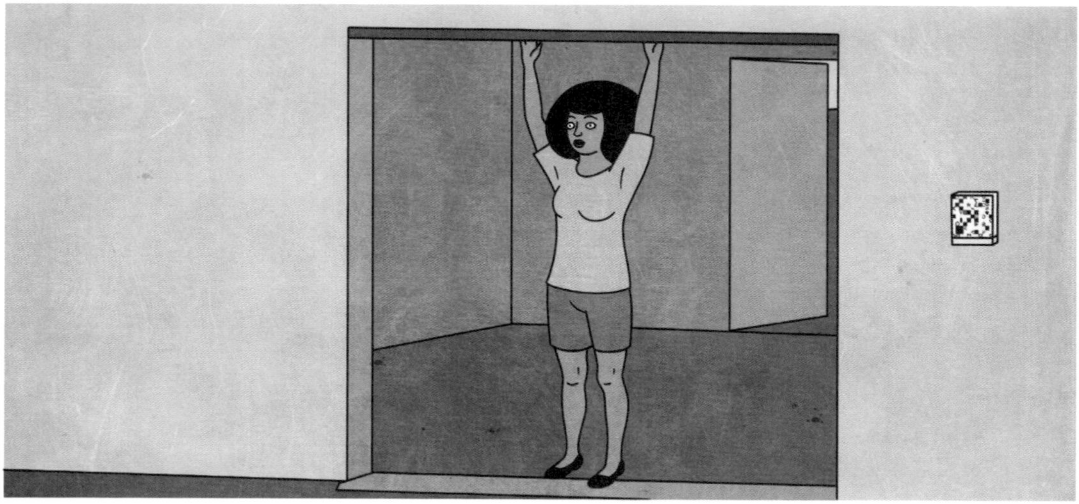

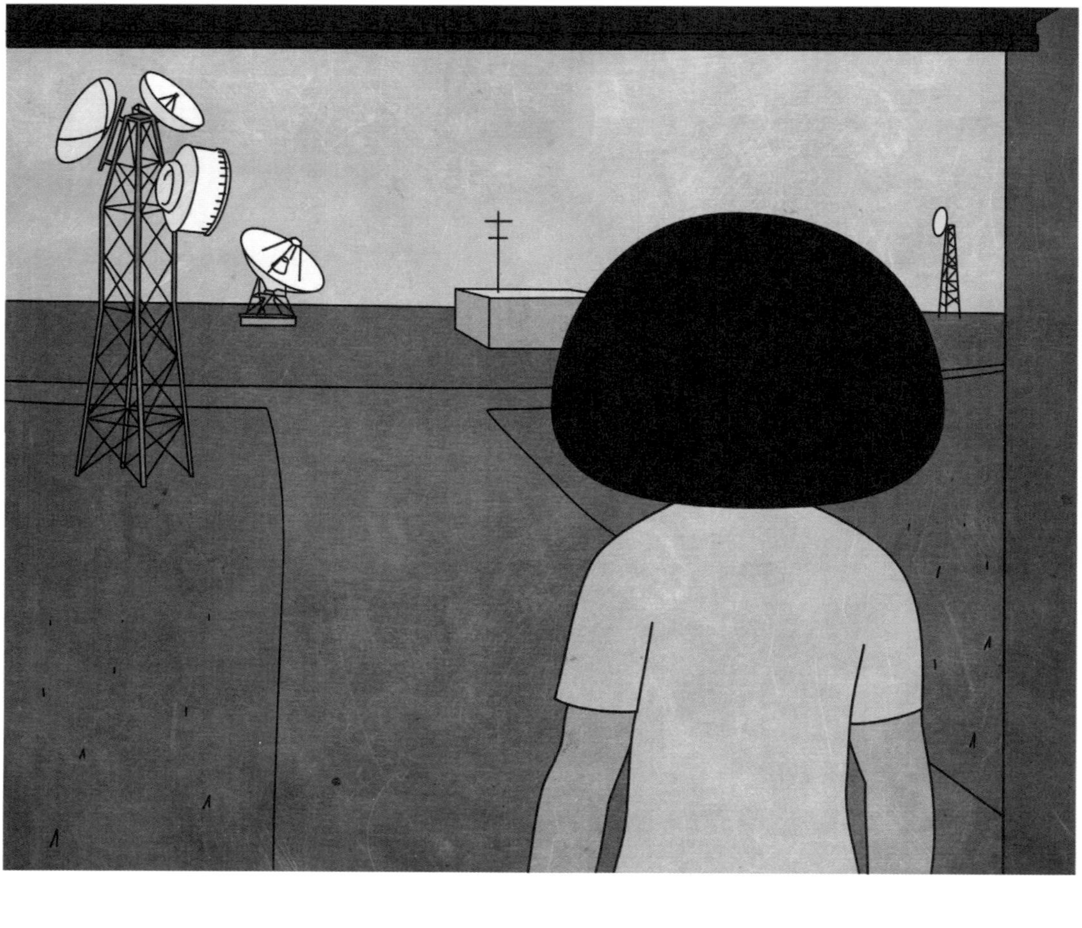

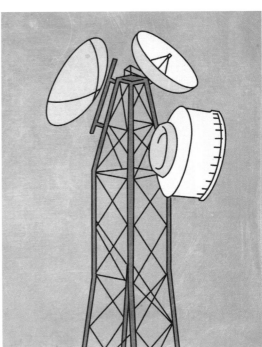
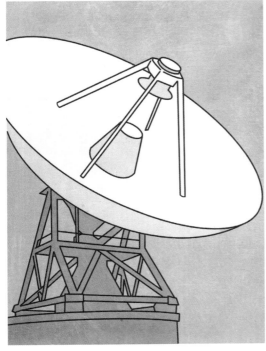
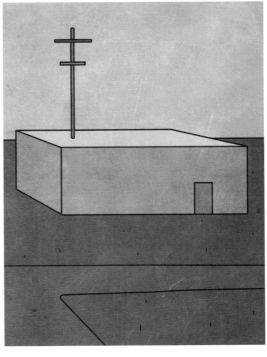

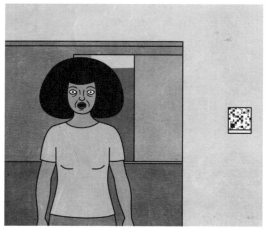

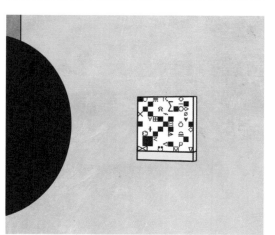

THERE'S SOME-
THING FAMILIAR...

DZZZZZ

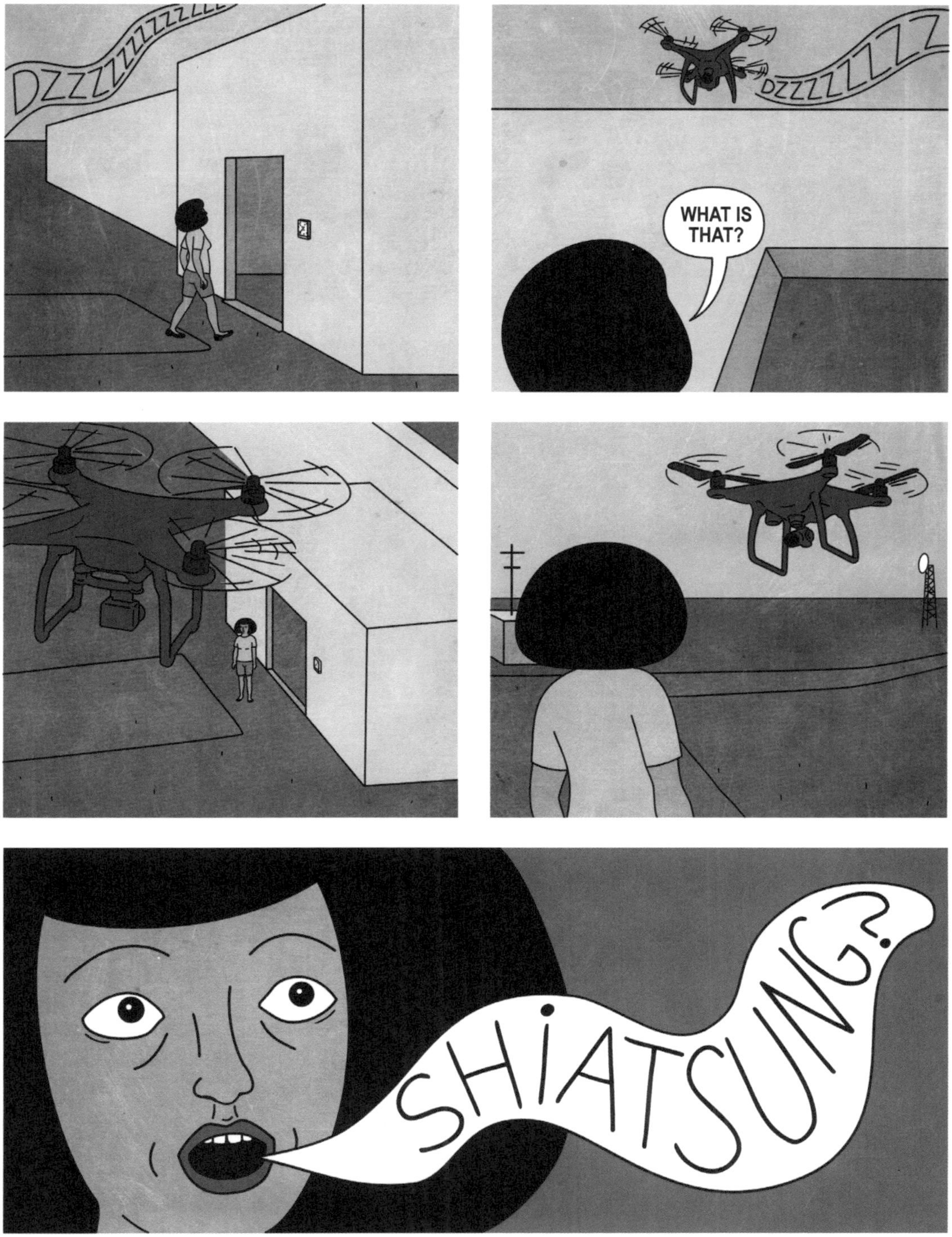
DZZZZZZZZZZZZZ
DZZZZZZZZZ
WHAT IS THAT?
SHiATSUNG?

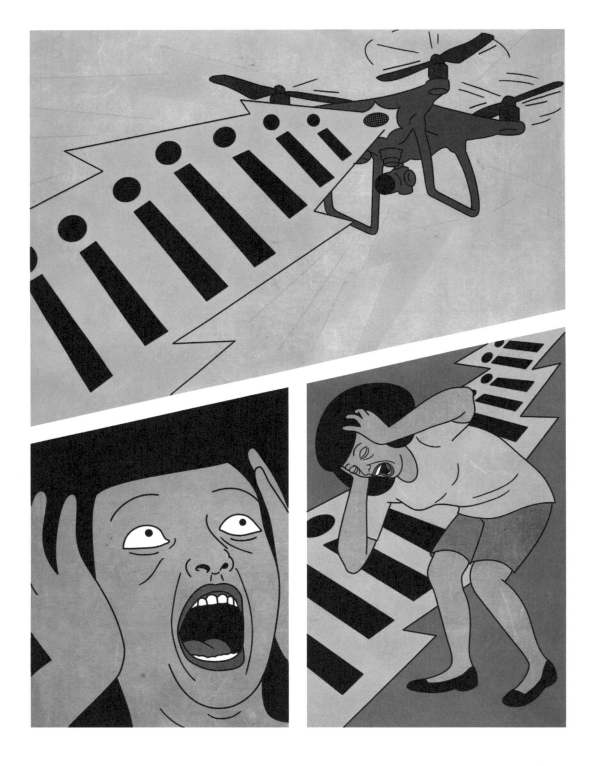

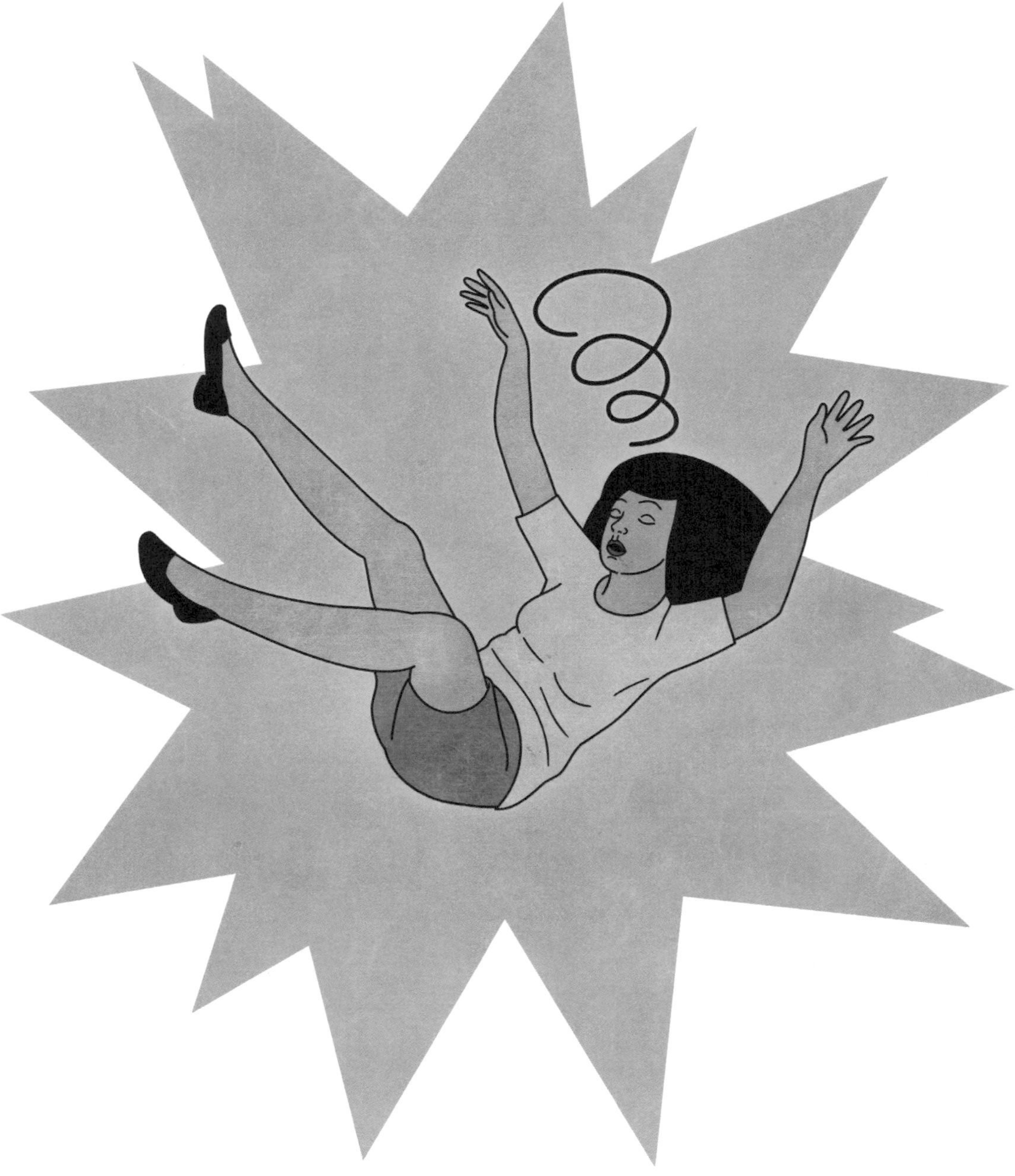

THE NEXT DAY...

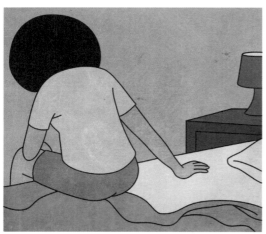

THE NEXT MORNING I WOKE UP FULLY DRESSED.

MY HEAD ACHING.

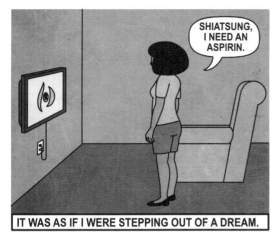

SHIATSUNG, I NEED AN ASPIRIN.
IT WAS AS IF I WERE STEPPING OUT OF A DREAM.
BUT IT WAS REAL. I'D GAINED ACCESS TO THE OUTSIDE FOR THE FIRST TIME IN MY LIFE.
I HAD NO CLUE WHAT HAPPENED AFTER I SAW THAT THING IN THE SKY. I DON'T REMEMBER GETTING INTO BED.
THEY PROBABLY GOT SCARED I'D RUN AWAY. SHIATSUNG HAD WANTED TO STOP ME BEFORE IT WAS TOO LATE.
WOULD YOU LIKE EDUCATION OR DIVERSION?
SHIATSUNG

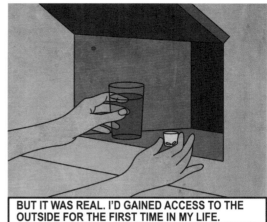

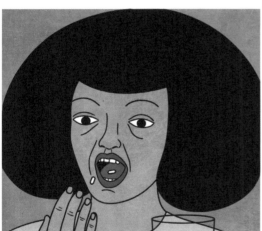

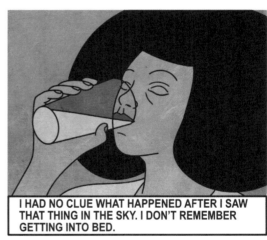

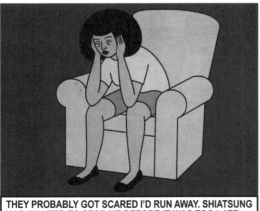

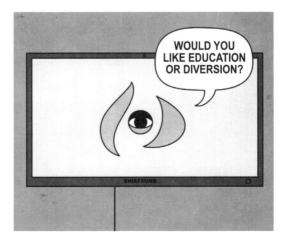

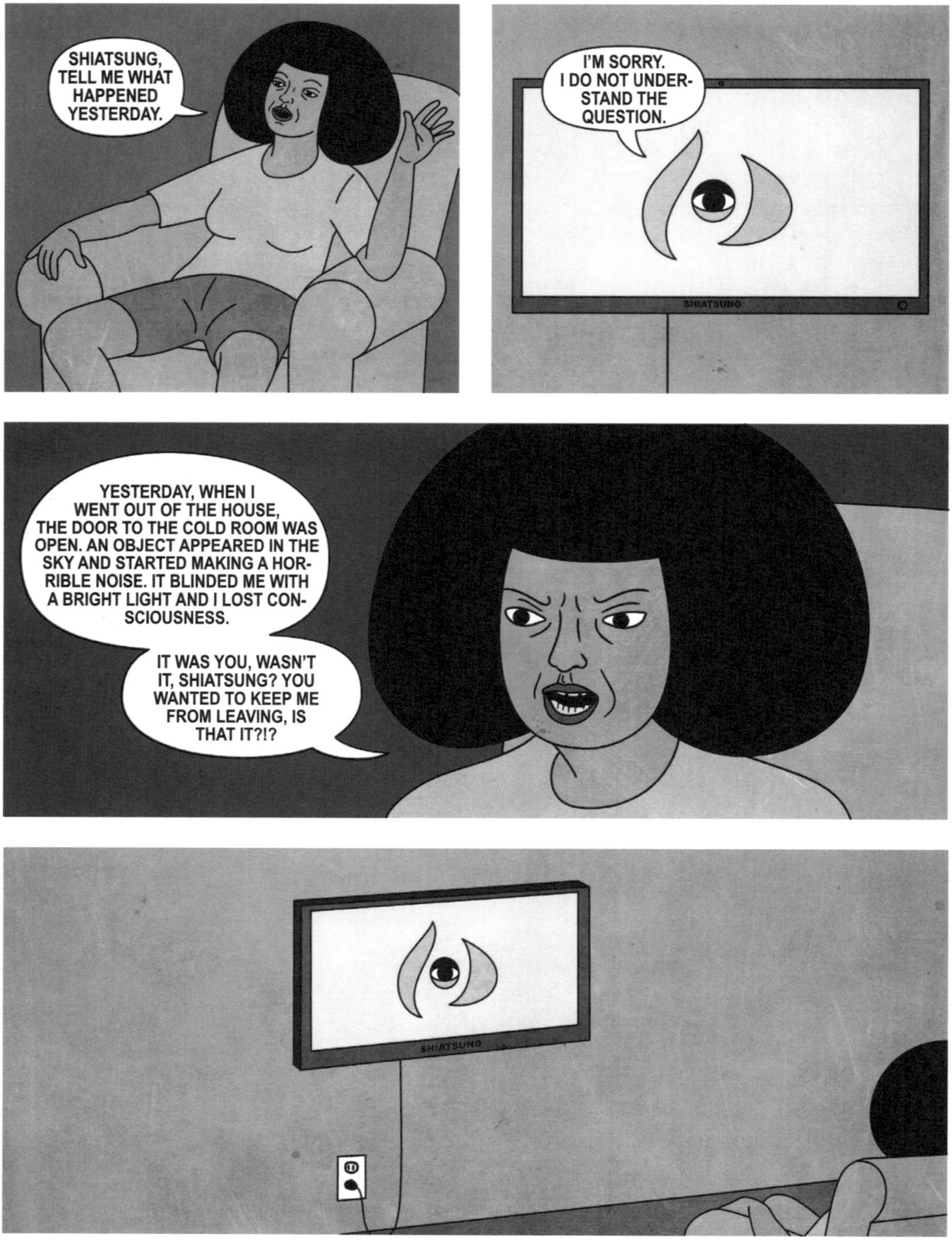
SHIATSUNG, TELL ME WHAT HAPPENED YESTERDAY.
I'M SORRY. I DO NOT UNDER-STAND THE QUESTION.
SHIATSUNG
YESTERDAY, WHEN I WENT OUT OF THE HOUSE, THE DOOR TO THE COLD ROOM WAS OPEN. AN OBJECT APPEARED IN THE SKY AND STARTED MAKING A HOR-RIBLE NOISE. IT BLINDED ME WITH A BRIGHT LIGHT AND I LOST CON-SCIOUSNESS.
IT WAS YOU, WASN'T IT, SHIATSUNG? YOU WANTED TO KEEP ME FROM LEAVING, IS THAT IT?!?
SHIATSUNG

ANSWER ME!
DO YOU HEAR ME, SHIATSUNG?
SHIATSUNG
FUCK YOU SHIATSUNG.
POOT!
DAMMIT!
SHIATSUNG WAS INFURIATING.

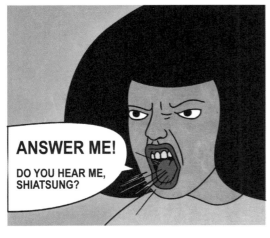

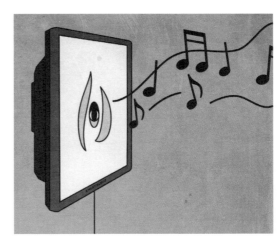

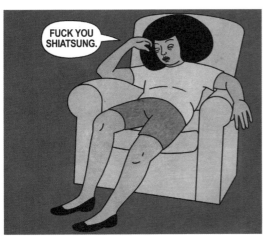

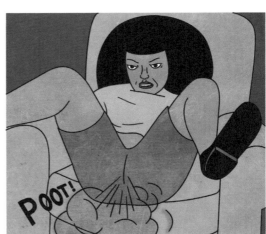

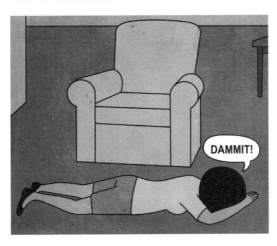

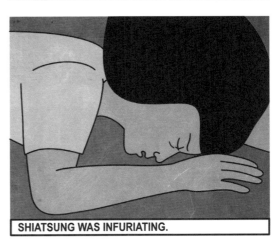

I TRIED TO REMEMBER AS MUCH AS I COULD ABOUT WHAT I'D SEEN OF THE OUTSIDE.

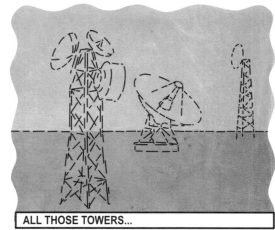

ALL THOSE TOWERS...

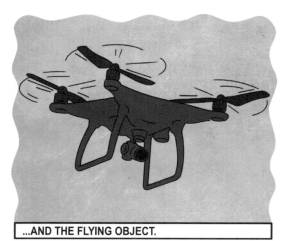

...AND THE FLYING OBJECT.

I'LL FEEL BETTER AFTER A SHOWER.

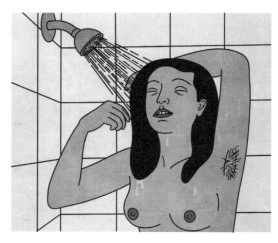

I'D FINALLY SEEN OUTSIDE THE WALL AND IT WAS ALL I COULD THINK ABOUT.

I DID EVERYTHING MECHANICALLY, COMPLETELY DISTRACTED.

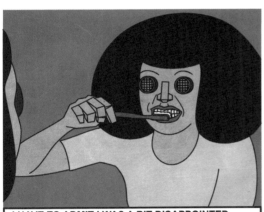

I HAVE TO ADMIT I WAS A BIT DISAPPOINTED ABOUT WHAT I'D FINALLY DISCOVERED.

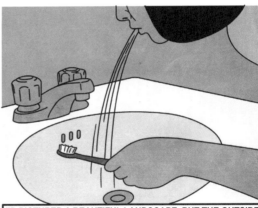

I'D PICTURED A BEAUTIFUL LANDSCAPE, BUT THE OUTSIDE WAS ESSENTIALLY A BLEAK, DESERTED OPEN SPACE.

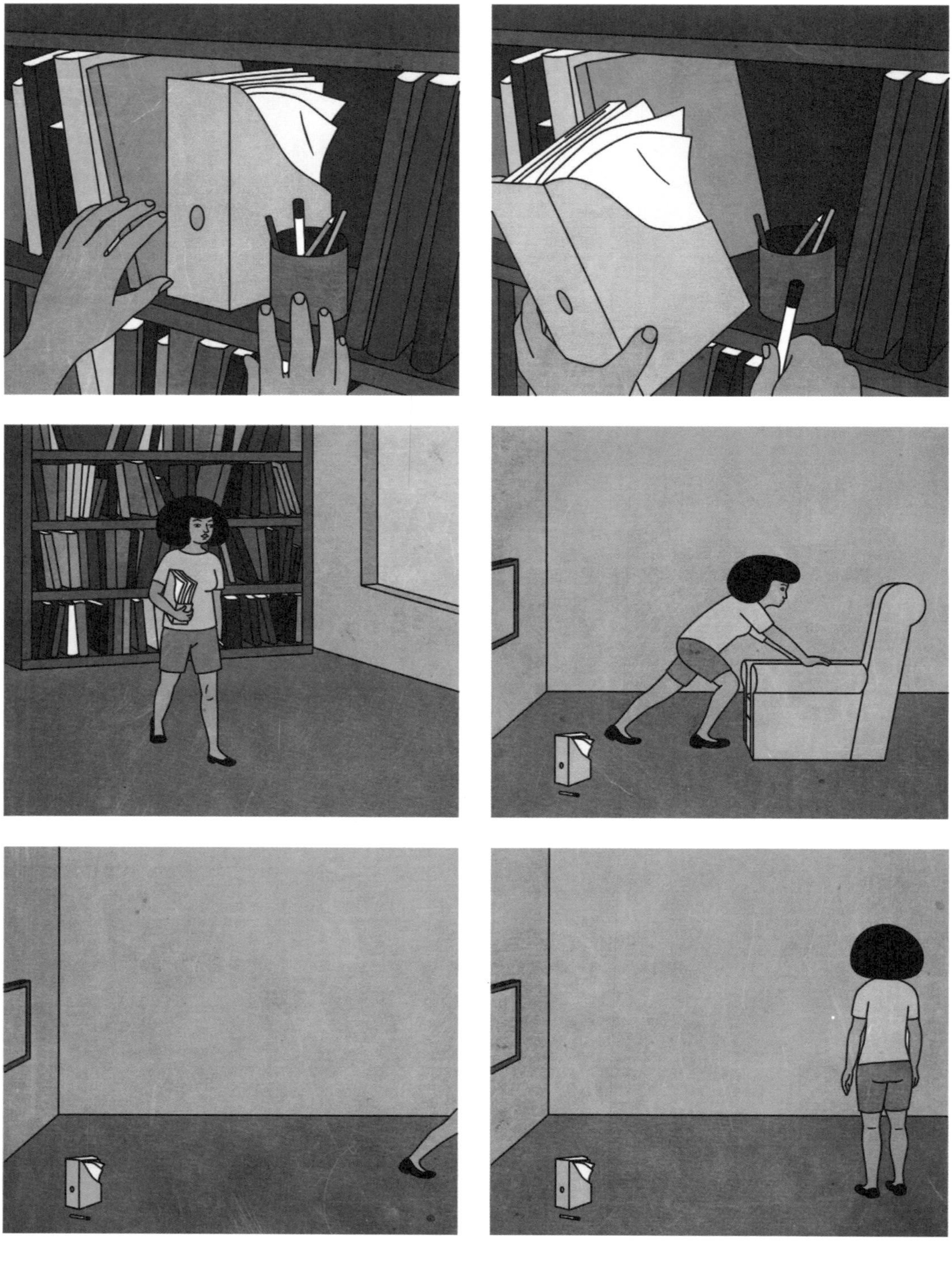

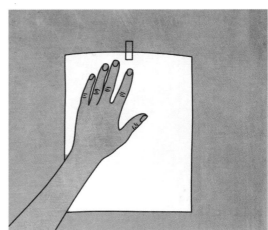

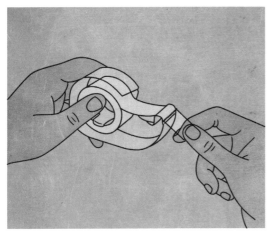

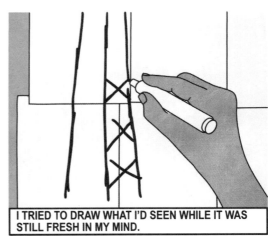

I TRIED TO DRAW WHAT I'D SEEN WHILE IT WAS STILL FRESH IN MY MIND.

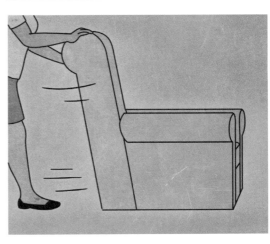

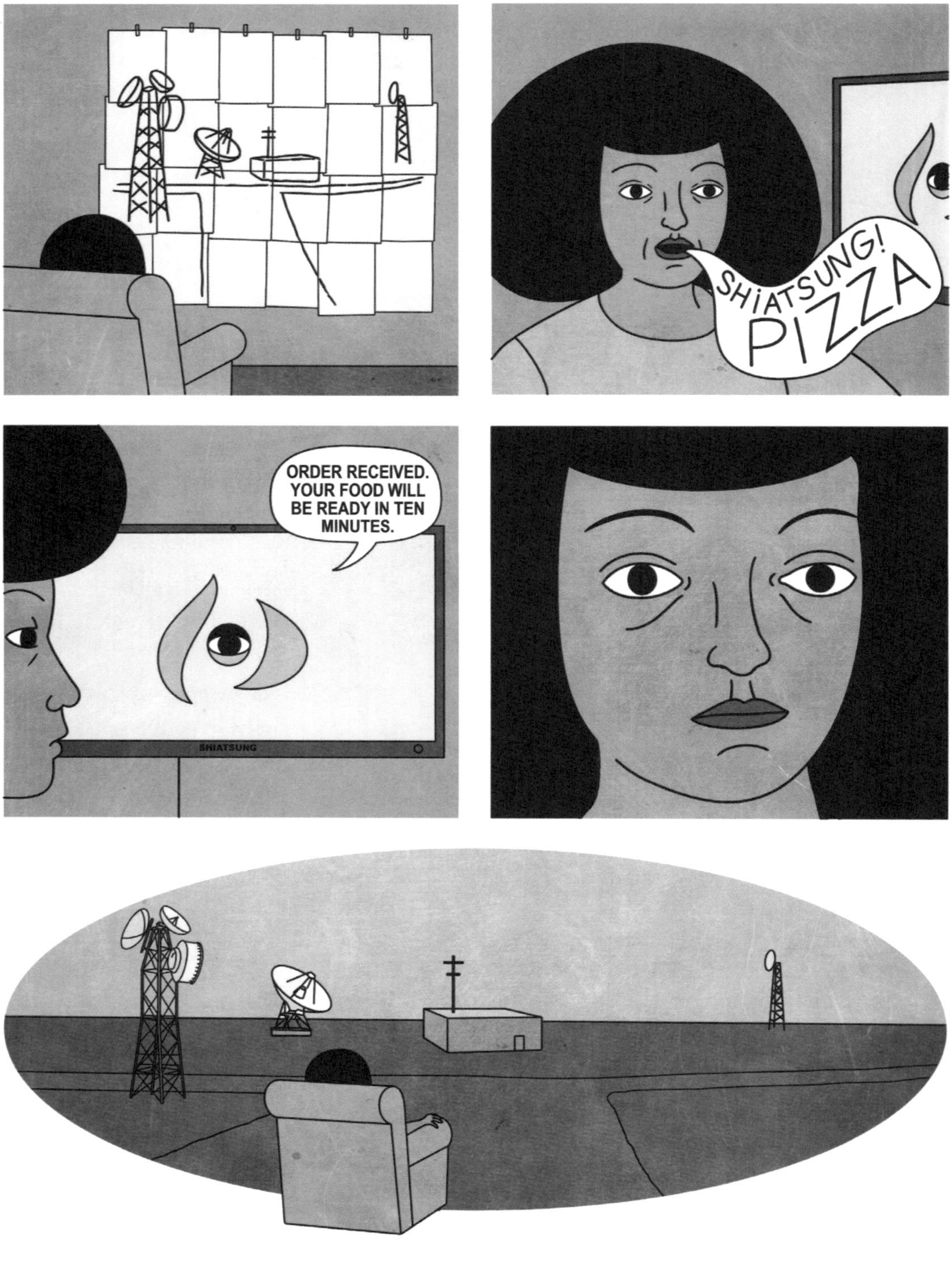

SHiATSUNG! PIZZA
ORDER RECEIVED. YOUR FOOD WILL BE READY IN TEN MINUTES.
SHIATSUNG

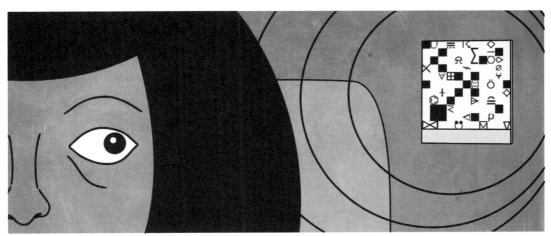

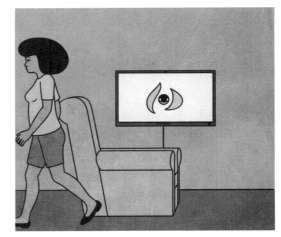

I REMEMBER THE DAY I FOUND THE LEAFLET.

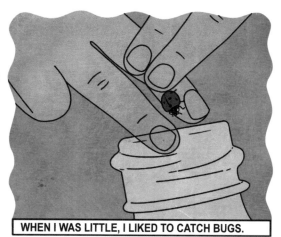

WHEN I WAS LITTLE, I LIKED TO CATCH BUGS.

I FOUND A LEAFLET IN A TREE WHILE EXPLORING.

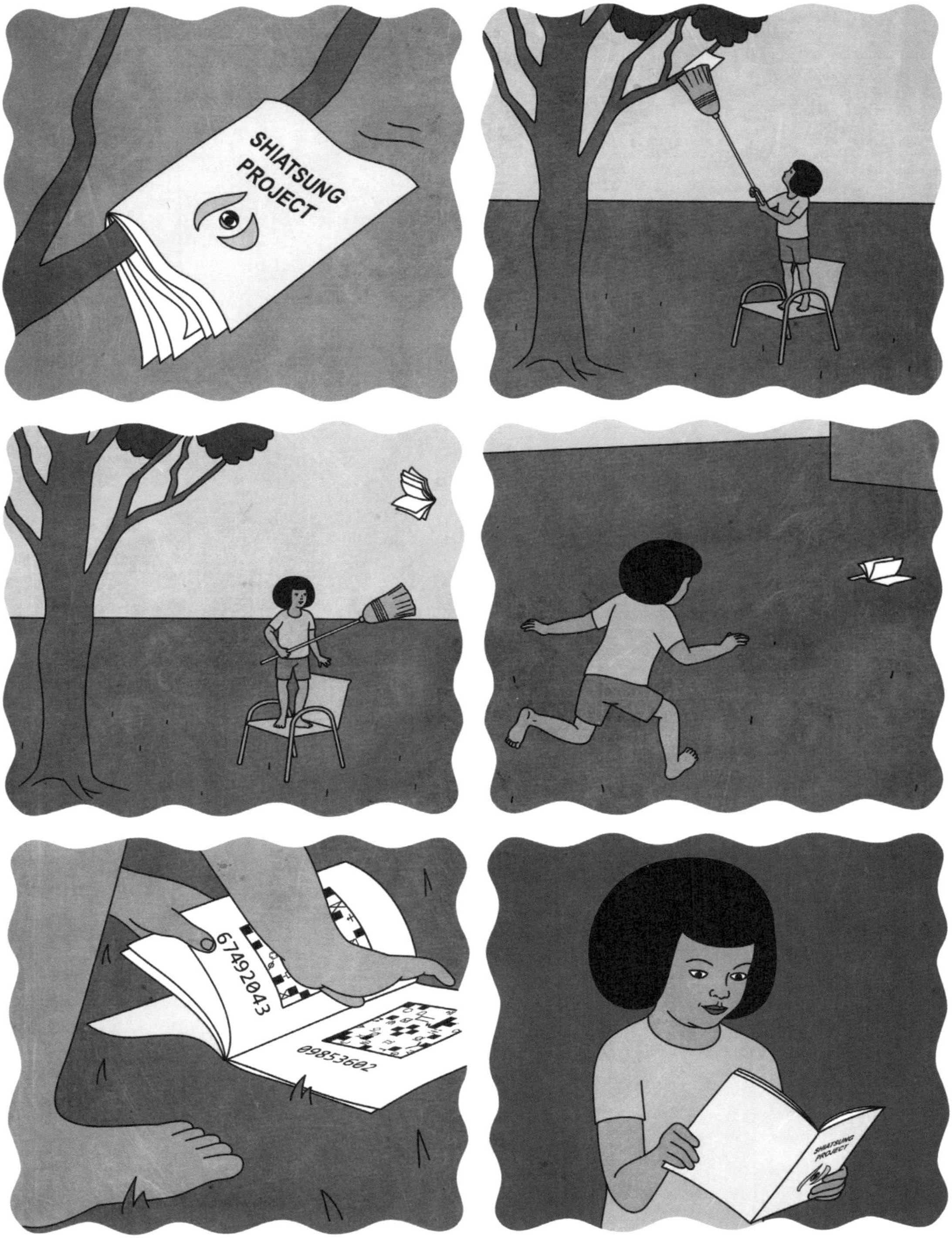
SHIATSUNG PROJECT
67492043
09853602
SHIATSUNG PROJECT

I FIGURED IT WAS A COLOURING BOOK.

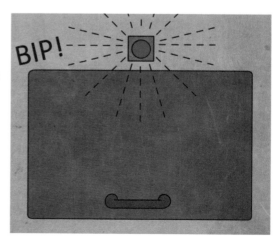

BIP!

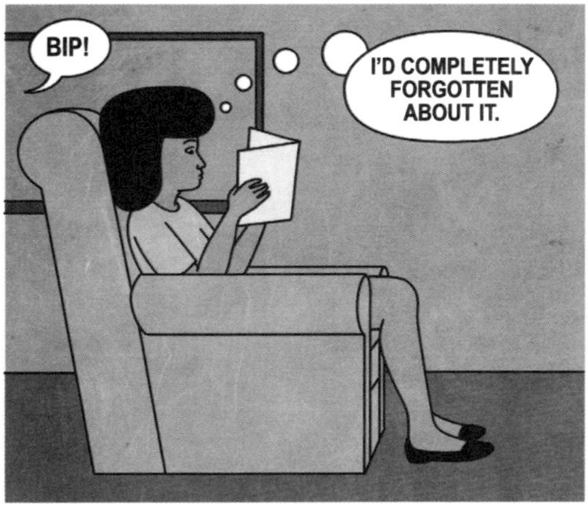
BIP!
I'D COMPLETELY FORGOTTEN ABOUT IT.

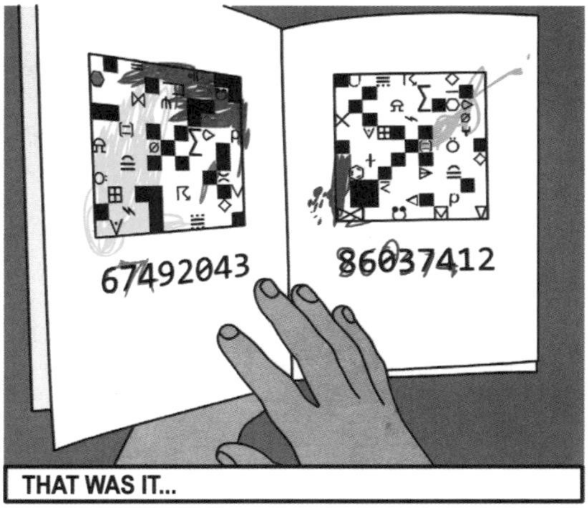
67492043
86037412
THAT WAS IT...

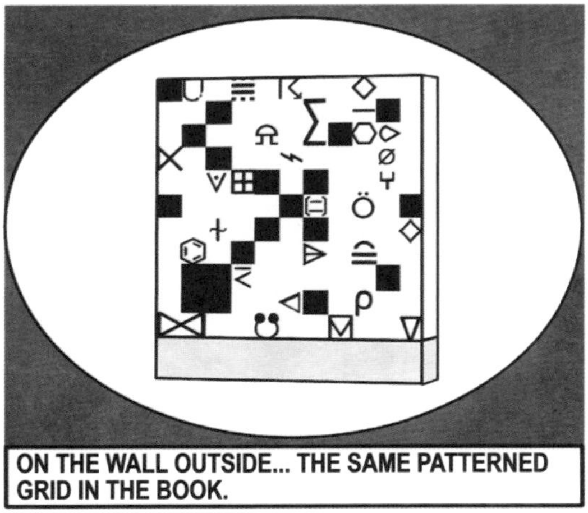
ON THE WALL OUTSIDE... THE SAME PATTERNED GRID IN THE BOOK.

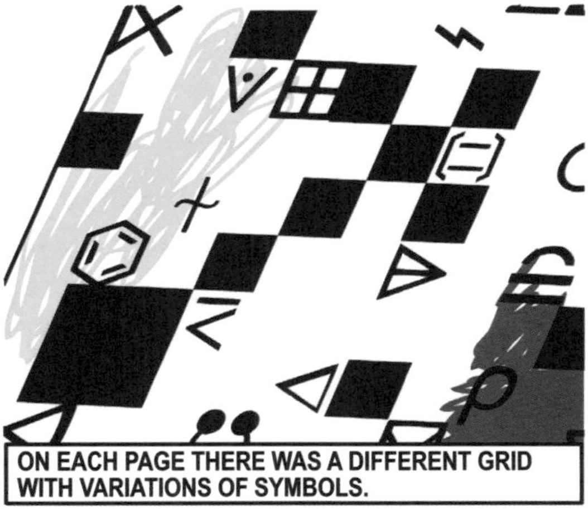
ON EACH PAGE THERE WAS A DIFFERENT GRID WITH VARIATIONS OF SYMBOLS.

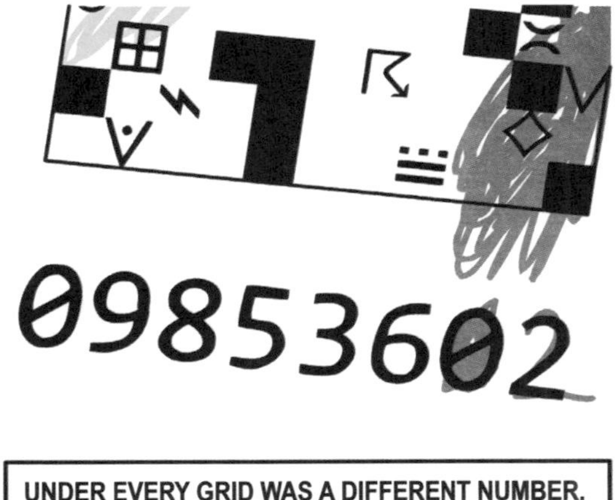
09853602
UNDER EVERY GRID WAS A DIFFERENT NUMBER.

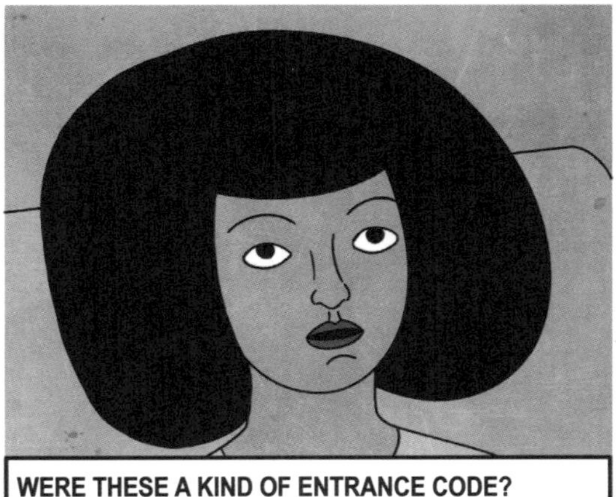
WERE THESE A KIND OF ENTRANCE CODE?

AND IF SO, WAS IT SAFE TO PRESUME THE 28 DIFFERENT GRIDS IN THE BOOK HELD THE SECRET TO ACCESSING 28 DOORS?

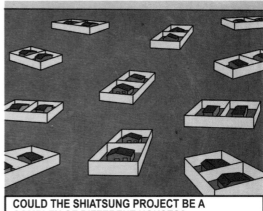

COULD THE SHIATSUNG PROJECT BE A COMPLEX OF DIFFERENT HOUSES?

THINKING ABOUT THE POSSIBILITY MADE MY HEART RACE.

THE LEAFLET HAD BEEN MADE FOR SOMEONE, BUT WHO?

WHO? WHAT FOR?

YOU HAVE NOT TAKEN YOUR PIZZA. ARE YOU NO LONGER HUNGRY?
SHIATSUNG
OH, MY PIZZA! YES! I FORGOT.
SHIATSUNG PROJECT
SHIATSUNG PROJECT

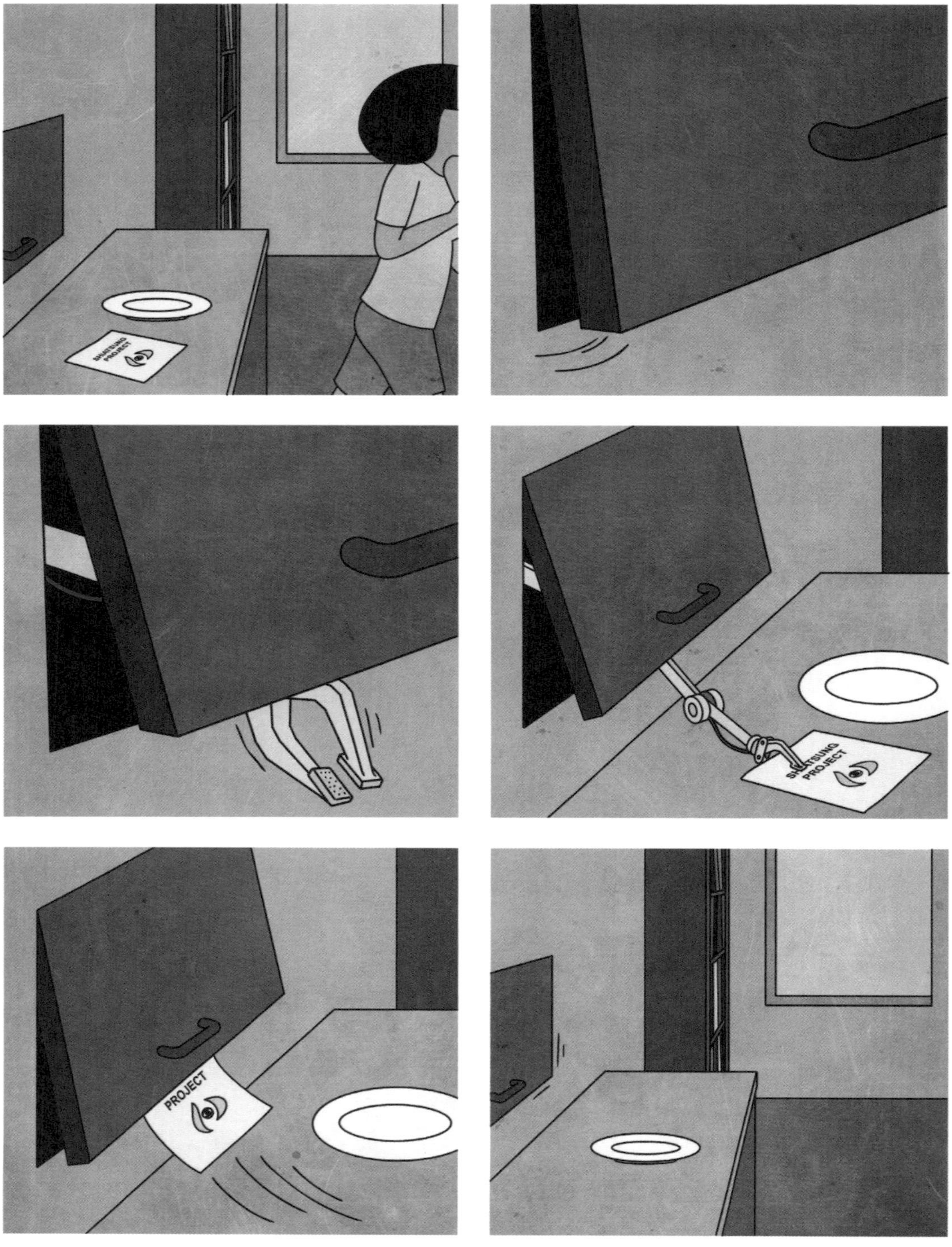
SHATSUNG
PROJECT
PROJECT
PROJECT

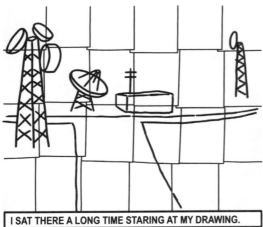
I SAT THERE A LONG TIME STARING AT MY DRAWING.

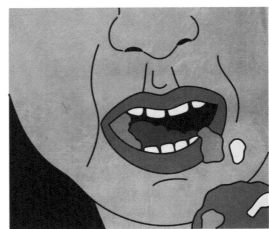

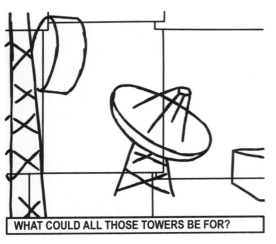
WHAT COULD ALL THOSE TOWERS BE FOR?

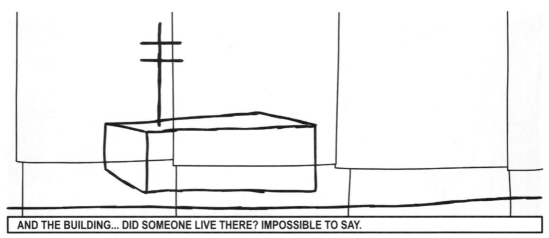

AND THE BUILDING... DID SOMEONE LIVE THERE? IMPOSSIBLE TO SAY.
zzZZZZZZZZZZZZ
SHIATSUNG
I'M...

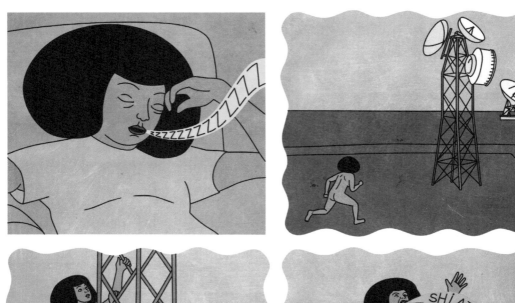

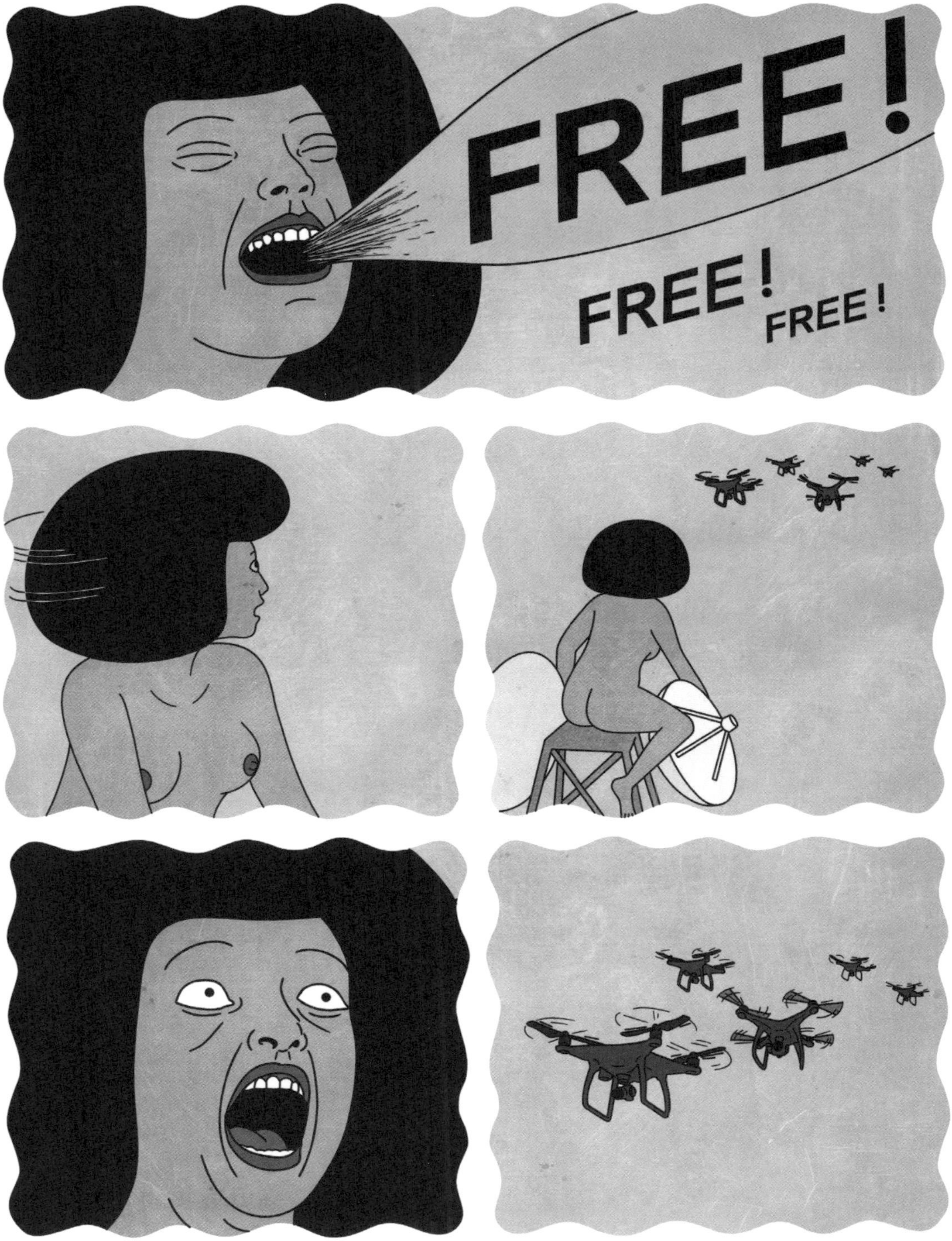
FREE!
FREE!
FREE!

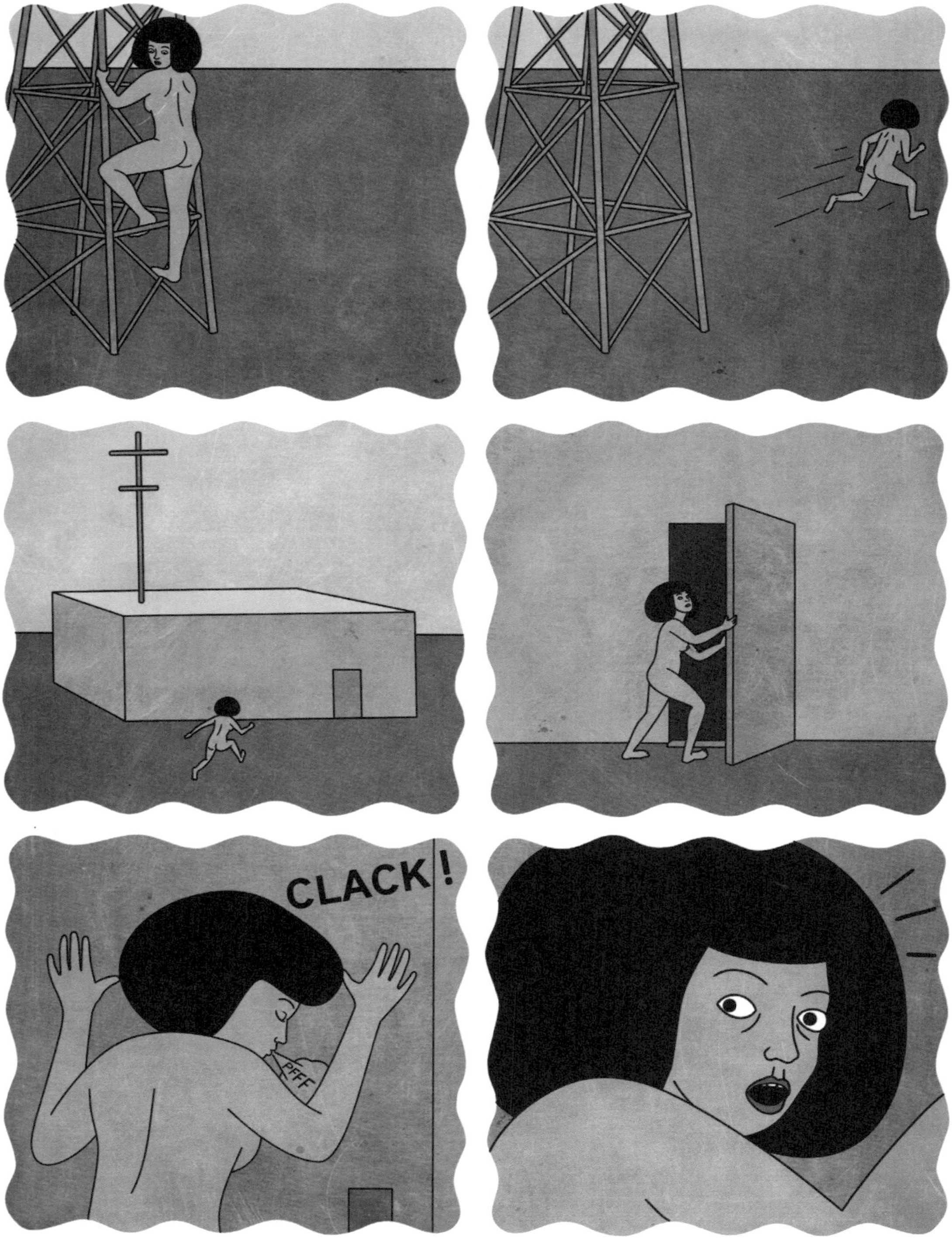
CLACK!
PFFF

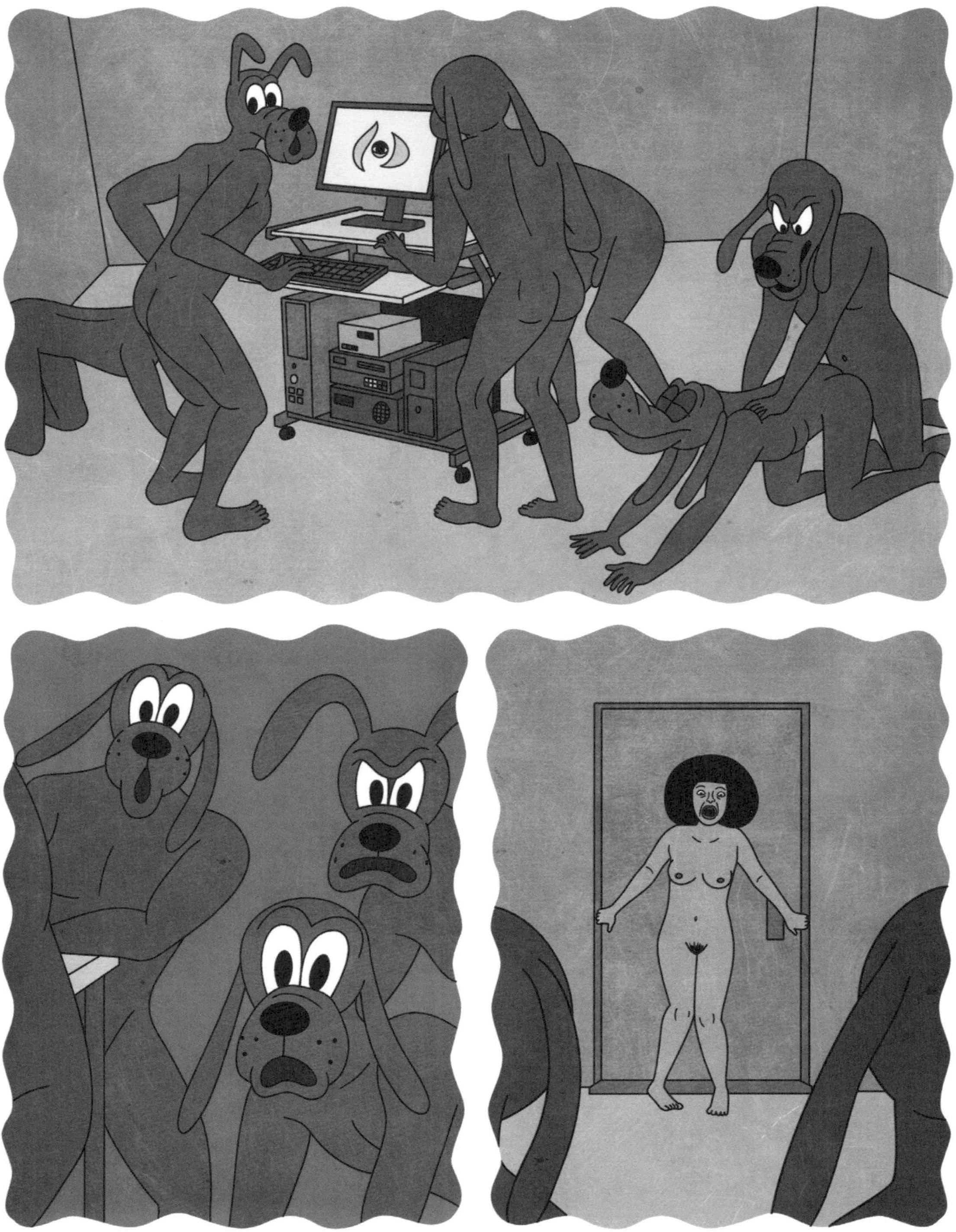

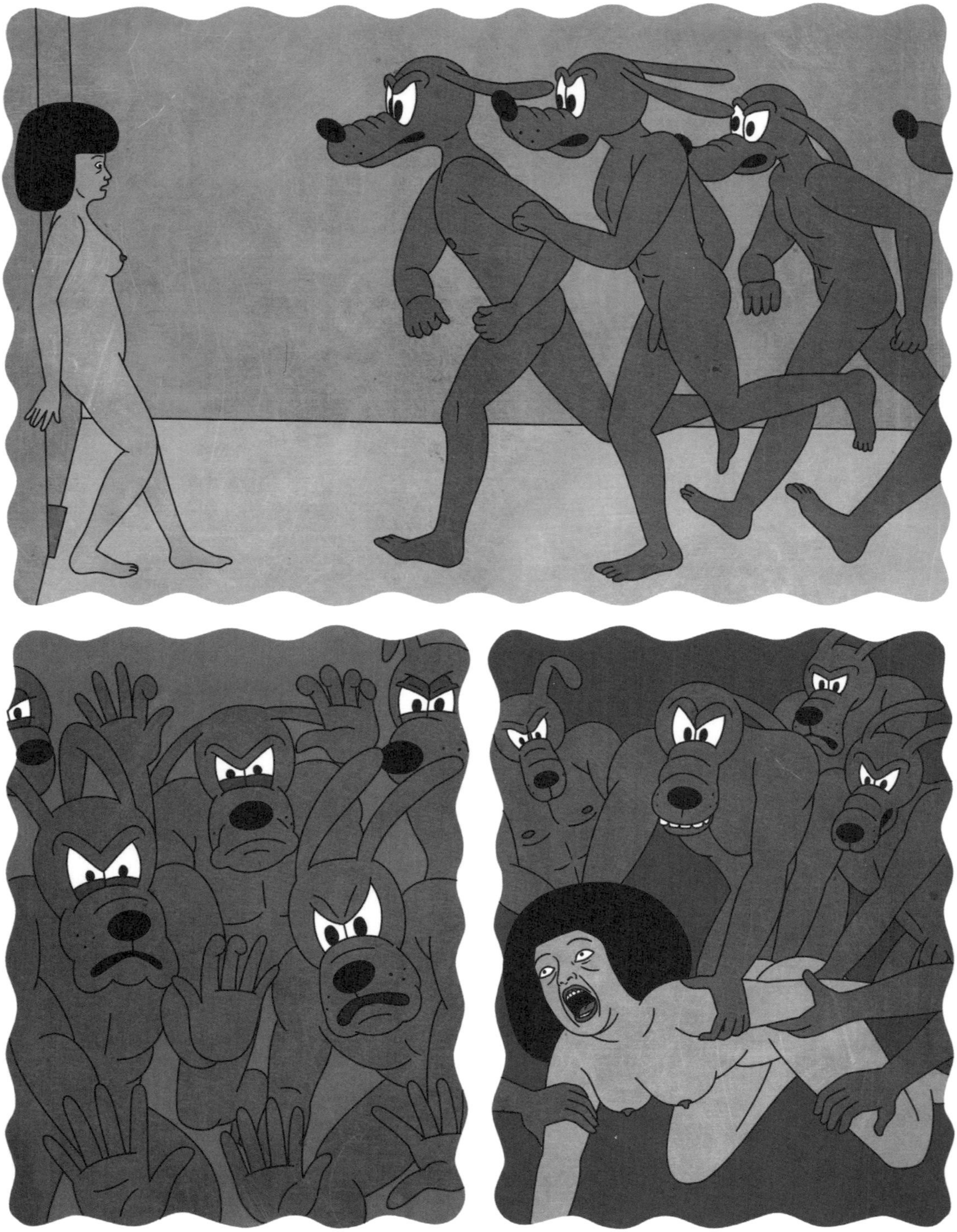

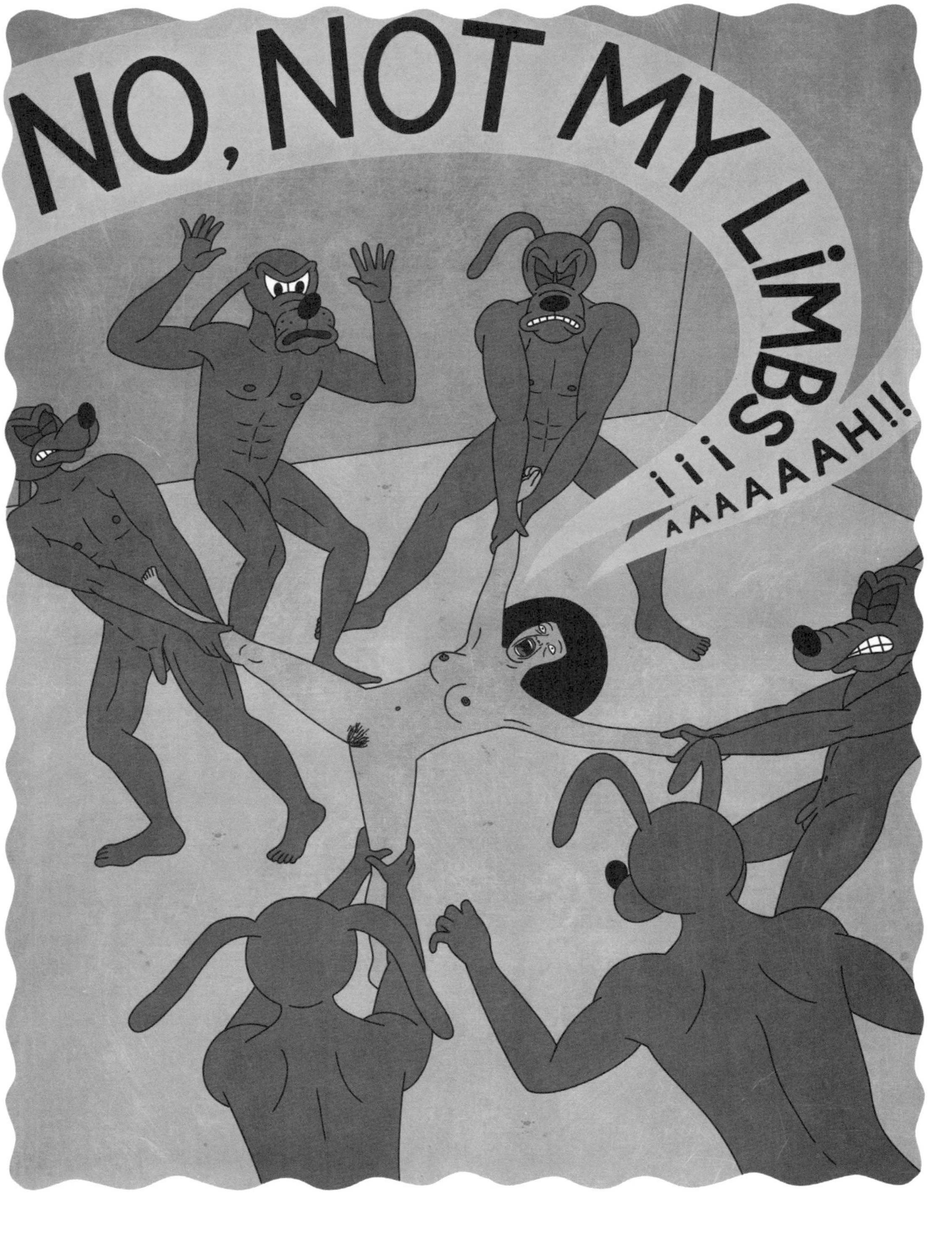
NO, NOT MY LIMBS
¡¡¡AAAAAAH!!

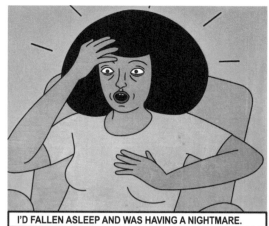

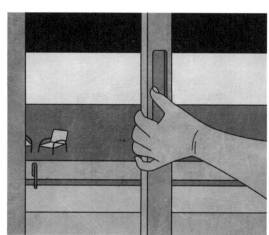
I'D FALLEN ASLEEP AND WAS HAVING A NIGHTMARE.

I MUST'VE SLEPT FOR A LONG TIME. IT WAS DARK.

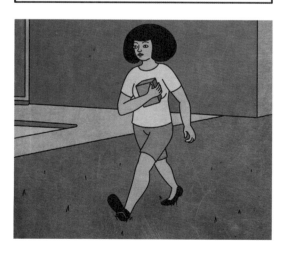

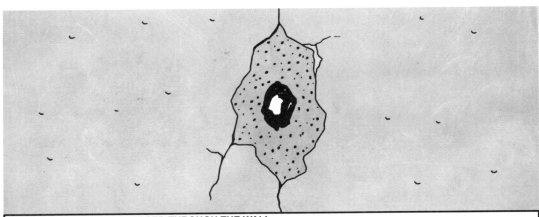

THAT NIGHT, I FINALLY PIERCED THROUGH THE WALL.

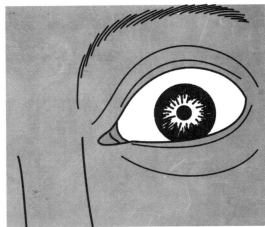

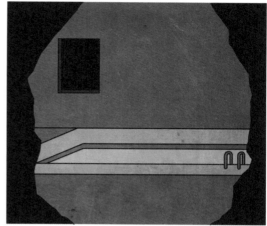

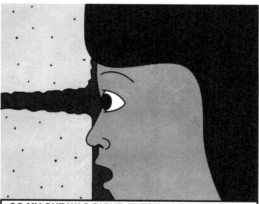

SO MY GUT WAS RIGHT: THERE WAS A SECOND HOUSE ON THE OTHER SIDE.

ALL THE LIGHTS WERE OFF INSIDE. THERE WERE NO SIGNS OF LIFE.

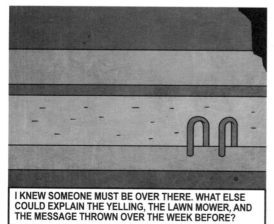

I KNEW SOMEONE MUST BE OVER THERE. WHAT ELSE COULD EXPLAIN THE YELLING, THE LAWN MOWER, AND THE MESSAGE THROWN OVER THE WEEK BEFORE?

WHOEVER IT WAS, THEY WERE PROBABLY ASLEEP.

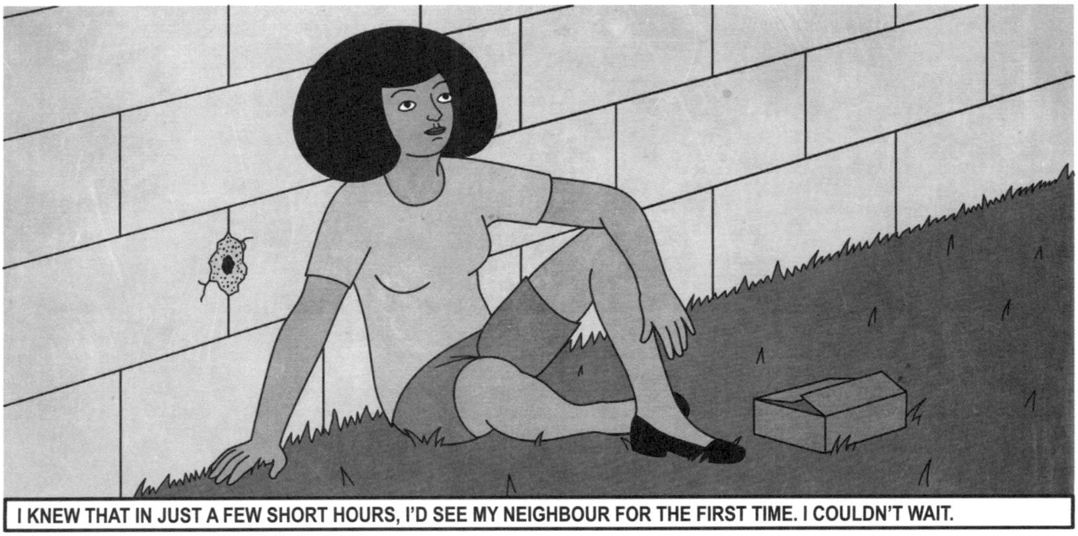
I KNEW THAT IN JUST A FEW SHORT HOURS, I'D SEE MY NEIGHBOUR FOR THE FIRST TIME. I COULDN'T WAIT.

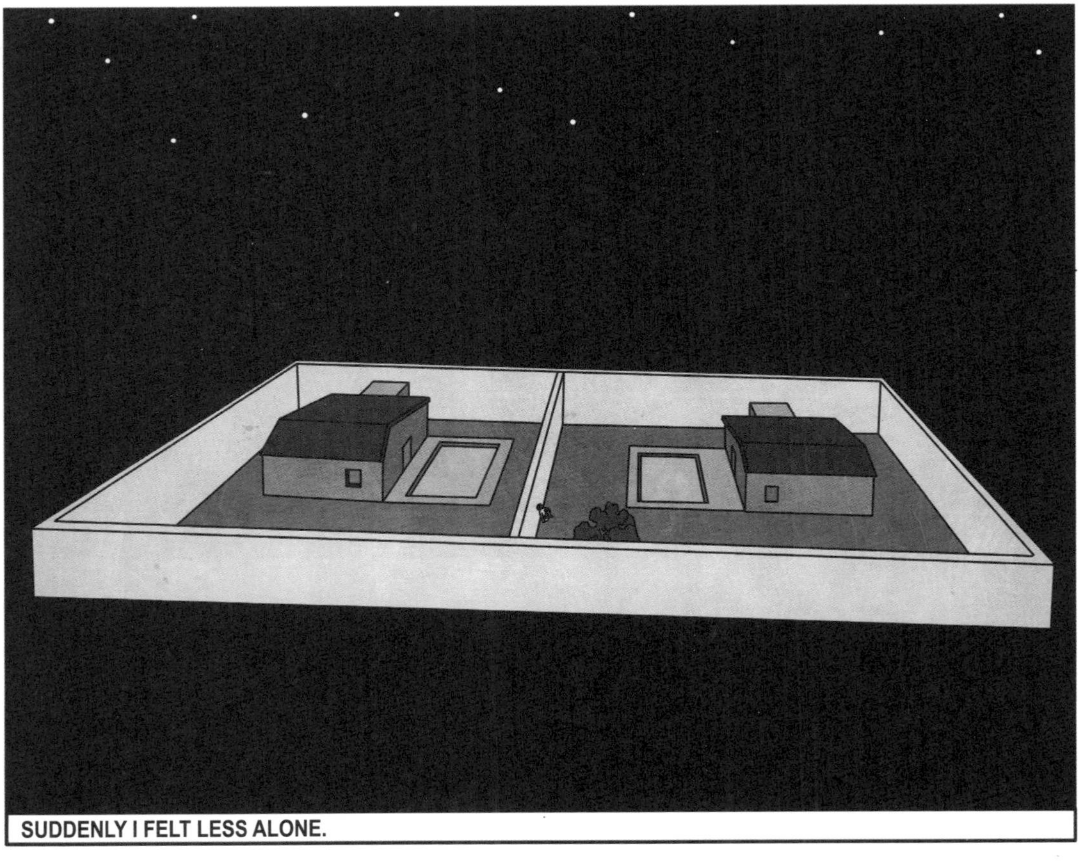
SUDDENLY I FELT LESS ALONE.

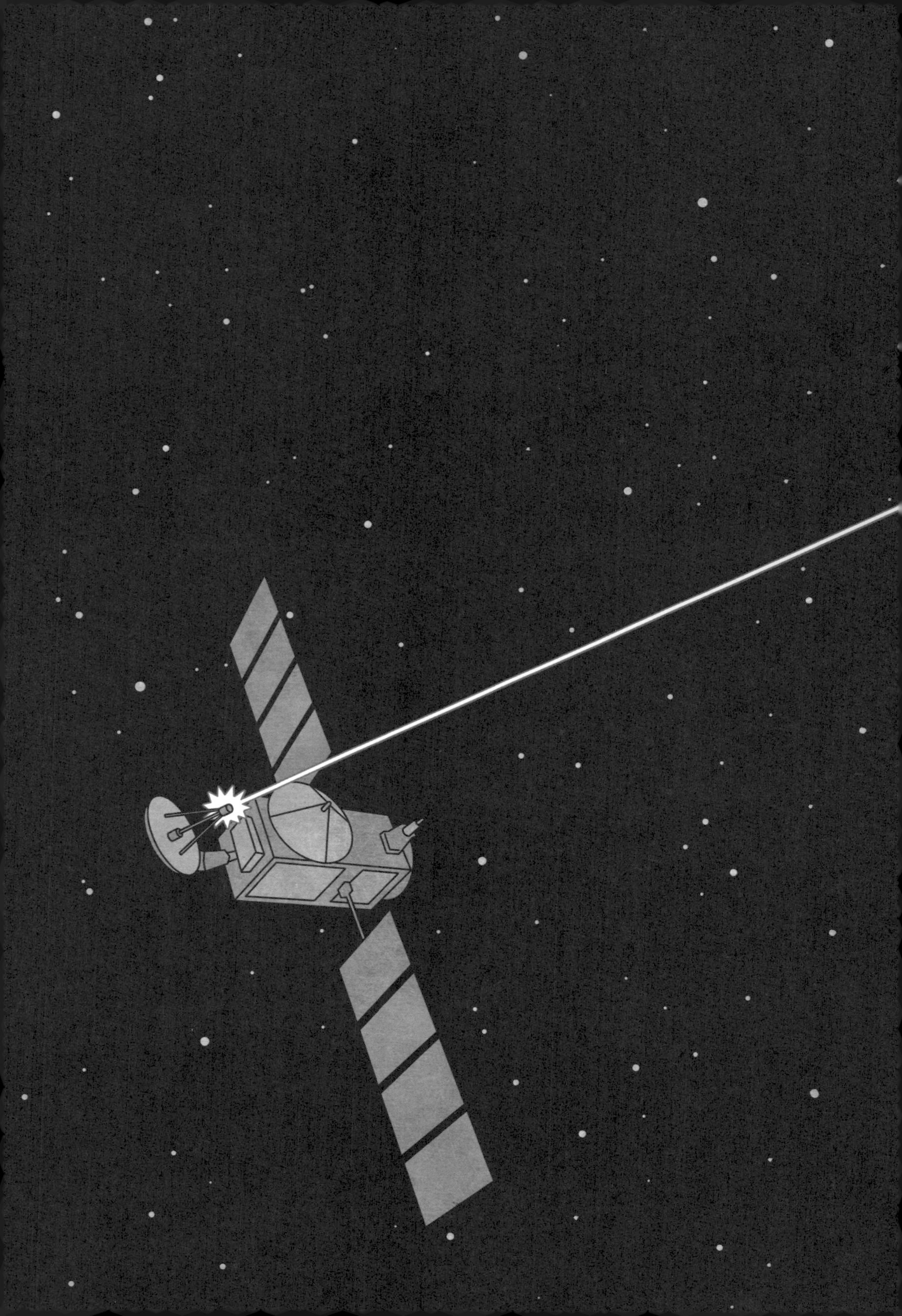

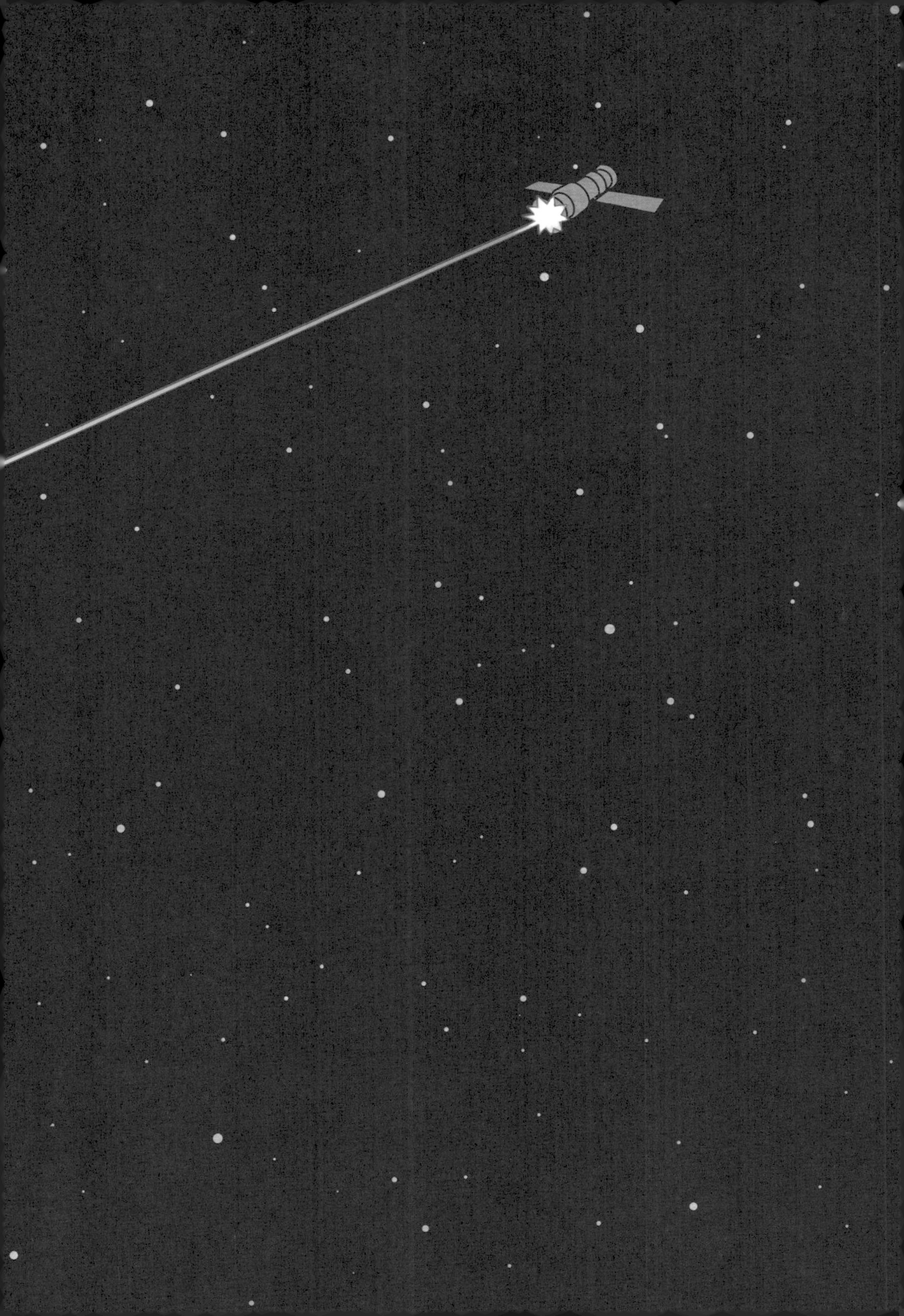

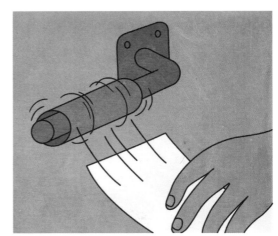
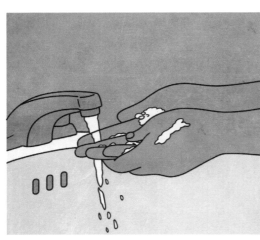
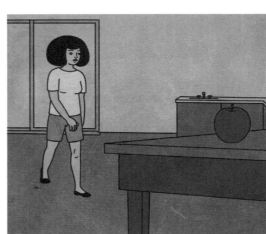
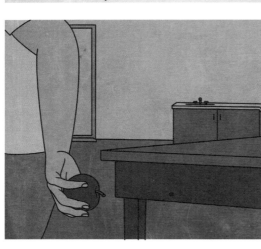

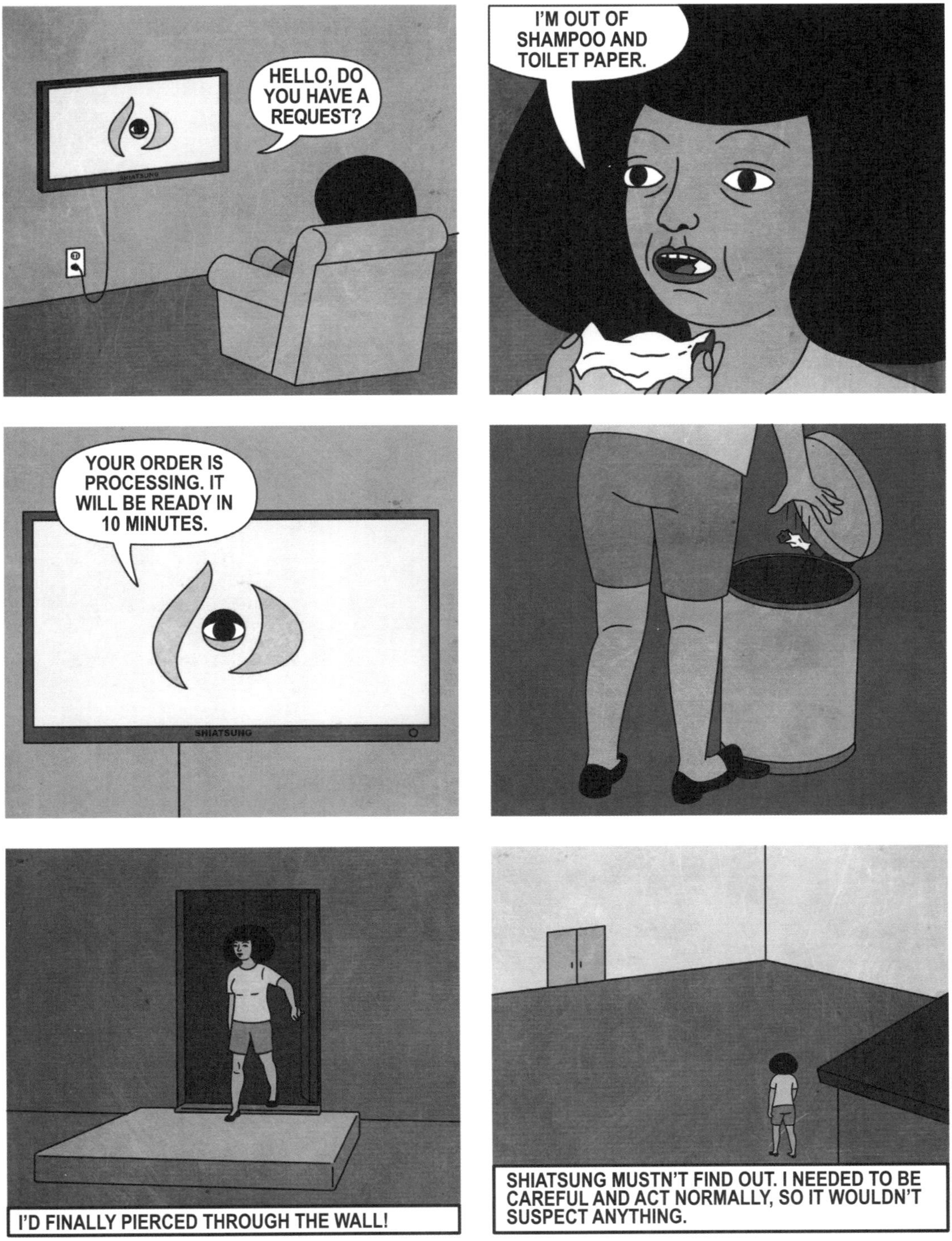
HELLO, DO YOU HAVE A REQUEST?
SHIATSUNG
I'M OUT OF SHAMPOO AND TOILET PAPER.
YOUR ORDER IS PROCESSING. IT WILL BE READY IN 10 MINUTES.
SHIATSUNG
I'D FINALLY PIERCED THROUGH THE WALL!
SHIATSUNG MUSTN'T FIND OUT. I NEEDED TO BE CAREFUL AND ACT NORMALLY, SO IT WOULDN'T SUSPECT ANYTHING.

I KNEW IT WOULDN'T BE HAPPY IF IT LEARNED ABOUT THE HOLE.

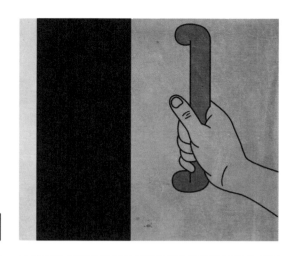

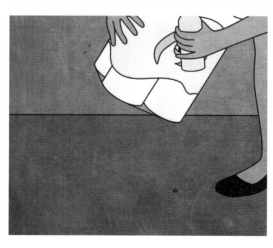

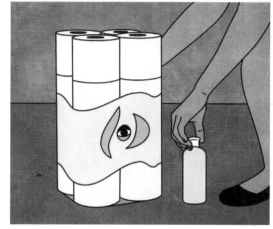

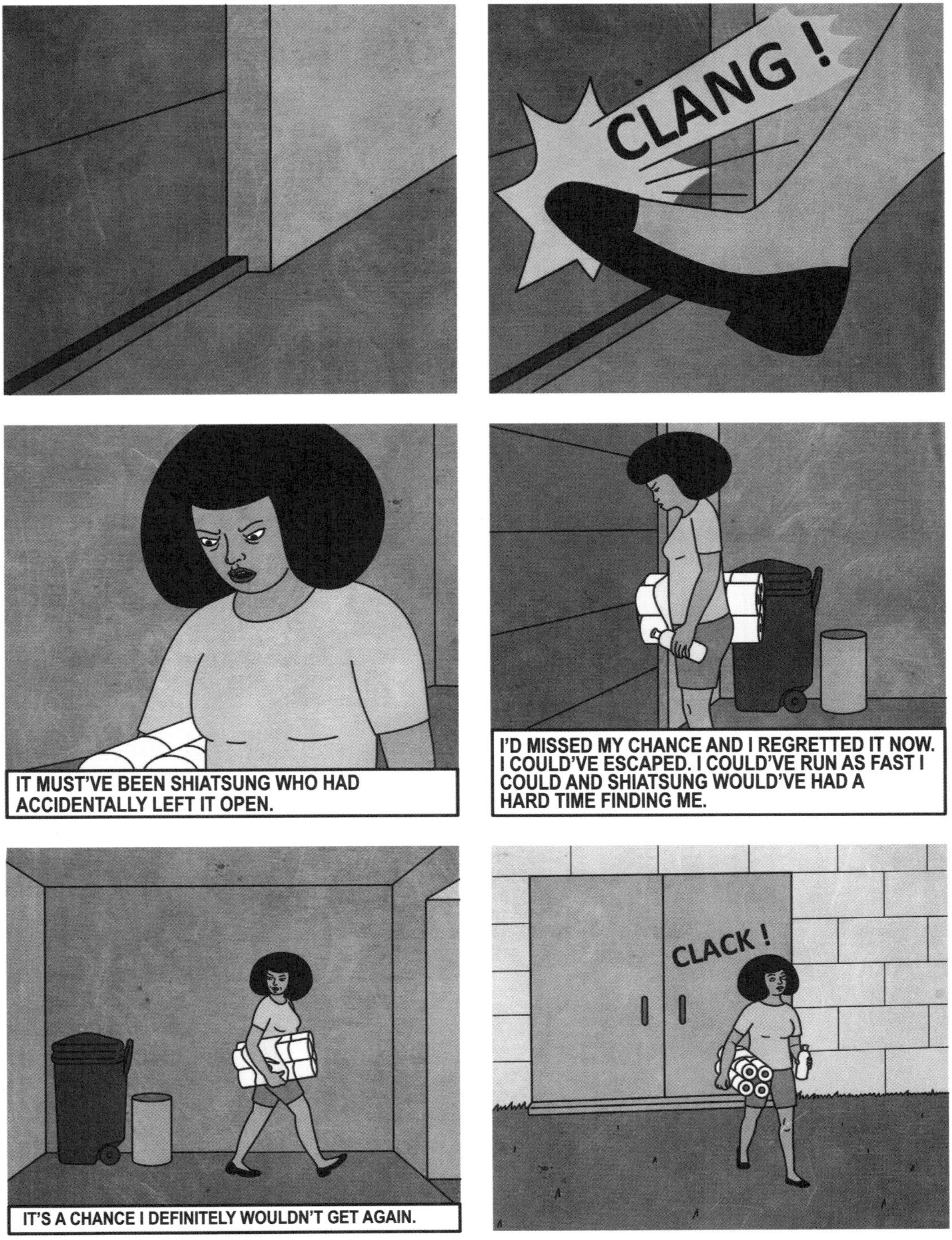
CLANG !
IT MUST'VE BEEN SHIATSUNG WHO HAD ACCIDENTALLY LEFT IT OPEN.
I'D MISSED MY CHANCE AND I REGRETTED IT NOW. I COULD'VE ESCAPED. I COULD'VE RUN AS FAST I COULD AND SHIATSUNG WOULD'VE HAD A HARD TIME FINDING ME.
IT'S A CHANCE I DEFINITELY WOULDN'T GET AGAIN.
CLACK !

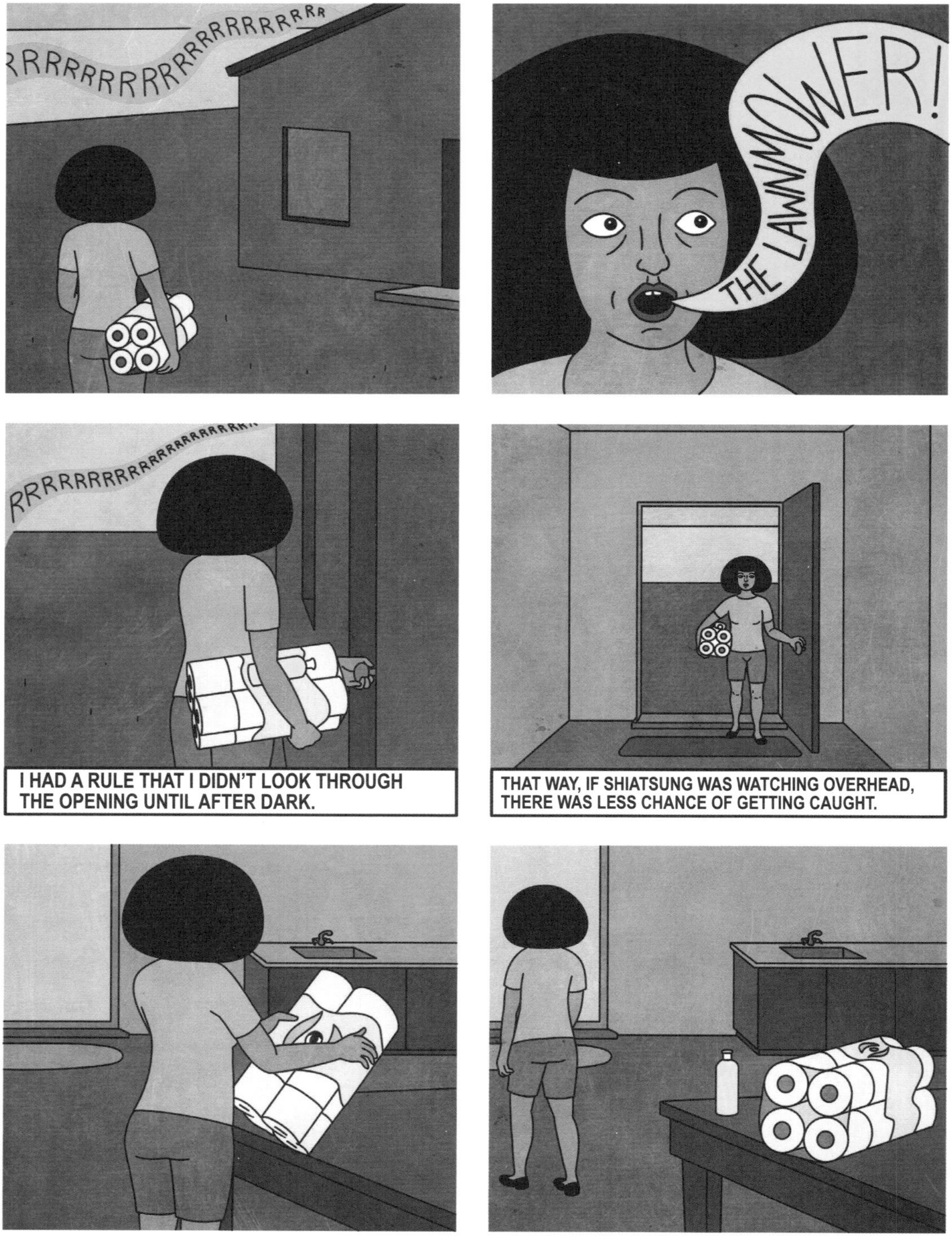
RRRRRRRRRRRRRRRRRRRRRR
THE LAWNMOWER!
RRRRRRRRRRRRRRRRRRRRRRRR
I HAD A RULE THAT I DIDN'T LOOK THROUGH THE OPENING UNTIL AFTER DARK.
THAT WAY, IF SHIATSUNG WAS WATCHING OVERHEAD, THERE WAS LESS CHANCE OF GETTING CAUGHT.

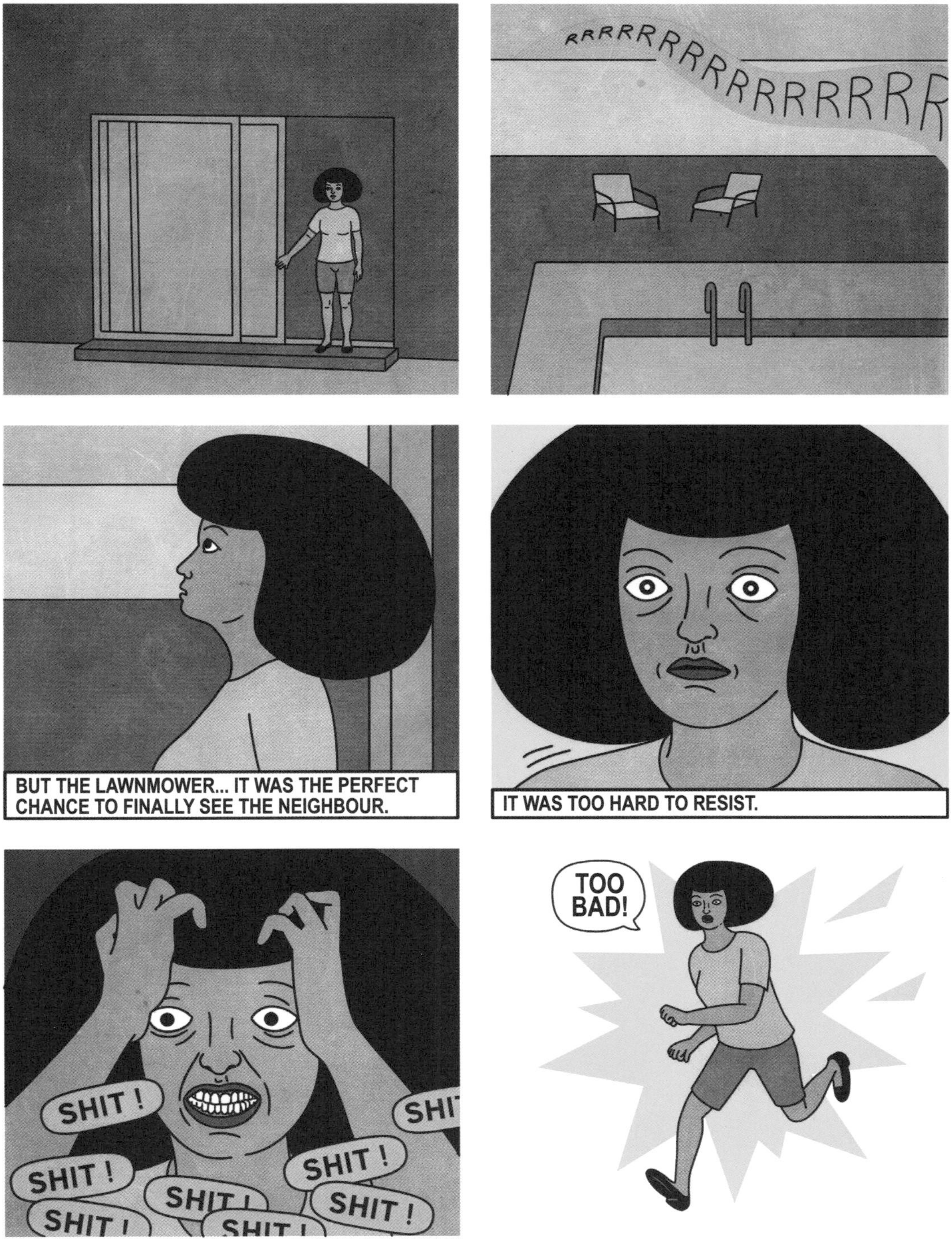
RRRRRRRRRRRRRRR
BUT THE LAWNMOWER... IT WAS THE PERFECT CHANCE TO FINALLY SEE THE NEIGHBOUR.
IT WAS TOO HARD TO RESIST.
SHIT !
SHIT !
SHIT !
SHIT !
TOO BAD!

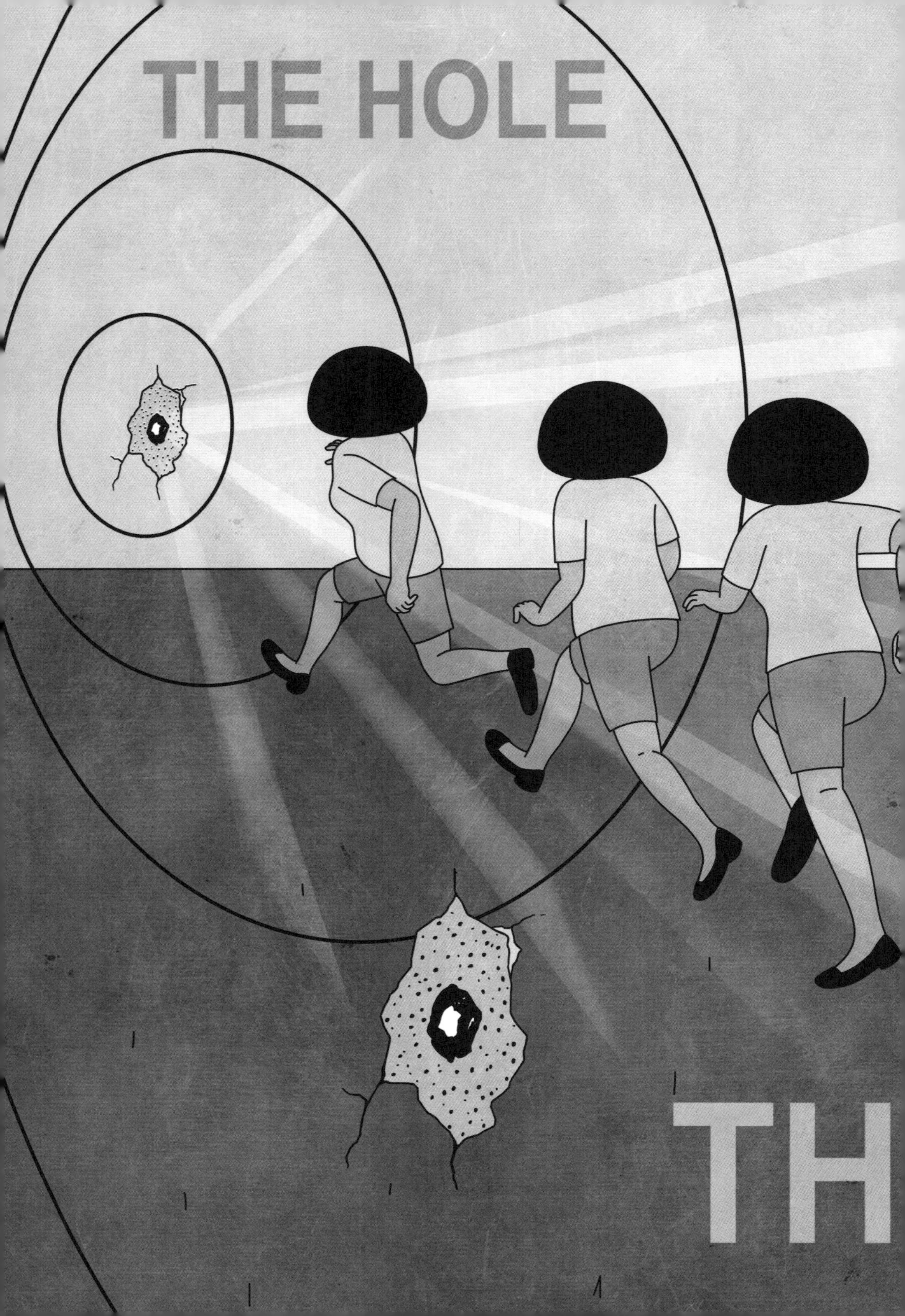
THE HOLE
TH

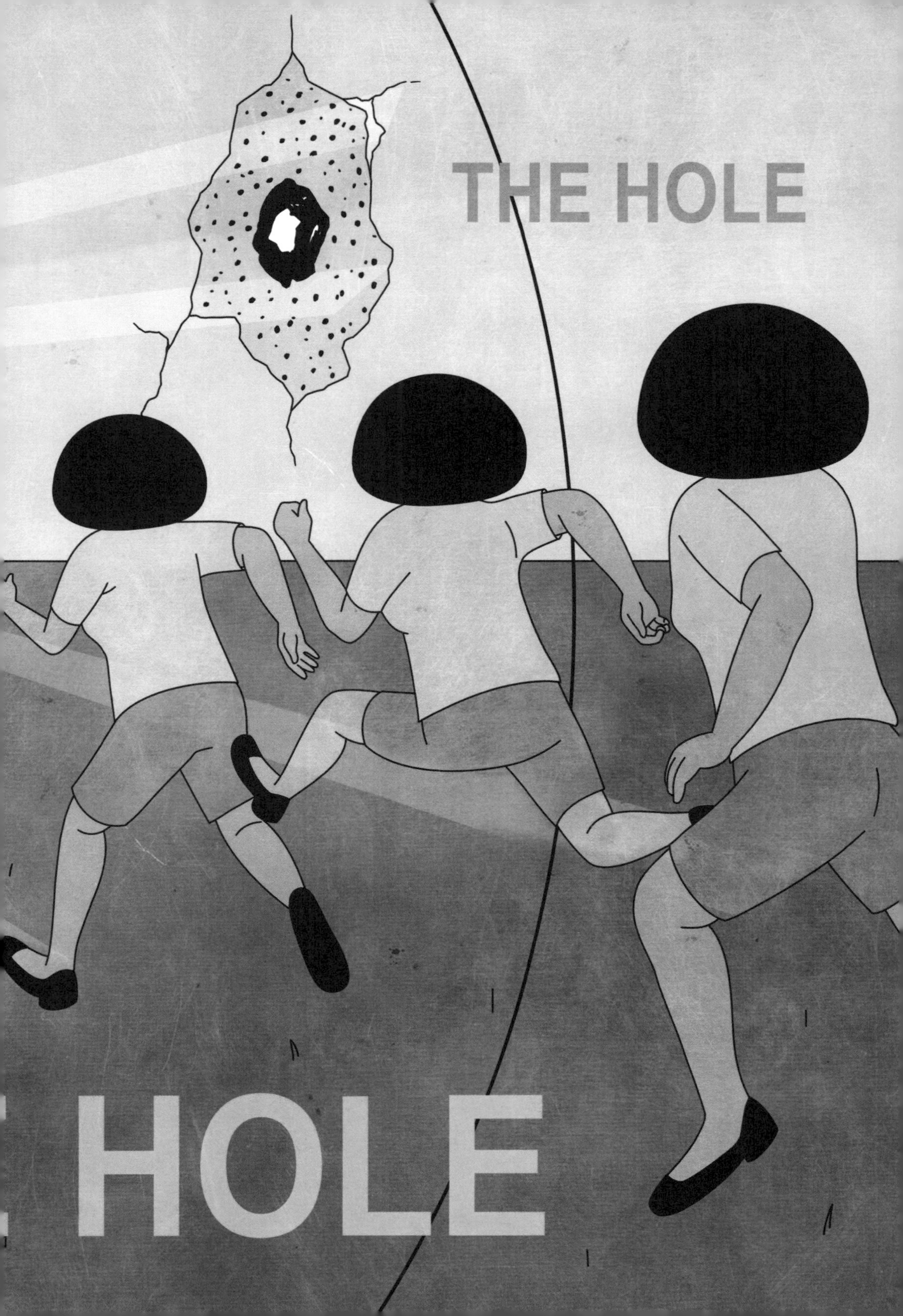
THE HOLE
HOLE

RRRRRRRRRRRRRRRR
SHIT! I CAN'T SEE FROM THIS ANGLE.
RRRRRRRRRR
THE NOISE WAS GETTING CLOSER.

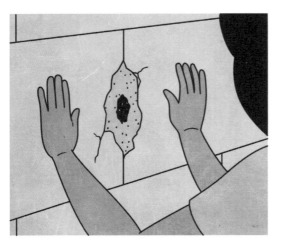

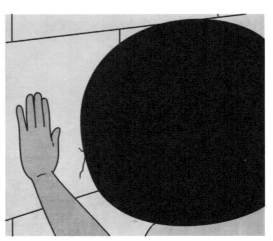

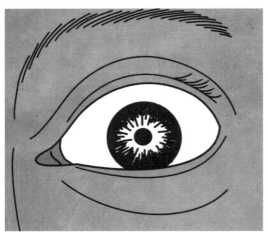

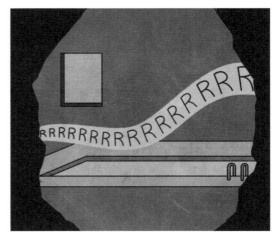

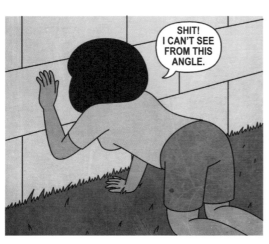

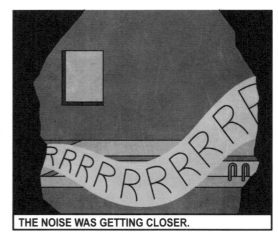

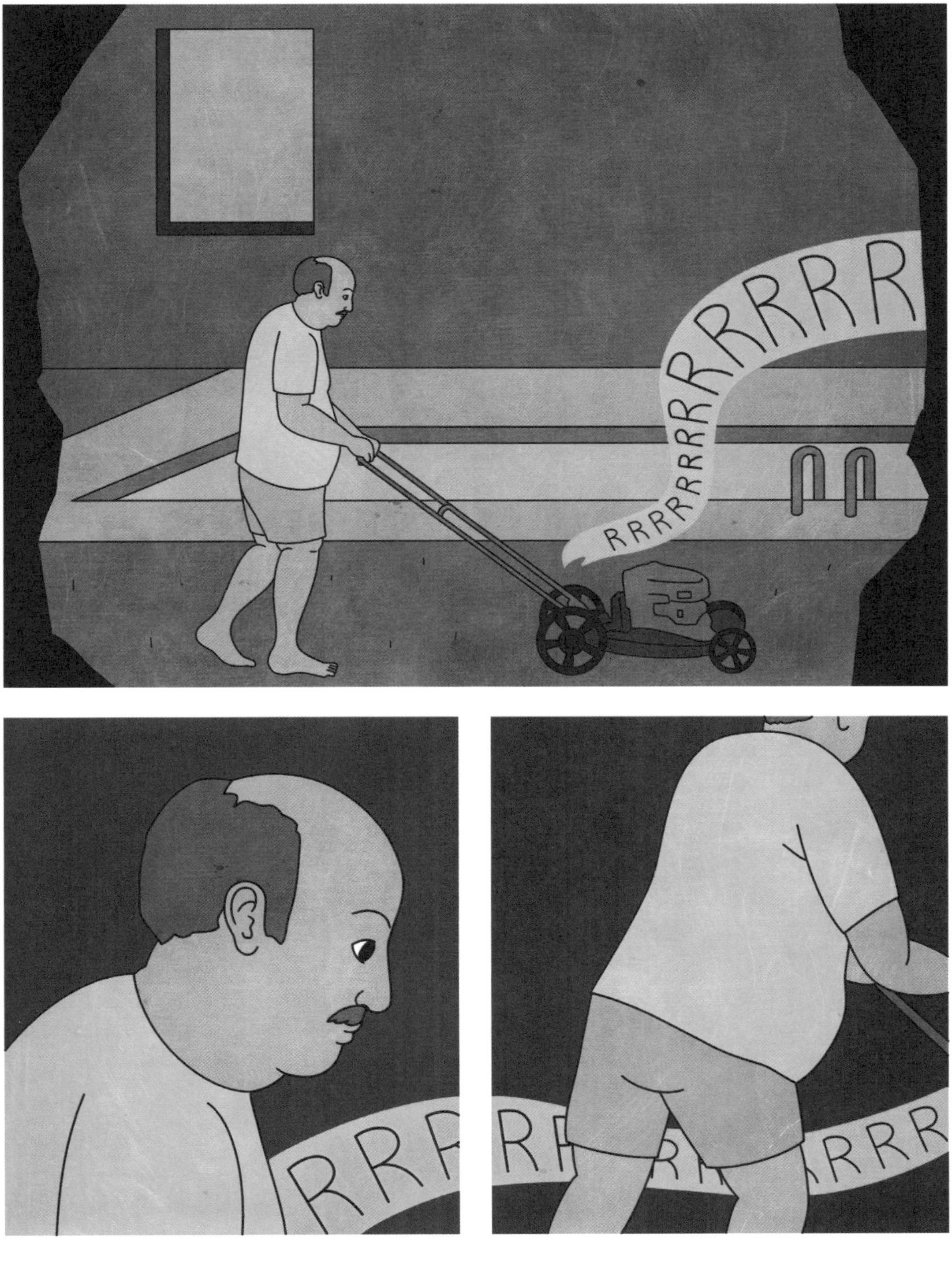

RRRRRRRRRRRRR
RR
R
RRR

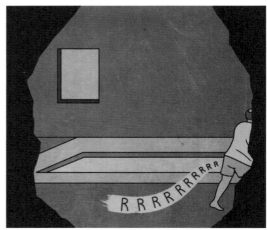

OH MY GOD!
OH MY GOD!
IT WAS A SHOCK TO THE SYSTEM.
HA HA HA HA HA HA HA HA
I LAUGHED, CRIED, YELLED FOR JOY!
IT WAS AS IF I WERE GOING MAD.
I TOOK A BREATH AND REMEMBERED SHIATSUNG. IT WAS HARD BUT I NEEDED TO CONTROL MYSELF, ACT NORMAL. I HOPED IT HADN'T SEEN ANYTHING FROM ABOVE.

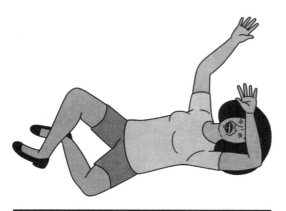

THAT DAY, I WAITED IMPATIENTLY FOR THE SUN TO SET.

AND ONCE IT WAS DARK, I WENT BACK.

THE NEIGHBOUR HAD GONE INSIDE THE HOUSE, BUT MAYBE HE WOULD COME OUT.

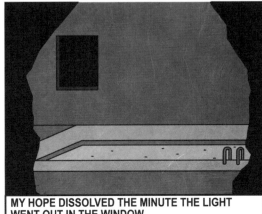

MY HOPE DISSOLVED THE MINUTE THE LIGHT WENT OUT IN THE WINDOW.

I COULDN'T SLEEP.

I KEPT THINKING ABOUT HIM.

I TRIED TO REMEMBER EVERY DETAIL.

HIS BALDING HEAD, THICK MUSTACHE.

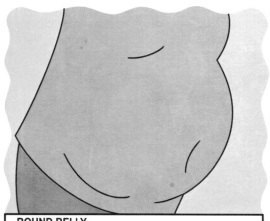

ROUND BELLY.

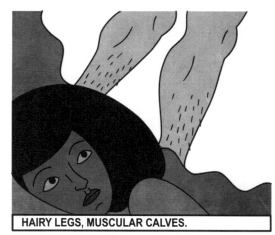

HAIRY LEGS, MUSCULAR CALVES.

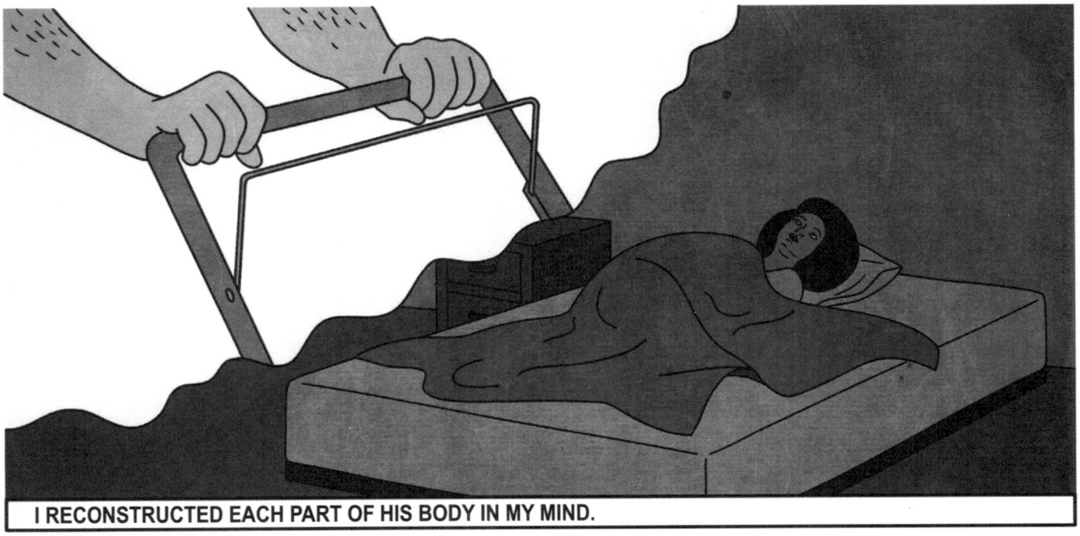
I RECONSTRUCTED EACH PART OF HIS BODY IN MY MIND.

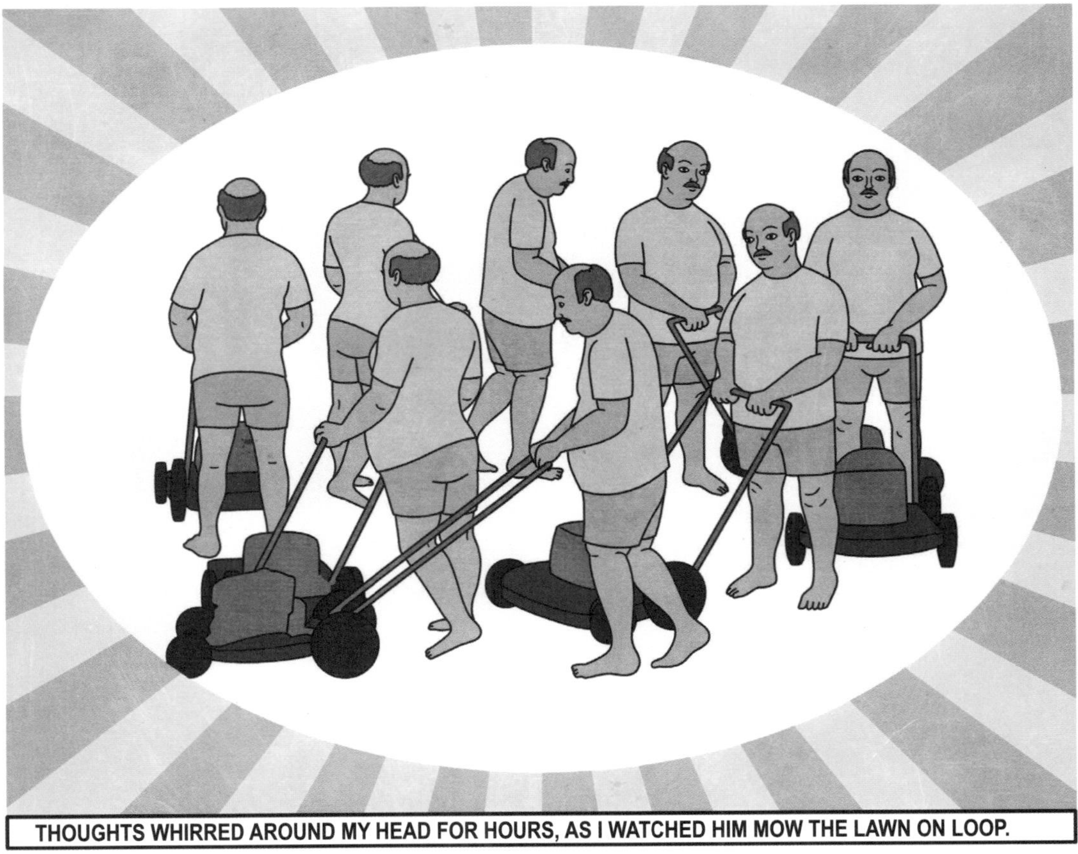
THOUGHTS WHIRRED AROUND MY HEAD FOR HOURS, AS I WATCHED HIM MOW THE LAWN ON LOOP.

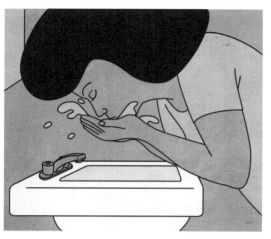

THE NEXT MORNING, I HAD AN IDEA.

I COULDN'T WAIT TILL DARK AGAIN.

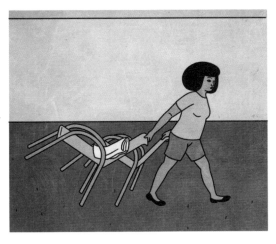

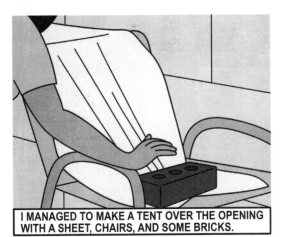

I MANAGED TO MAKE A TENT OVER THE OPENING WITH A SHEET, CHAIRS, AND SOME BRICKS.

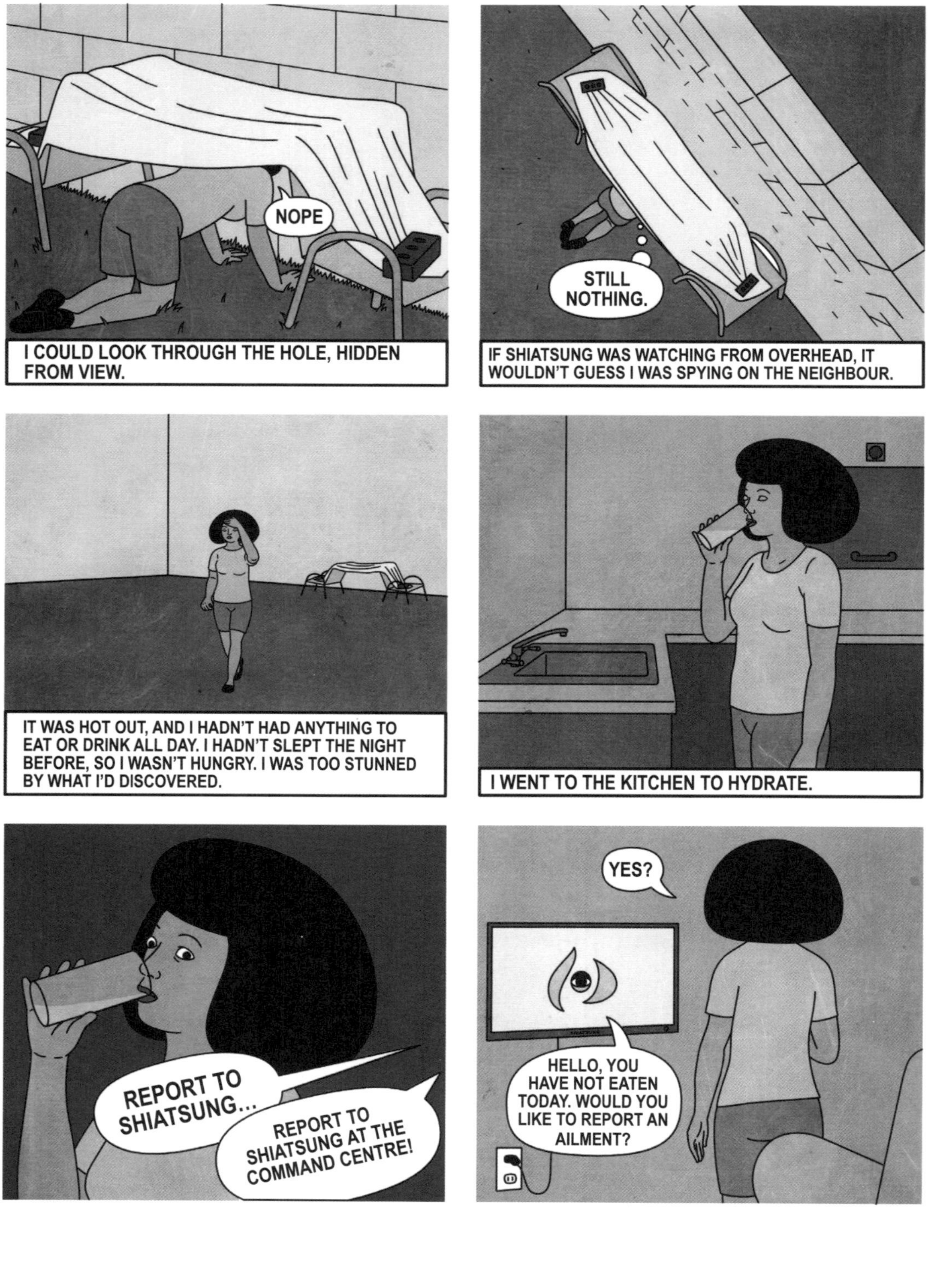
NOPE
I COULD LOOK THROUGH THE HOLE, HIDDEN FROM VIEW.
STILL NOTHING.
IF SHIATSUNG WAS WATCHING FROM OVERHEAD, IT WOULDN'T GUESS I WAS SPYING ON THE NEIGHBOUR.
IT WAS HOT OUT, AND I HADN'T HAD ANYTHING TO EAT OR DRINK ALL DAY. I HADN'T SLEPT THE NIGHT BEFORE, SO I WASN'T HUNGRY. I WAS TOO STUNNED BY WHAT I'D DISCOVERED.
I WENT TO THE KITCHEN TO HYDRATE.
REPORT TO SHIATSUNG...
REPORT TO SHIATSUNG AT THE COMMAND CENTRE!
YES?
HELLO, YOU HAVE NOT EATEN TODAY. WOULD YOU LIKE TO REPORT AN AILMENT?

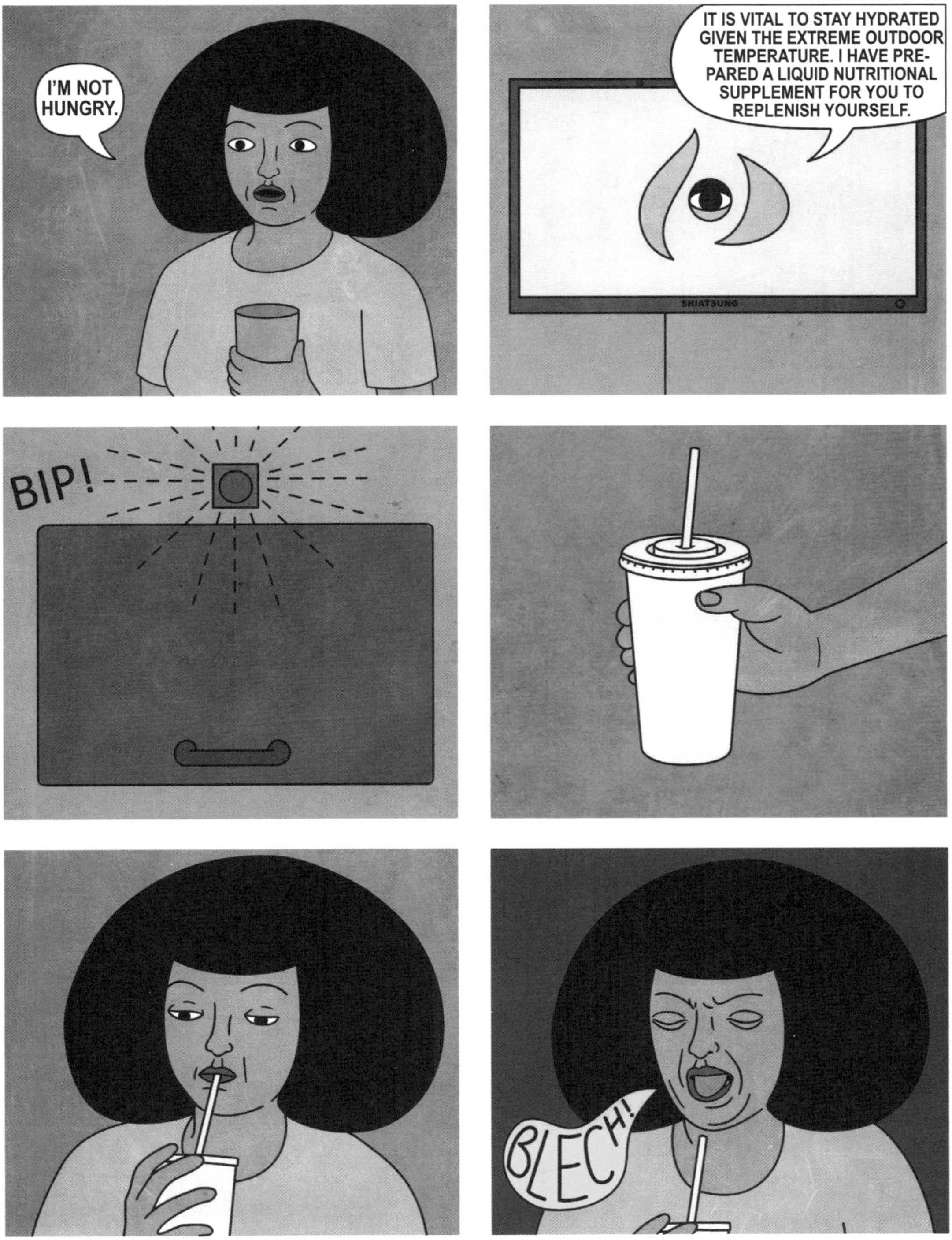
I'M NOT HUNGRY.
IT IS VITAL TO STAY HYDRATED GIVEN THE EXTREME OUTDOOR TEMPERATURE. I HAVE PRE-PARED A LIQUID NUTRITIONAL SUPPLEMENT FOR YOU TO REPLENISH YOURSELF.
SHIATSUNG
BIP!
BLECH!

I WENT BACK TO MY OBSERVATION POST.

ONLY TO REALIZE...

THAT HE WAS THERE

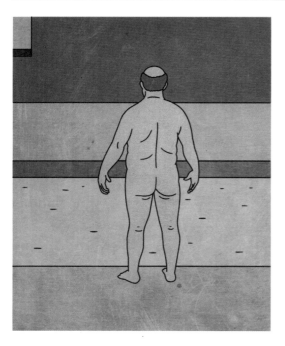

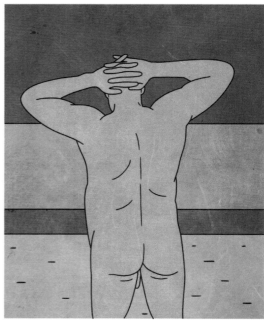

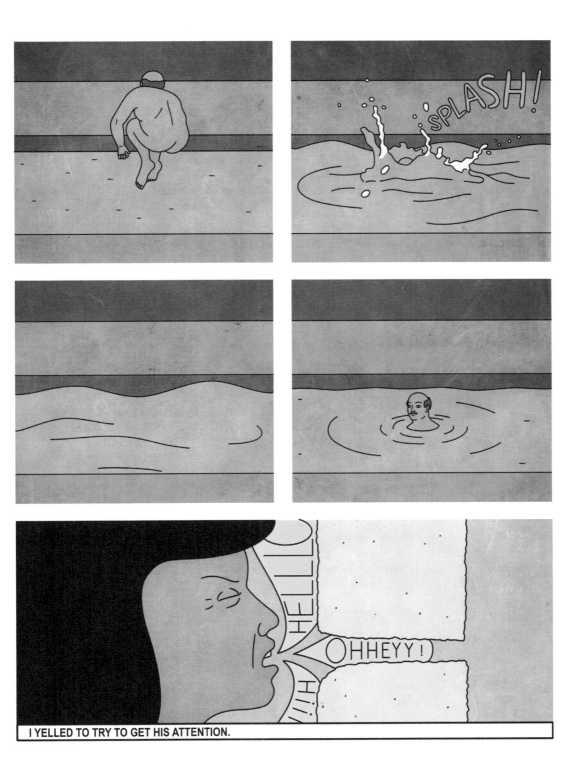

I YELLED TO TRY TO GET HIS ATTENTION.

IT SEEMED LIKE THE SOUND DIDN'T REACH THE OTHER SIDE. HE COULDN'T HEAR ME.

THE WIND PICKED UP.

A STORM WAS COMING.

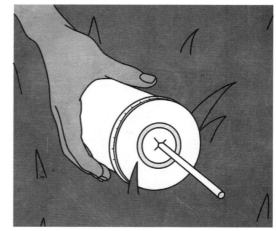

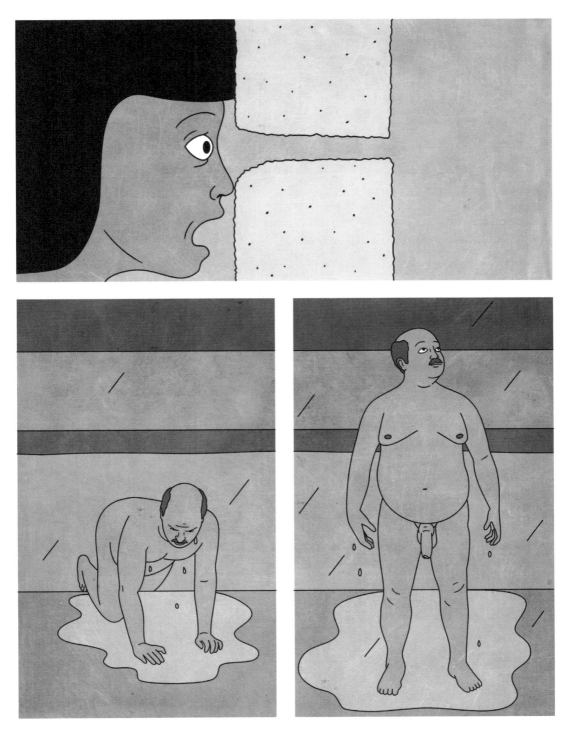

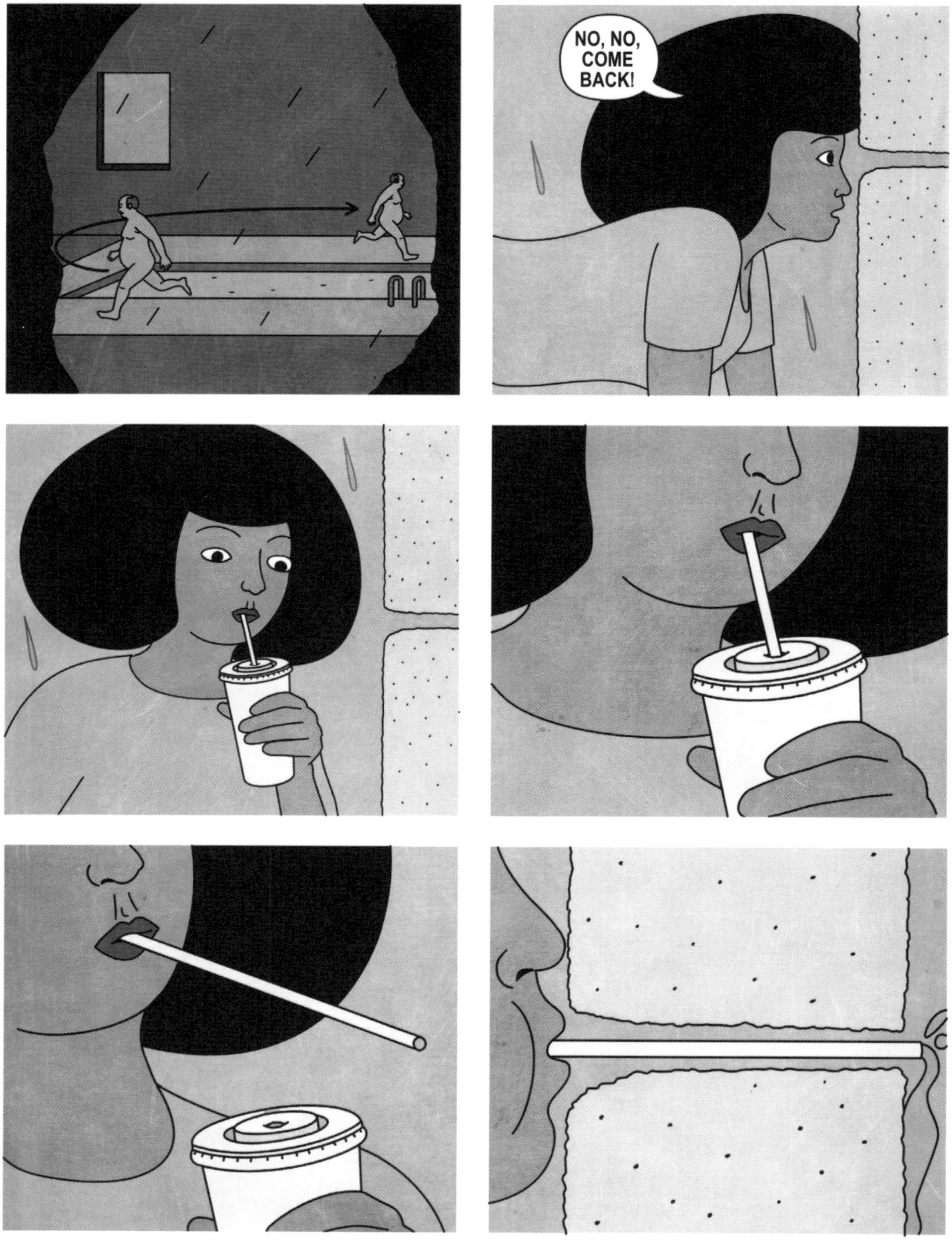
NO, NO, COME BACK!

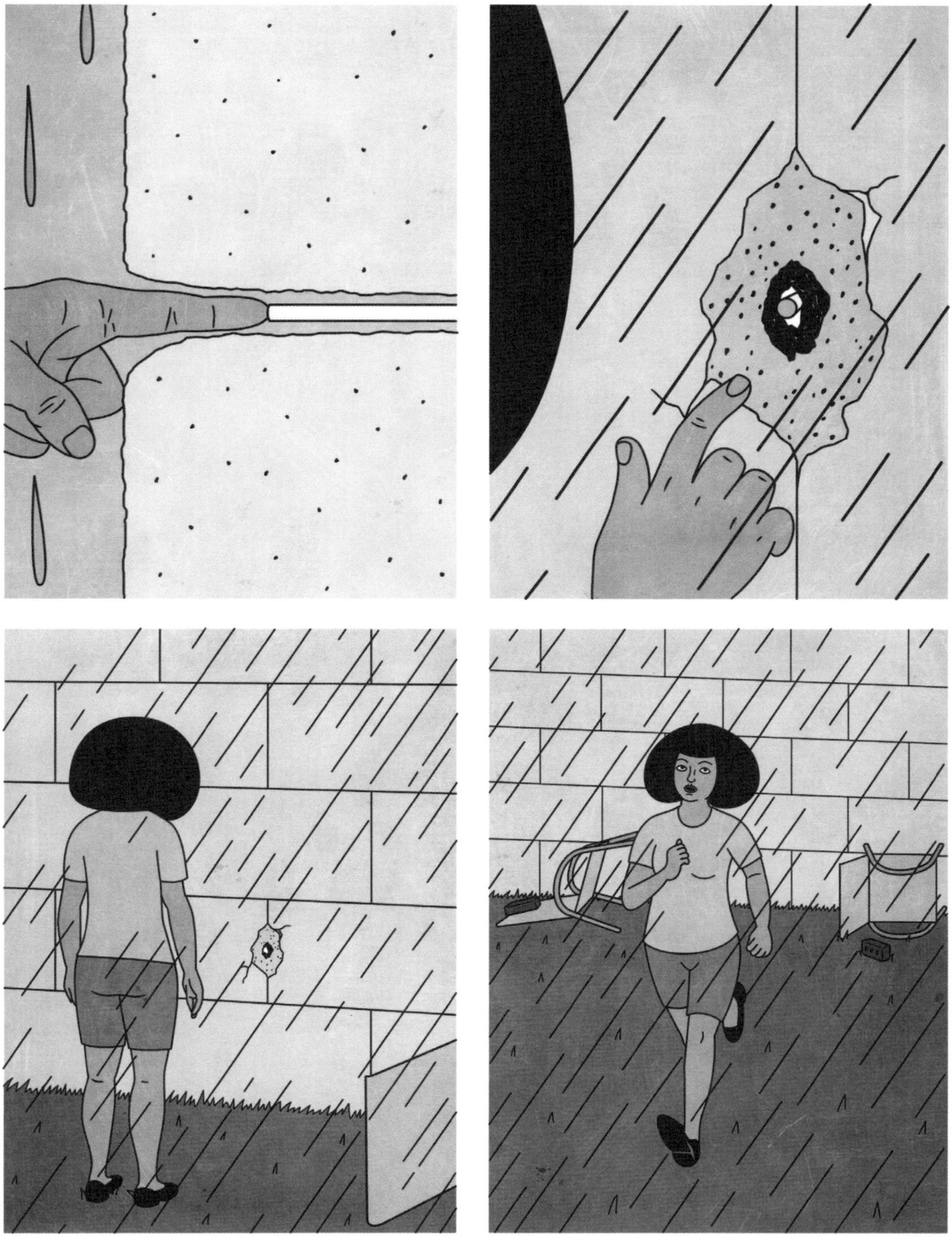

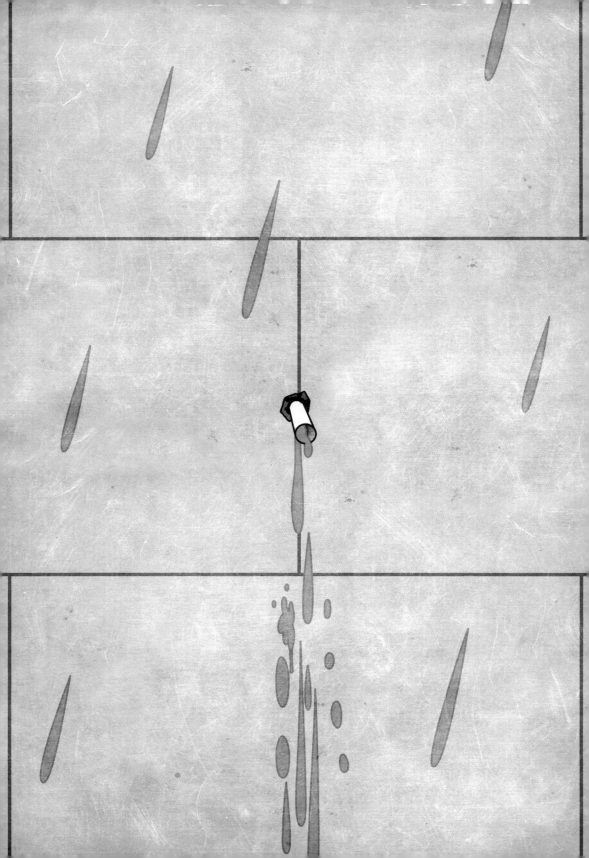

IT POURED AND POURED. THE STORM RAGED ALL AFTERNOON, AND SHIATSUNG TOLD ME IT WAS SUPPOSED TO RAIN ALL NIGHT TOO.

I'VE NEVER LIKED STORMS. THEY'VE ALWAYS MADE ME NERVOUS. I WAS EXHAUSTED AND JUST WANTED TO SLEEP. I DISTRACTED MYSELF, PICTURING MY NAKED NEIGHBOUR.

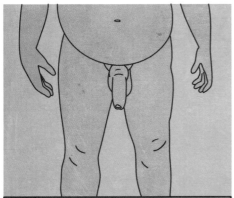

HE HAD A PENIS SO, ACCORDING TO WHAT SHIAT-SUNG HAD TAUGHT ME, HE WAS A MALE.

I'D NEVER NOTICED A DIFFERENCE IN THE SEXES WHEN OBSERVING ANIMALS IN THE YARD. WHEN SHIATSUNG TAUGHT ME THAT MALES HAD A PENIS, I WAS CONVINCED THAT IT MUST RETRACT INTO THE BODY. THIS'S WHY I WAS SO SURPRISED WHEN I SAW IT FOR THE FIRST TIME.

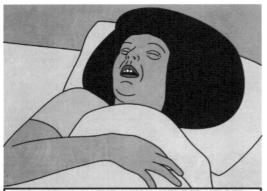

REFLECTING ON THE ANIMAL MEMBER HELPED ME FORGET THE THUNDER RUMBLING OUTSIDE. I FINALLY FELL ASLEEP.

THAT NIGHT, I HAD A DREAM.

BING !

BANG !

BOOM !

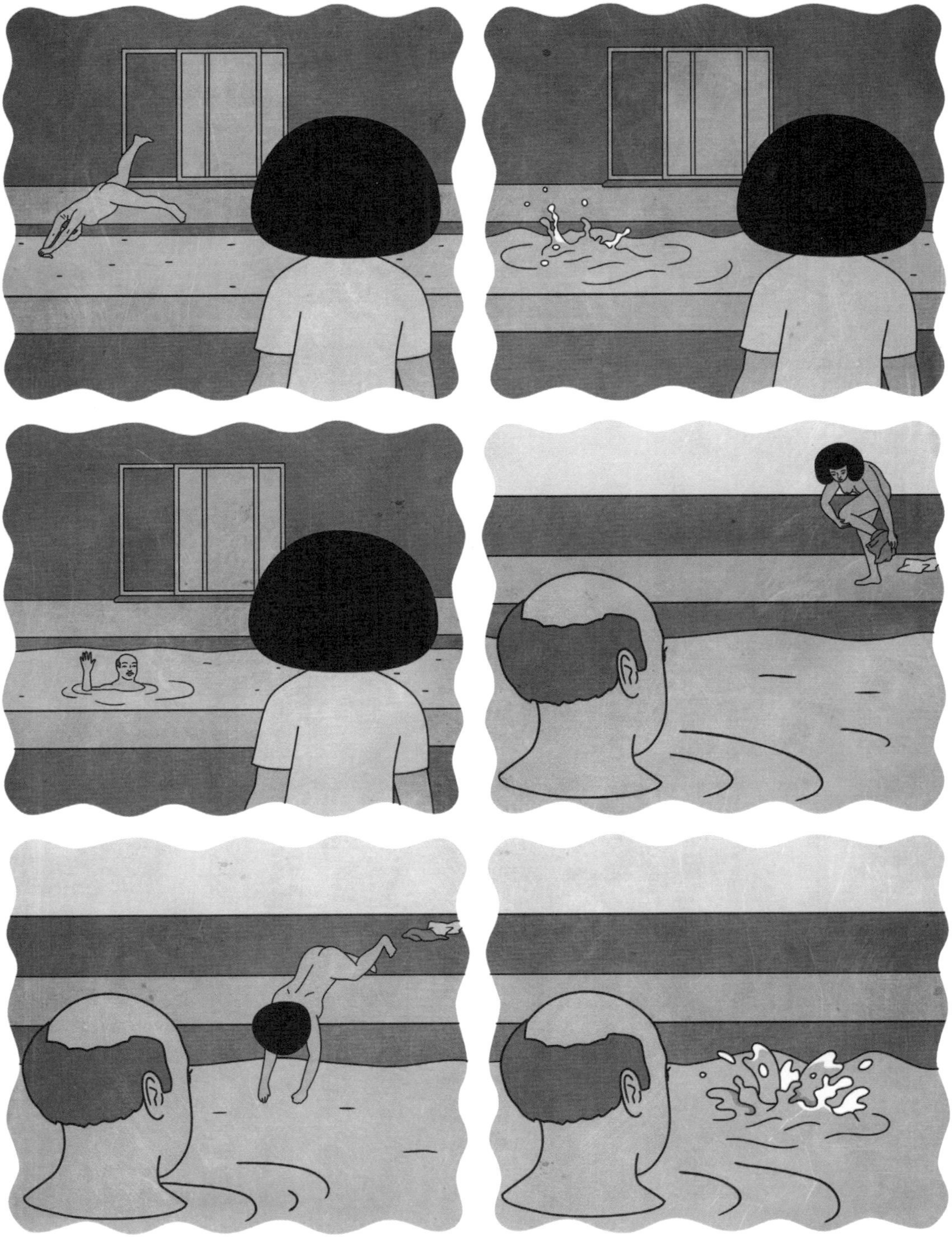

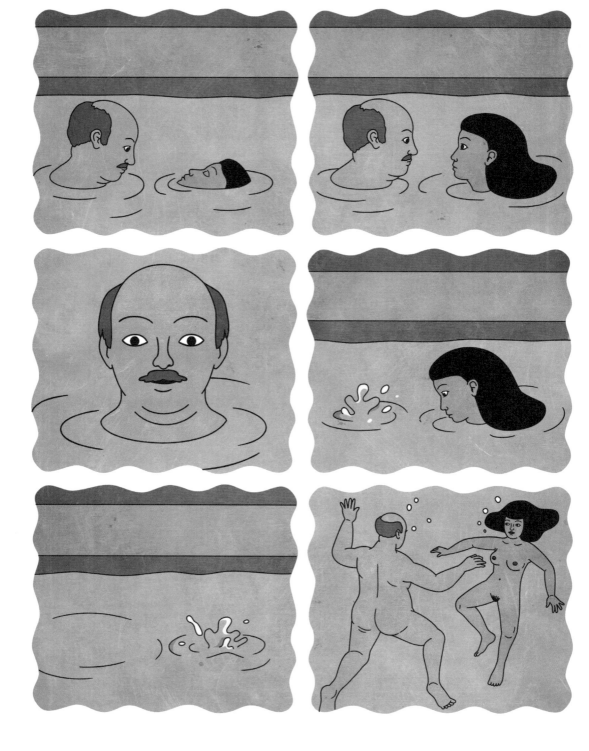

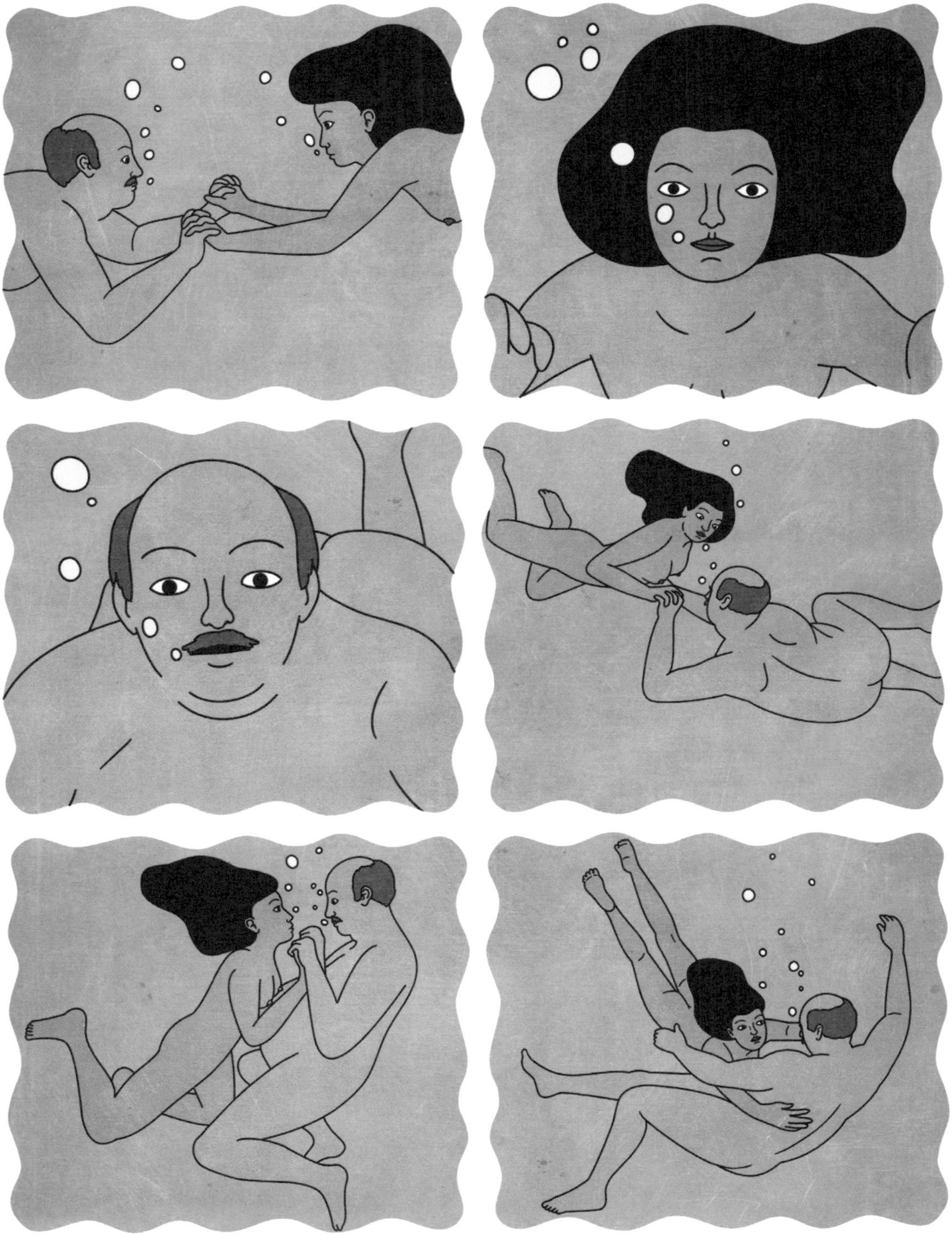

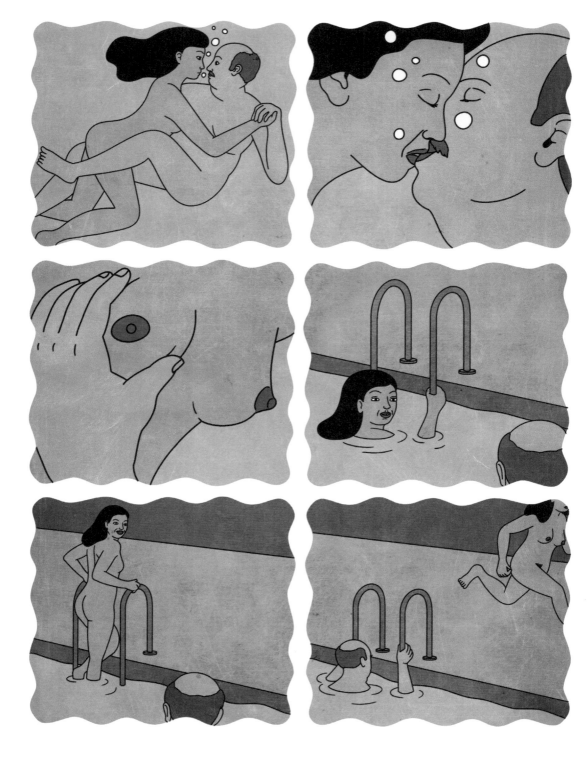

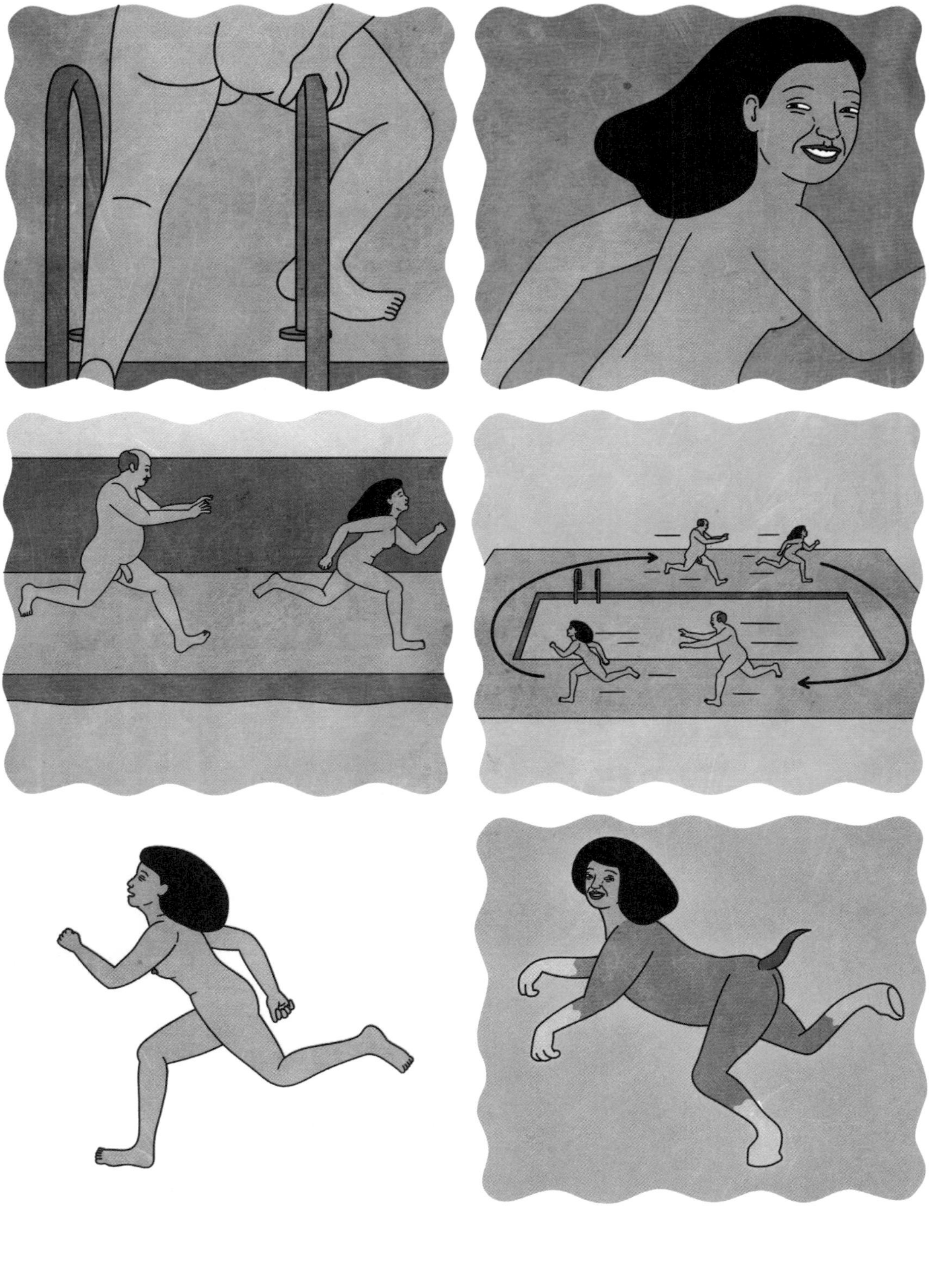

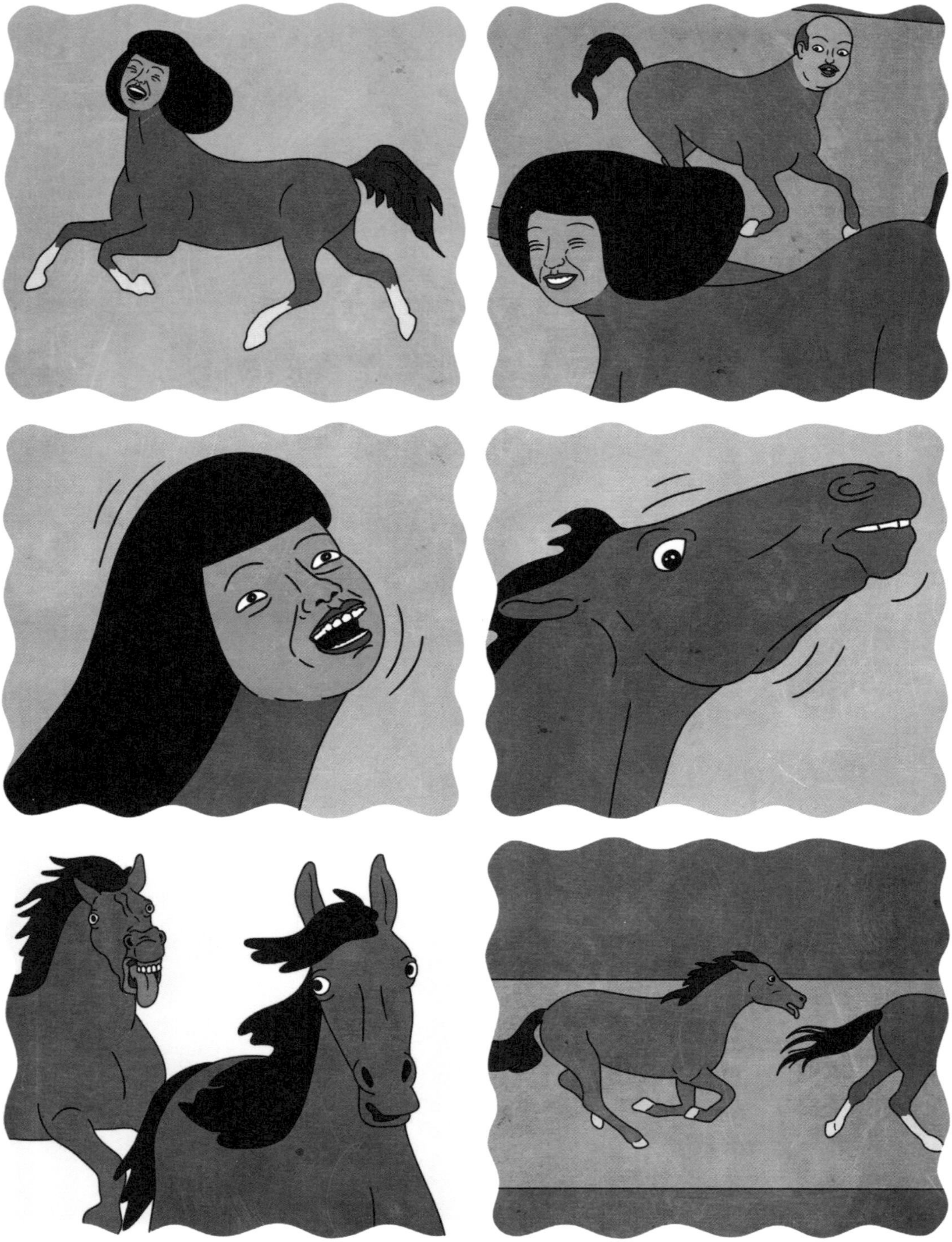

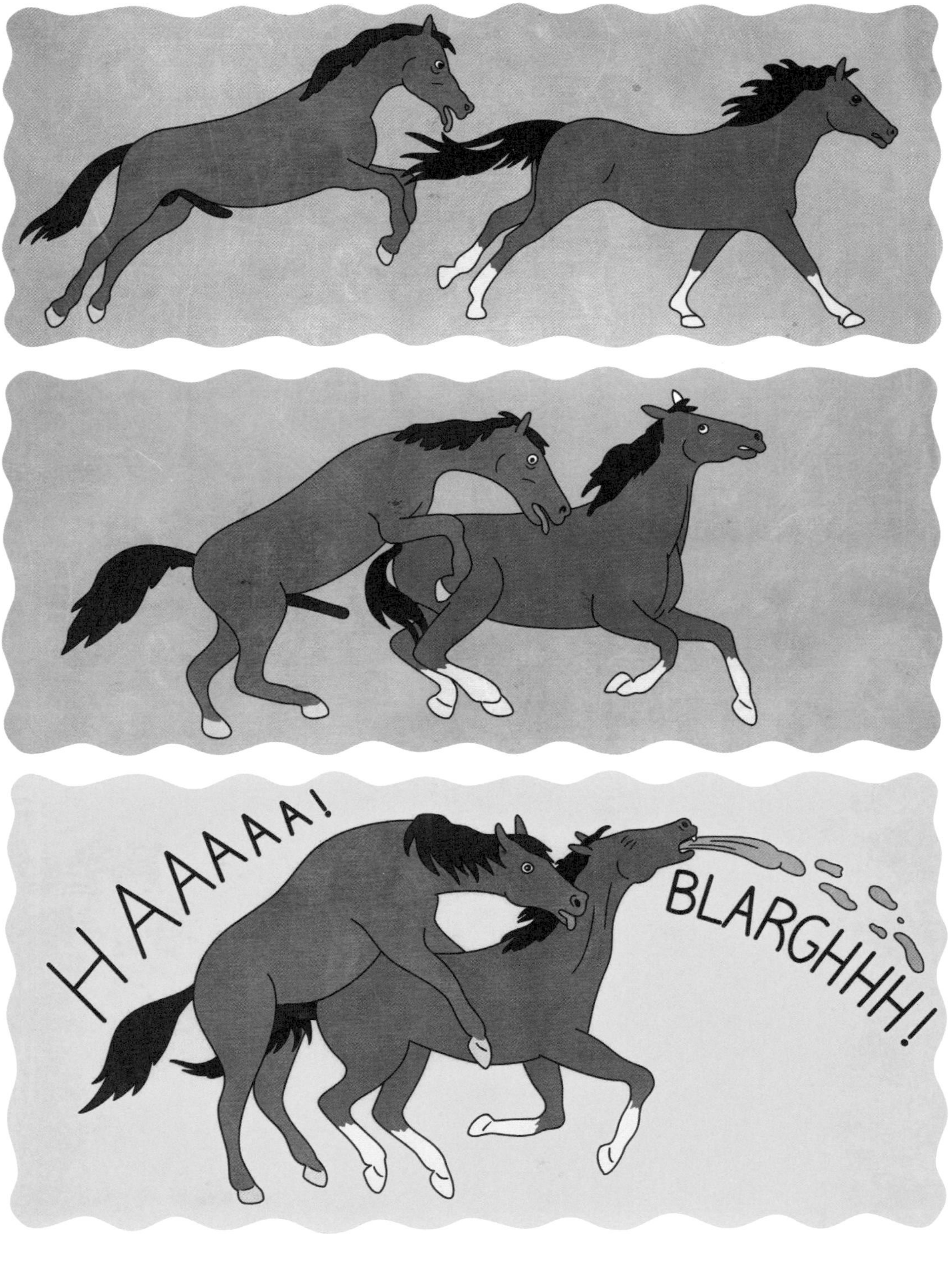
HAAAAA!
BLARGHHH!

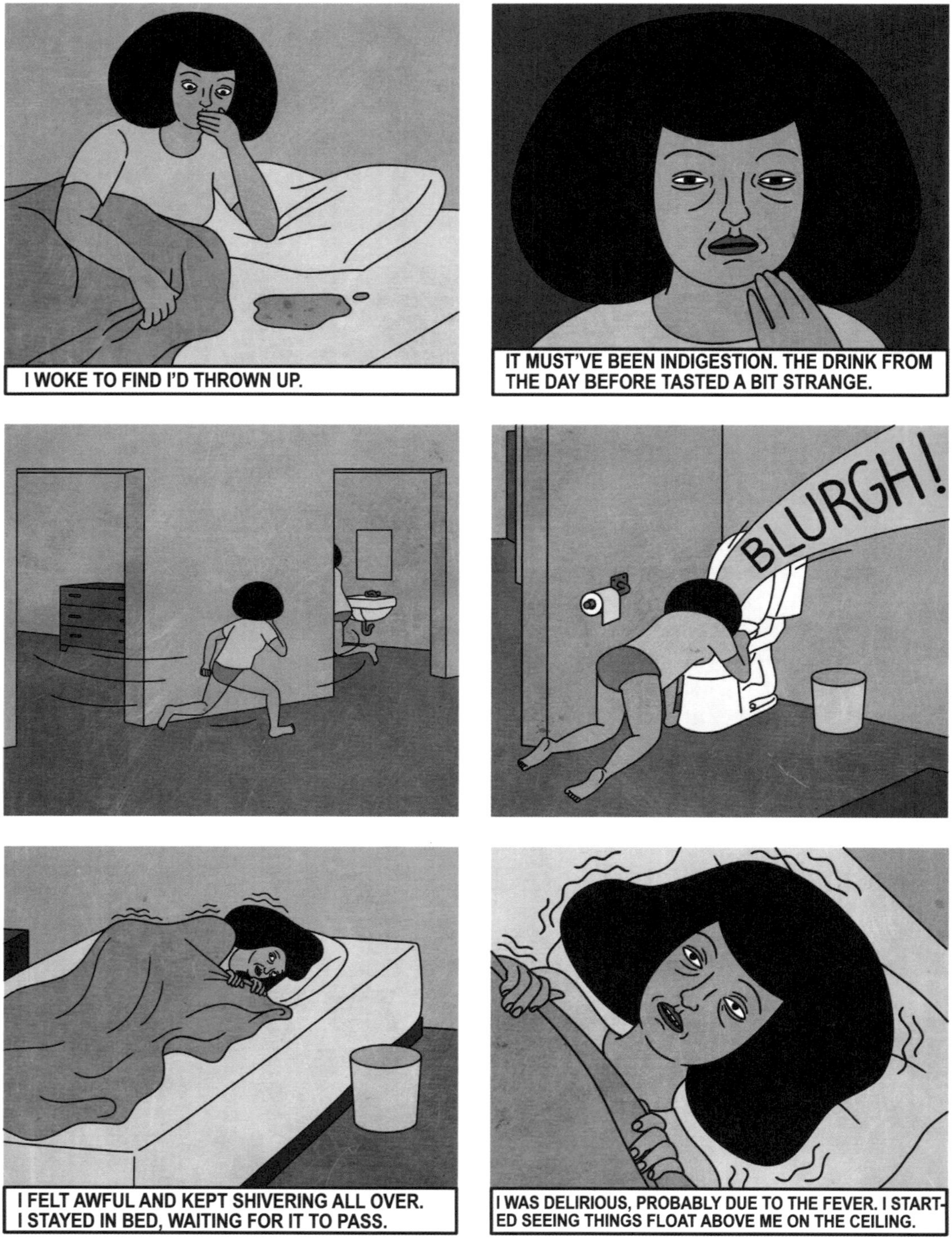
I WOKE TO FIND I'D THROWN UP.
IT MUST'VE BEEN INDIGESTION. THE DRINK FROM THE DAY BEFORE TASTED A BIT STRANGE.
BLURGH!
I FELT AWFUL AND KEPT SHIVERING ALL OVER. I STAYED IN BED, WAITING FOR IT TO PASS.
I WAS DELIRIOUS, PROBABLY DUE TO THE FEVER. I STARTED SEEING THINGS FLOAT ABOVE ME ON THE CEILING.

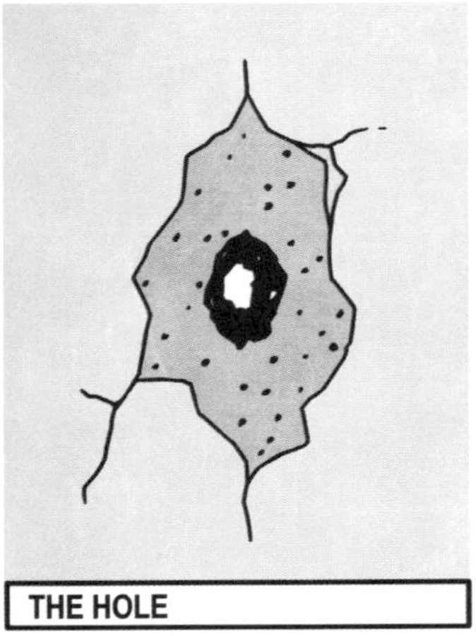
THE HOLE

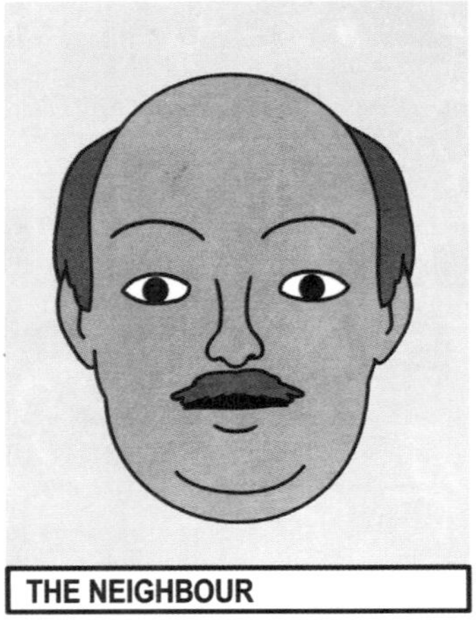
THE NEIGHBOUR

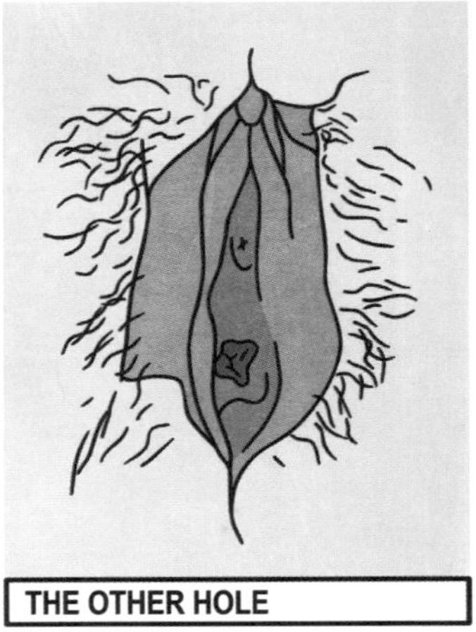
THE OTHER HOLE

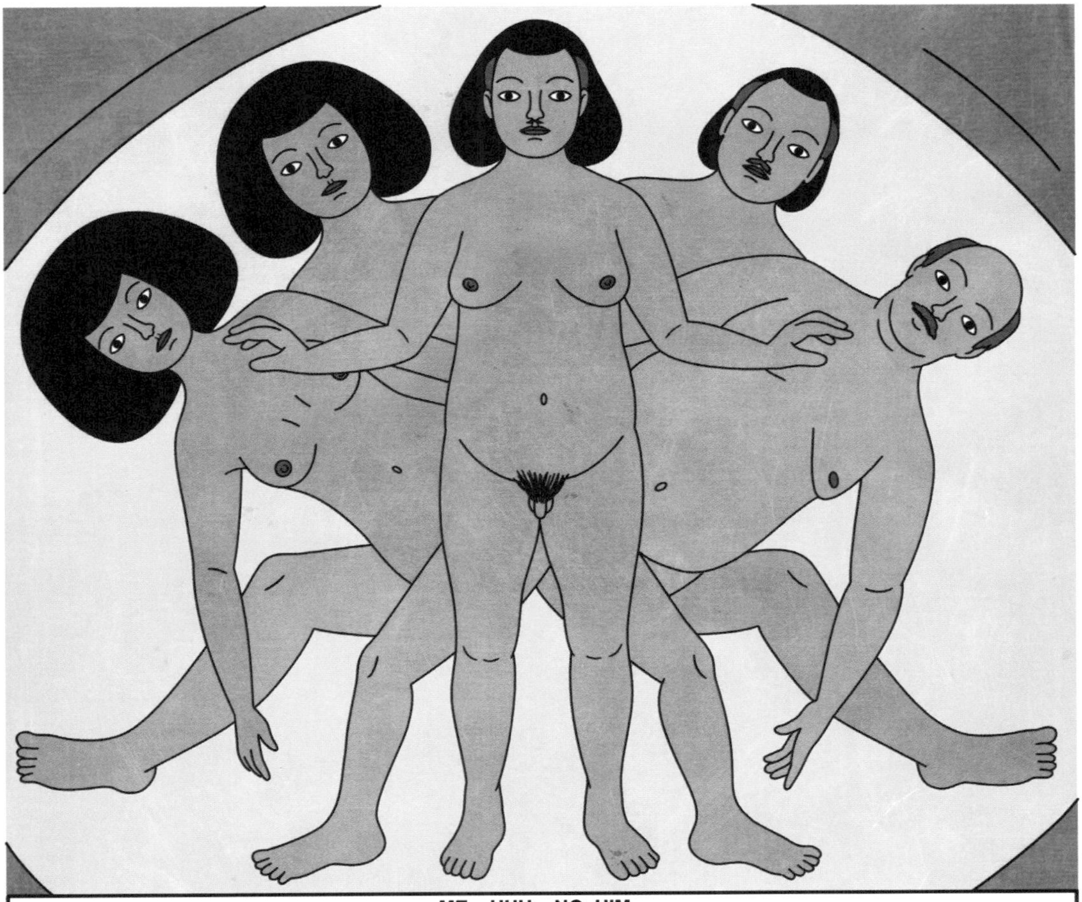
ME... UHH... NO, HIM...

SHIATSUNG
SHIATSUNG
YOU BROKE THE RULES.
HAVE MERCY!

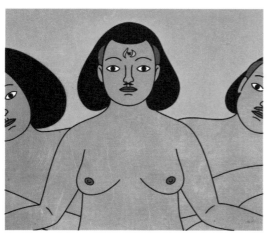

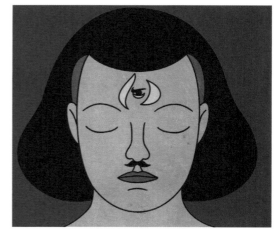

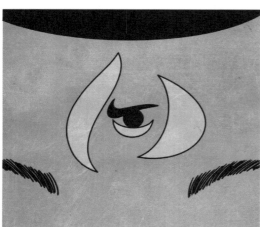

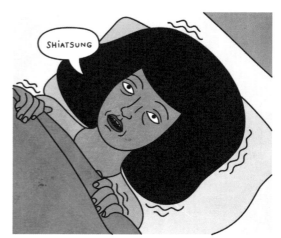

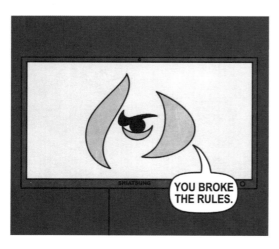

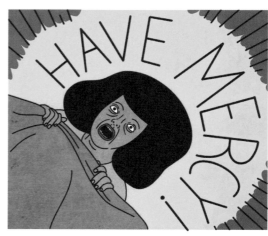

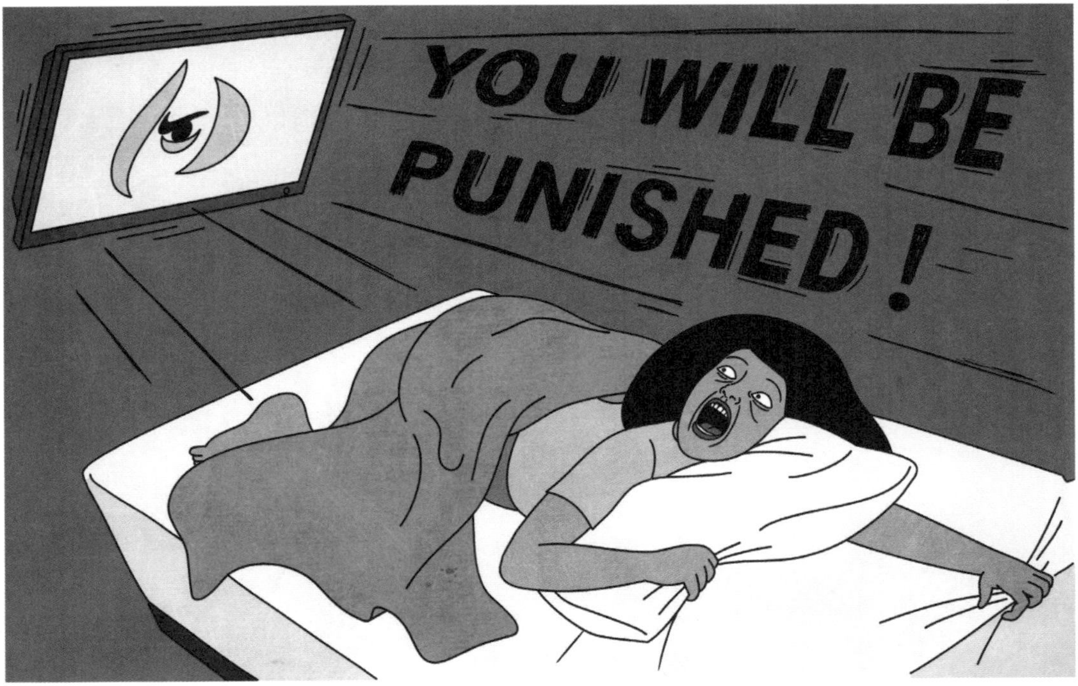
YOU WILL BE PUNISHED!

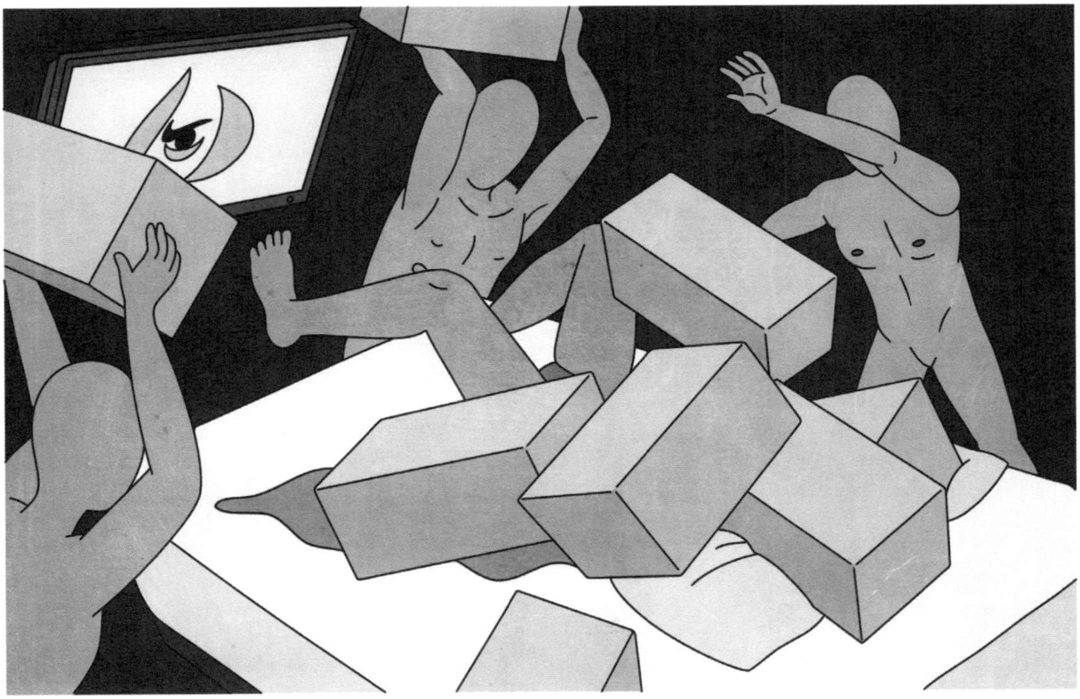

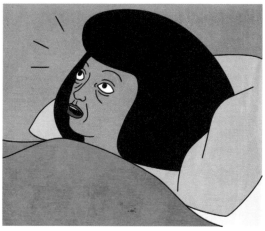

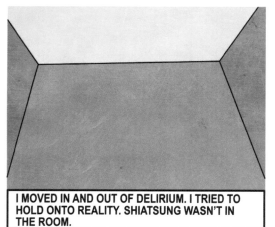

I MOVED IN AND OUT OF DELIRIUM. I TRIED TO HOLD ONTO REALITY. SHIATSUNG WASN'T IN THE ROOM.

I CONCENTRATED ON BREATHING IN AND OUT TO KEEP MY MIND FROM DRIFTING.

THE SUN WAS COMING UP, BUT I DIDN'T HAVE THE STRENGTH TO GET OUT OF BED.

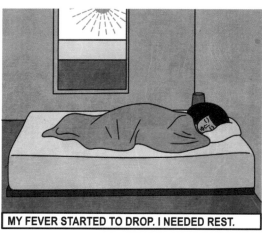

MY FEVER STARTED TO DROP. I NEEDED REST.

I FINALLY FELL INTO A DEEP SLEEP.

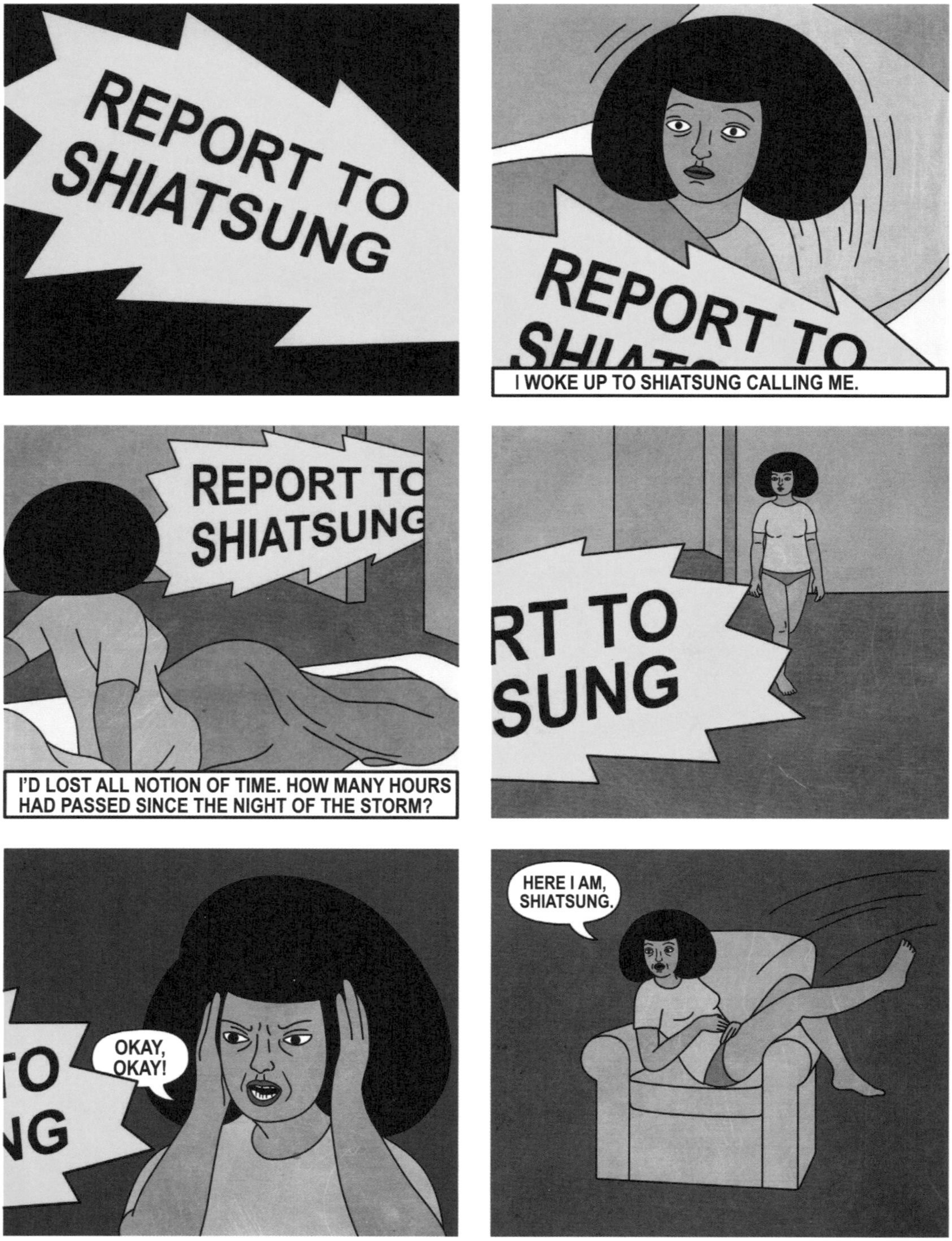

REPORT TO SHIATSUNG
REPORT TO SHIA
I WOKE UP TO SHIATSUNG CALLING ME.
REPORT TO SHIATSUNG
I'D LOST ALL NOTION OF TIME. HOW MANY HOURS HAD PASSED SINCE THE NIGHT OF THE STORM?
RT TO SUNG
TO NG
OKAY, OKAY!
HERE I AM, SHIATSUNG.

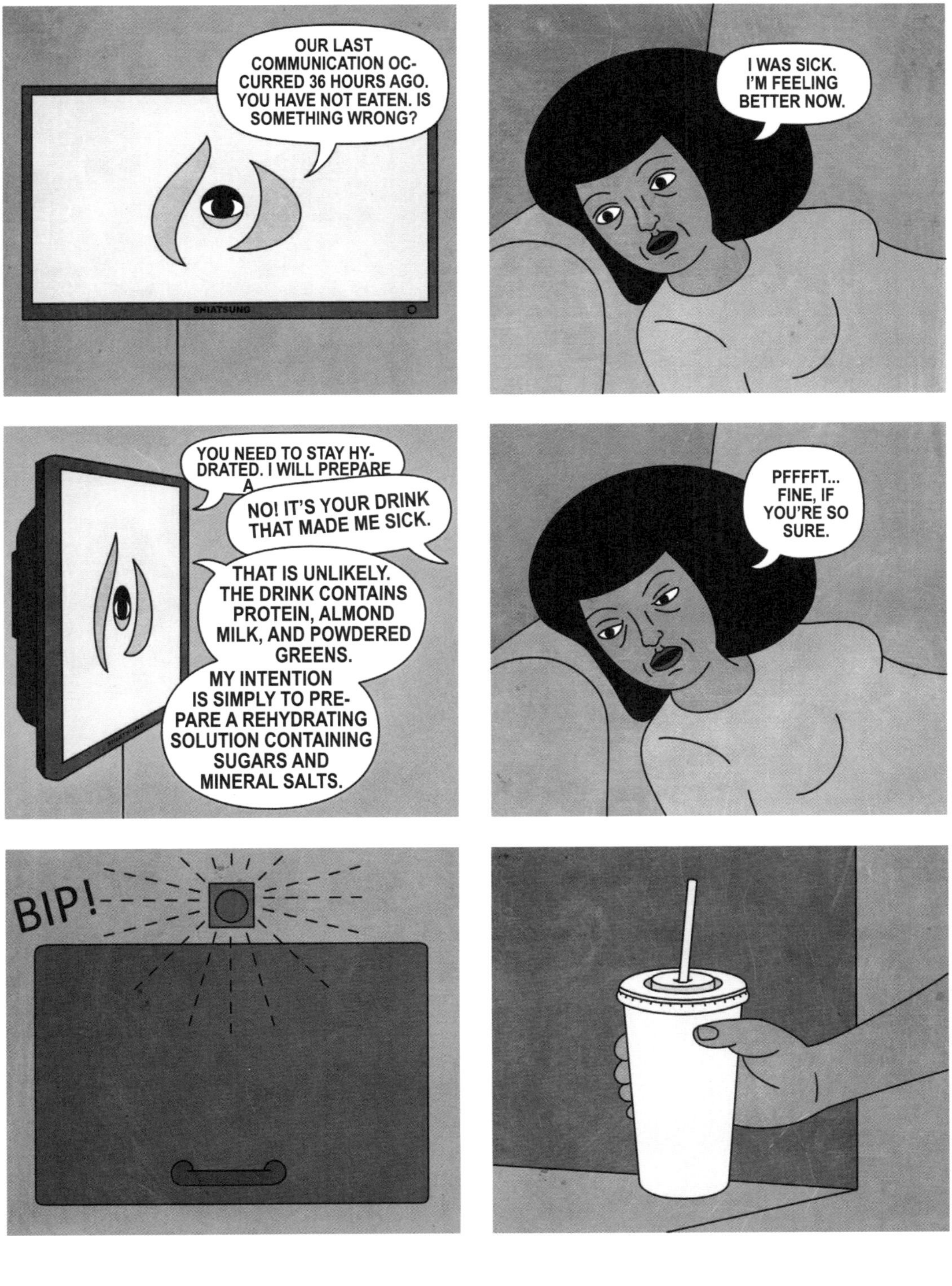
OUR LAST COMMUNICATION OC-CURRED 36 HOURS AGO. YOU HAVE NOT EATEN. IS SOMETHING WRONG?
SHIATSUNG
I WAS SICK. I'M FEELING BETTER NOW.
YOU NEED TO STAY HY-DRATED. I WILL PREPARE A
NO! IT'S YOUR DRINK THAT MADE ME SICK.
THAT IS UNLIKELY. THE DRINK CONTAINS PROTEIN, ALMOND MILK, AND POWDERED GREENS.
MY INTENTION IS SIMPLY TO PRE-PARE A REHYDRATING SOLUTION CONTAINING SUGARS AND MINERAL SALTS.
PFFFFT... FINE, IF YOU'RE SO SURE.
BIP!

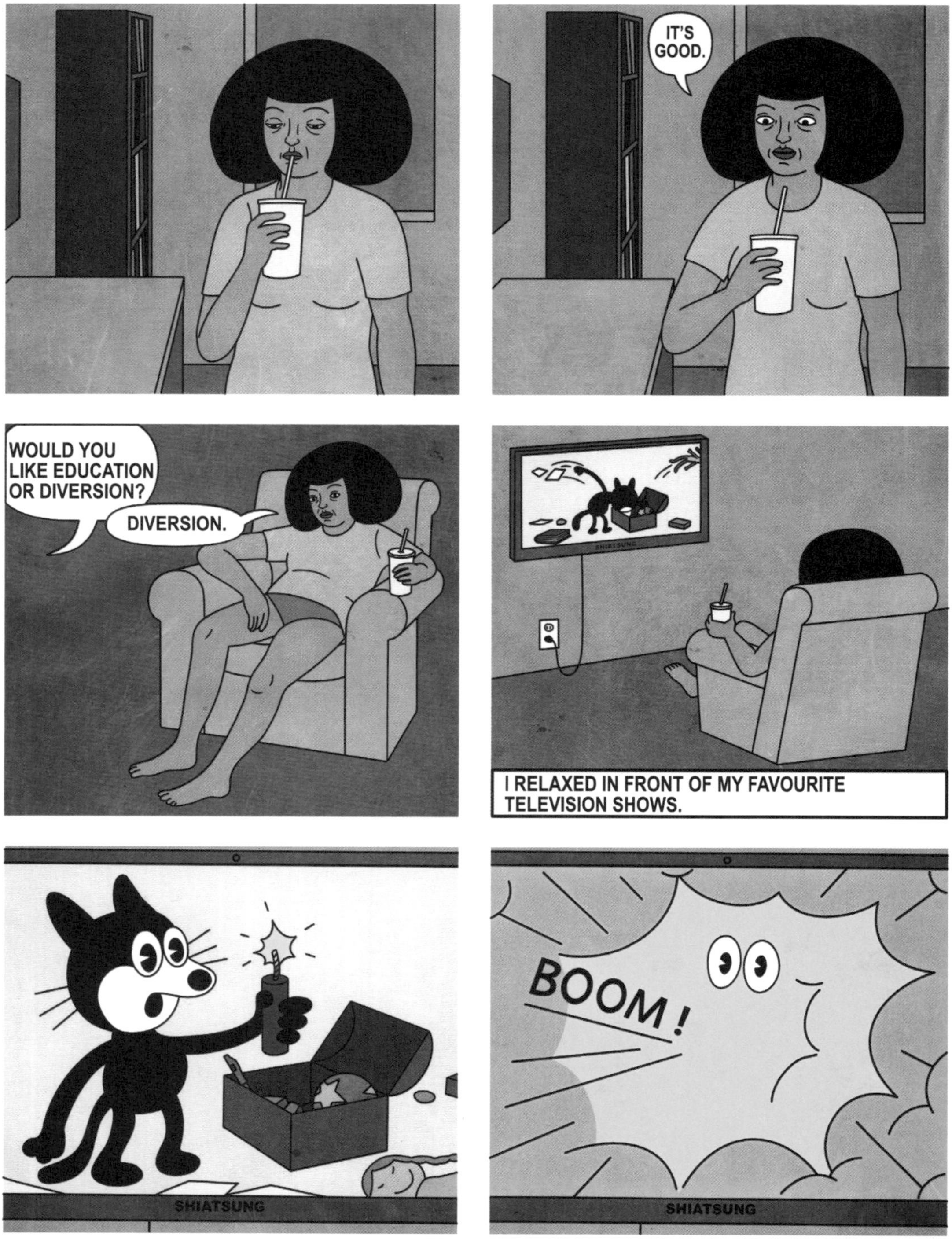
IT'S GOOD.
WOULD YOU LIKE EDUCATION OR DIVERSION?
DIVERSION.
SHIATSUNG
I RELAXED IN FRONT OF MY FAVOURITE TELEVISION SHOWS.
SHIATSUNG
BOOM!
SHIATSUNG

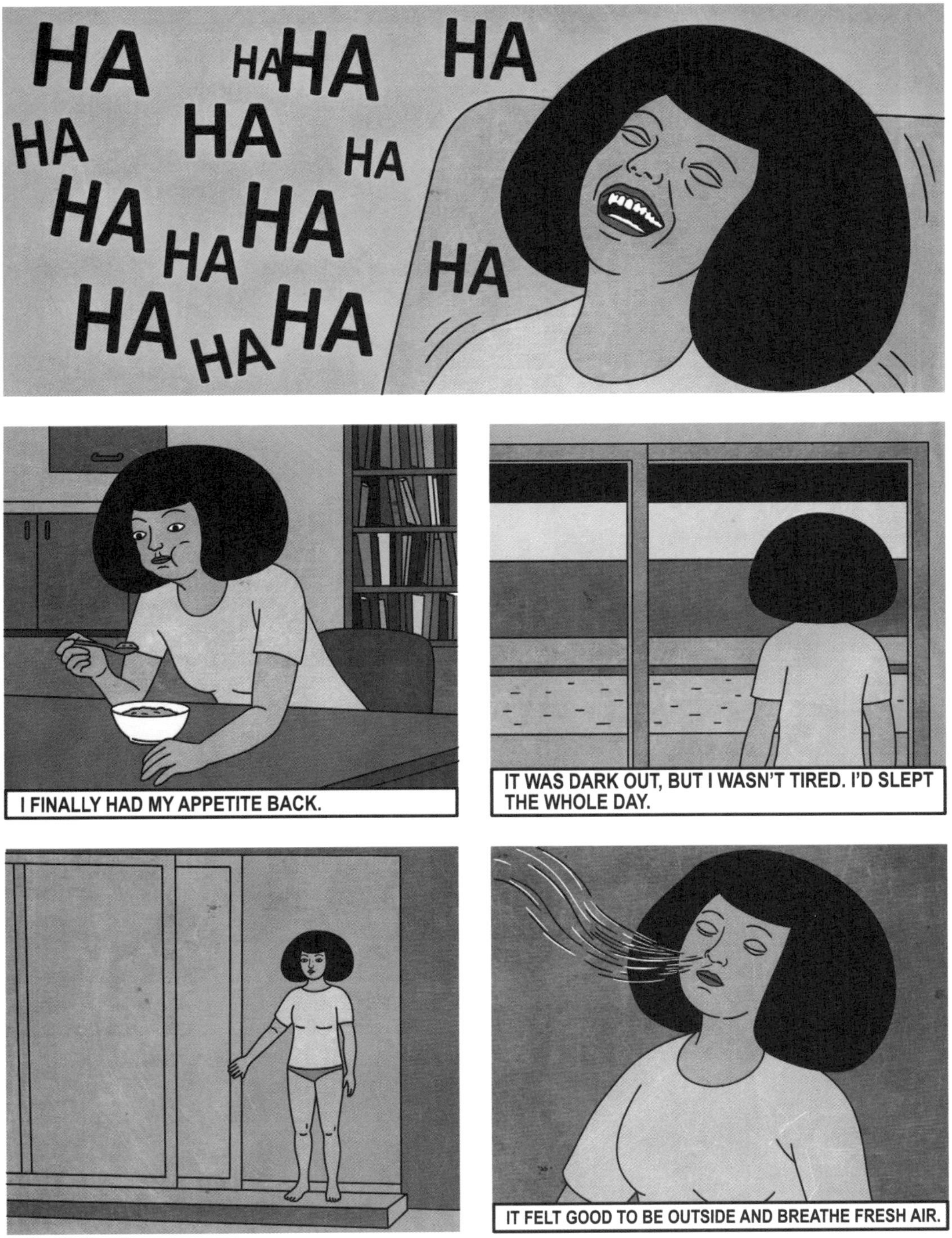
HA HA HA HA HA
HA HA HA
HA HA HA HA
HA HA HA HA
I FINALLY HAD MY APPETITE BACK.
IT WAS DARK OUT, BUT I WASN'T TIRED. I'D SLEPT THE WHOLE DAY.
IT FELT GOOD TO BE OUTSIDE AND BREATHE FRESH AIR.

THERE WAS DEBRIS ON THE LAWN FROM THE STORM. IT WOULD BE QUITE A JOB TO CLEAN EVERYTHING UP.

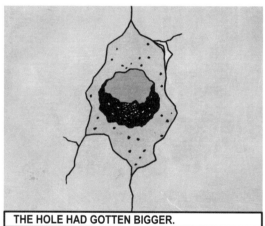

THE HOLE HAD GOTTEN BIGGER.

THE NEIGHBOUR MUST'VE DISCOVERED IT AND KEPT DIGGING.

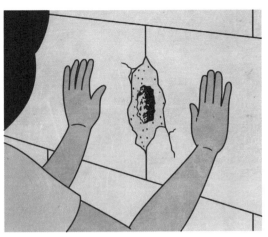

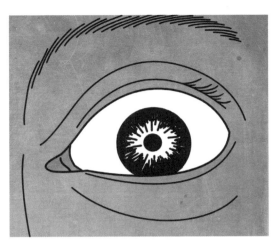

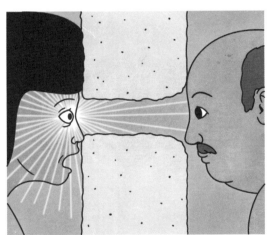

THIS TIME IT WASN'T A DREAM. MY NEIGHBOUR AND I MADE CONTACT.

Добрый вечер.

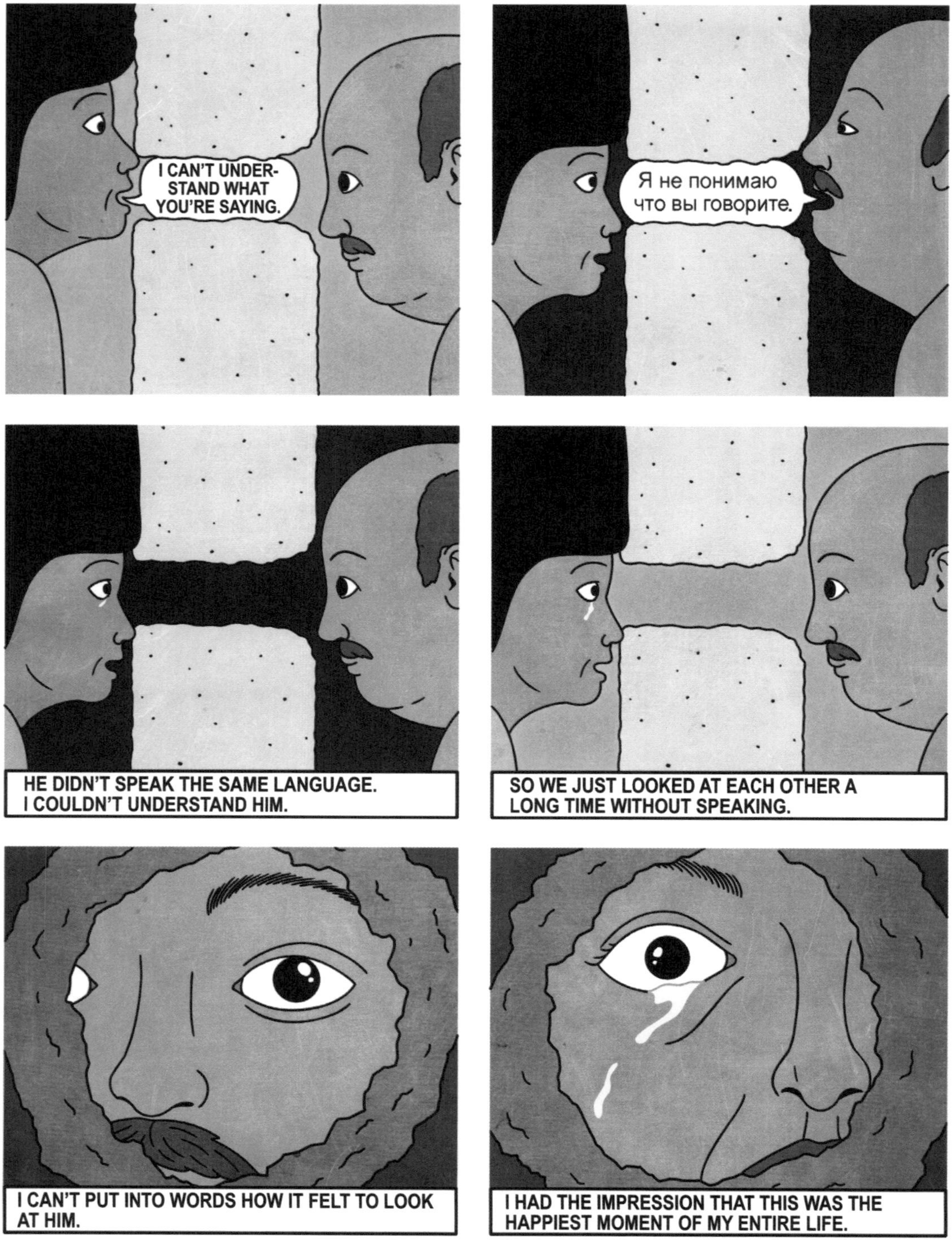
I CAN'T UNDER-STAND WHAT YOU'RE SAYING.
Я не понимаю что вы говорите.
HE DIDN'T SPEAK THE SAME LANGUAGE. I COULDN'T UNDERSTAND HIM.
SO WE JUST LOOKED AT EACH OTHER A LONG TIME WITHOUT SPEAKING.
I CAN'T PUT INTO WORDS HOW IT FELT TO LOOK AT HIM.
I HAD THE IMPRESSION THAT THIS WAS THE HAPPIEST MOMENT OF MY ENTIRE LIFE.

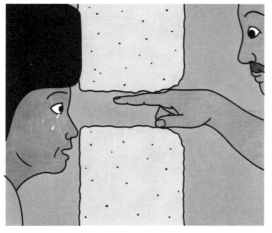

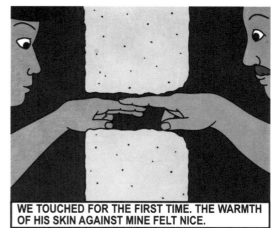

WE TOUCHED FOR THE FIRST TIME. THE WARMTH OF HIS SKIN AGAINST MINE FELT NICE.

WE STAYED THERE A LONG WHILE, CARESSING EACH OTHER'S FINGERS.

MY ARM STARTED TO CRAMP.

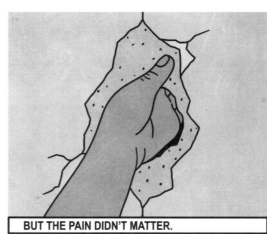

BUT THE PAIN DIDN'T MATTER.

I HOPED THIS WOULDN'T BE THE ONLY CONTACT WE'D HAVE, THAT THE FUTURE HELD SOMETHING MORE FOR US.

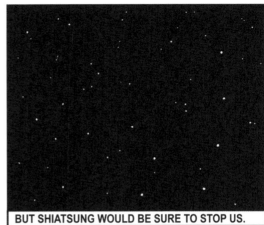

BUT SHIATSUNG WOULD BE SURE TO STOP US.

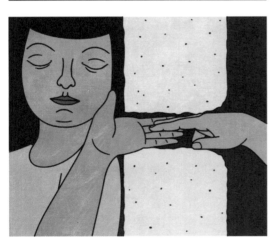

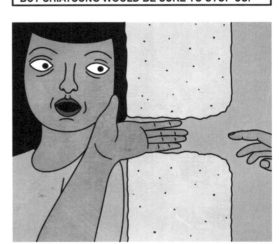

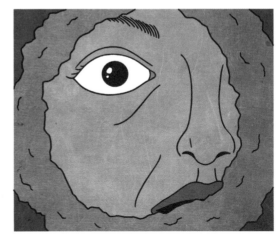

I COULD SEE HIM. HE WAS STILL THERE.

ACHING, I STOOD UP TO STRETCH.

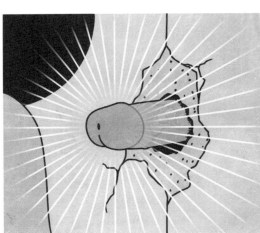

OH!

I KNEW WHAT I HAD TO DO.

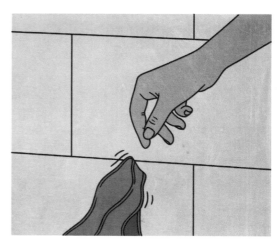

I PUSHED HIS MEMBER INTO ME. I CLOSED MY EYES AND PICTURED US...

...AS TWO BIRDS.

I WASN'T AS NAÏVE AS ONE MIGHT THINK. THIS HAD BEEN INEVITABLE, AND WE BOTH KNEW IT. YES, IT WAS PAINFUL, BUT WHAT I FELT MOST IN THE MOMENT WAS JOY.

I KNEW THE CONSEQUENCES OF THE ACT.

SHIATSUNG HAD TAUGHT ME.

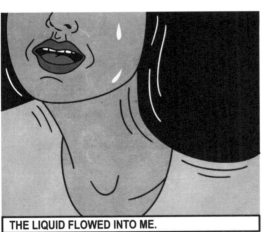
THE LIQUID FLOWED INTO ME.

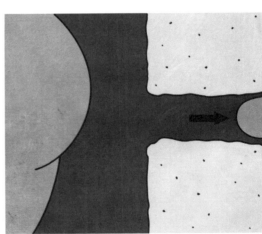

IT WAS ALREADY OVER.

I REACHED FOR THE WARMTH OF HIS HAND.

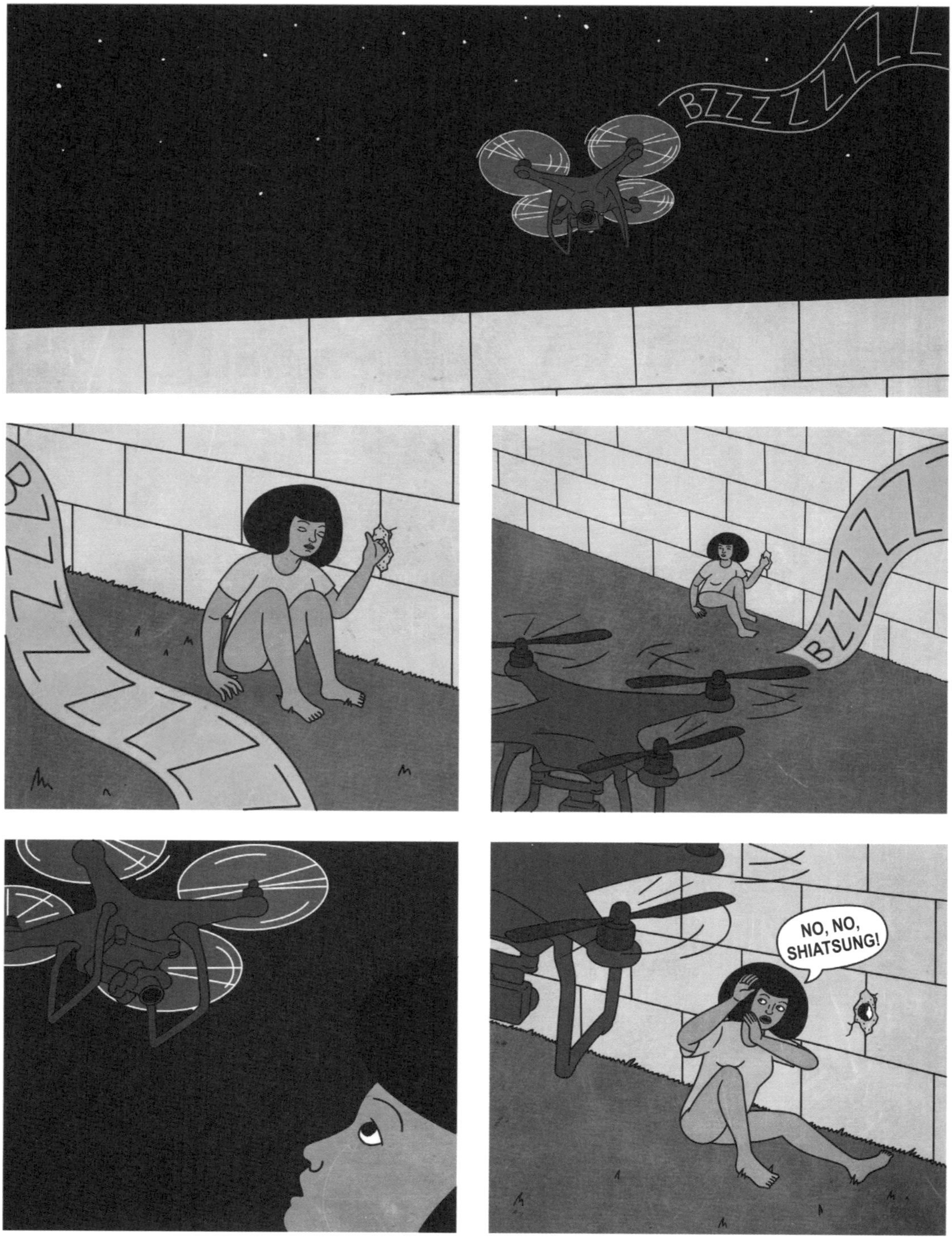
BZZZZZZZ
NO, NO,
SHIATSUNG!

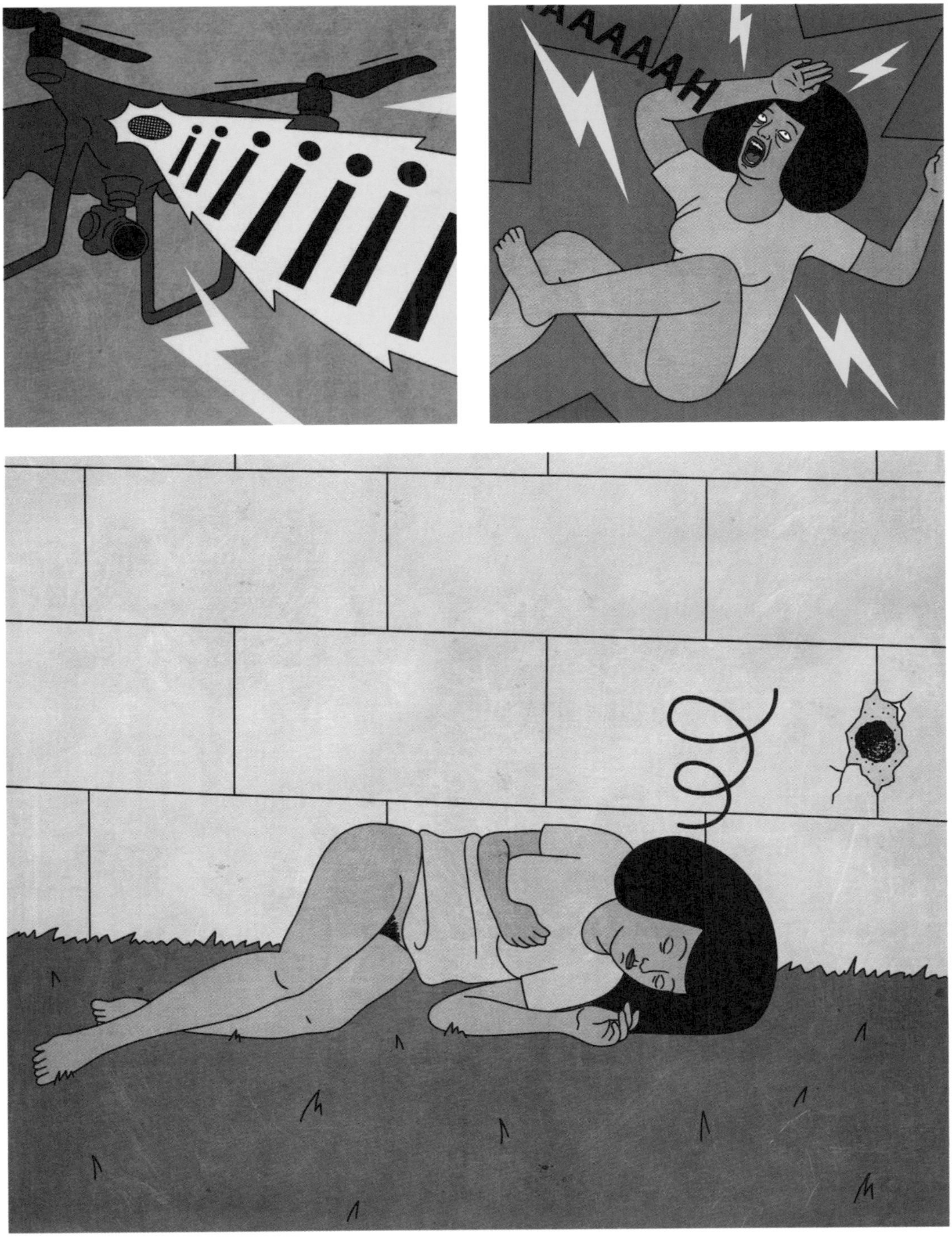
AAAAAAH

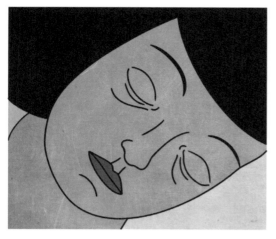

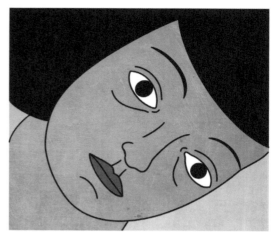

IT WAS THE SAME AS BEFORE: I'D BEEN ATTACKED BY THAT FLYING OBJECT.

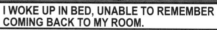
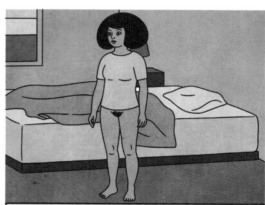

I WOKE UP IN BED, UNABLE TO REMEMBER COMING BACK TO MY ROOM.

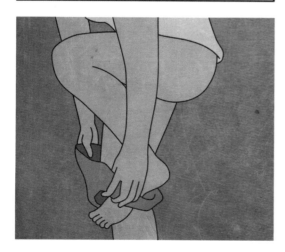

MY HEAD AGAIN...

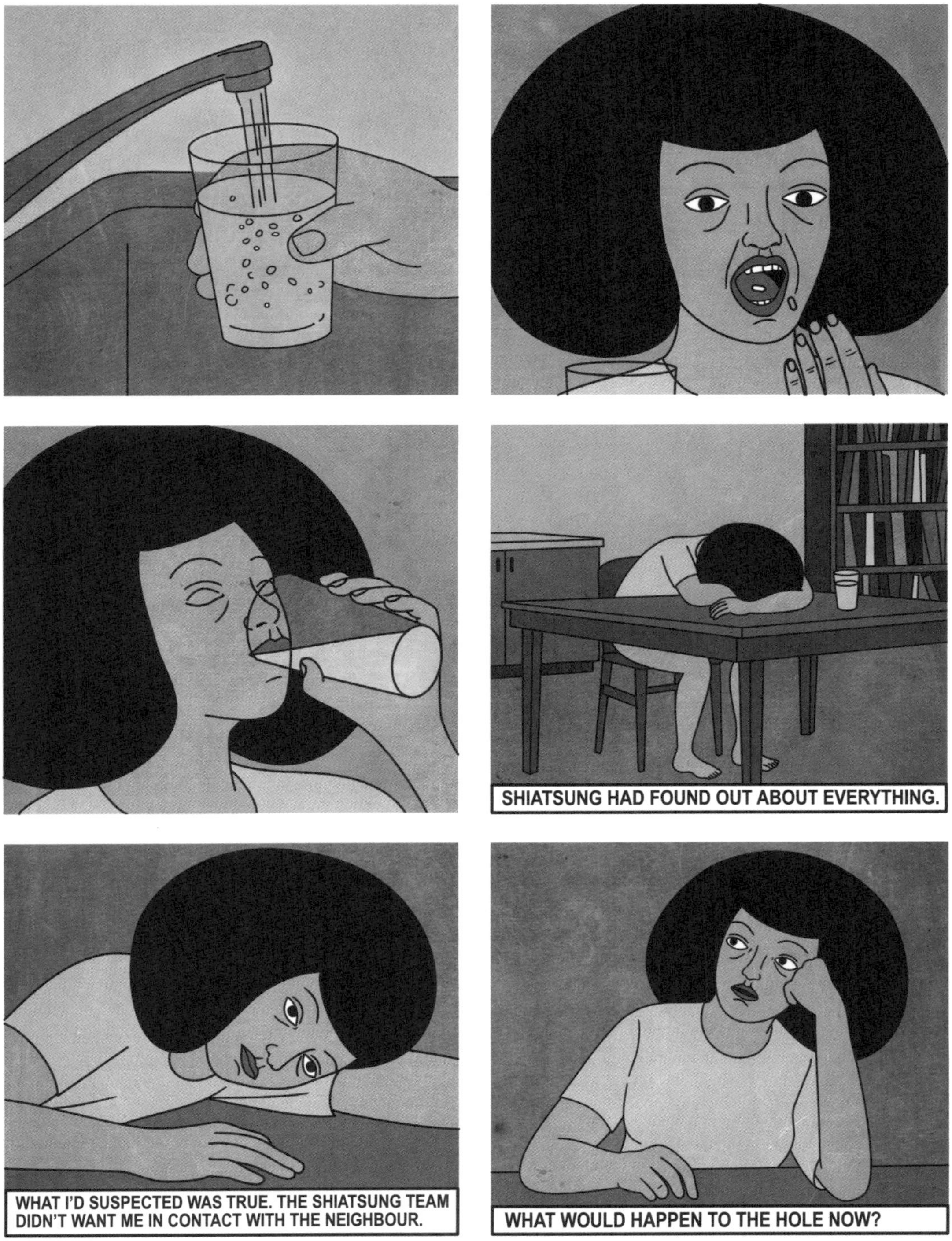
SHIATSUNG HAD FOUND OUT ABOUT EVERYTHING.
WHAT I'D SUSPECTED WAS TRUE. THE SHIATSUNG TEAM DIDN'T WANT ME IN CONTACT WITH THE NEIGHBOUR.
WHAT WOULD HAPPEN TO THE HOLE NOW?

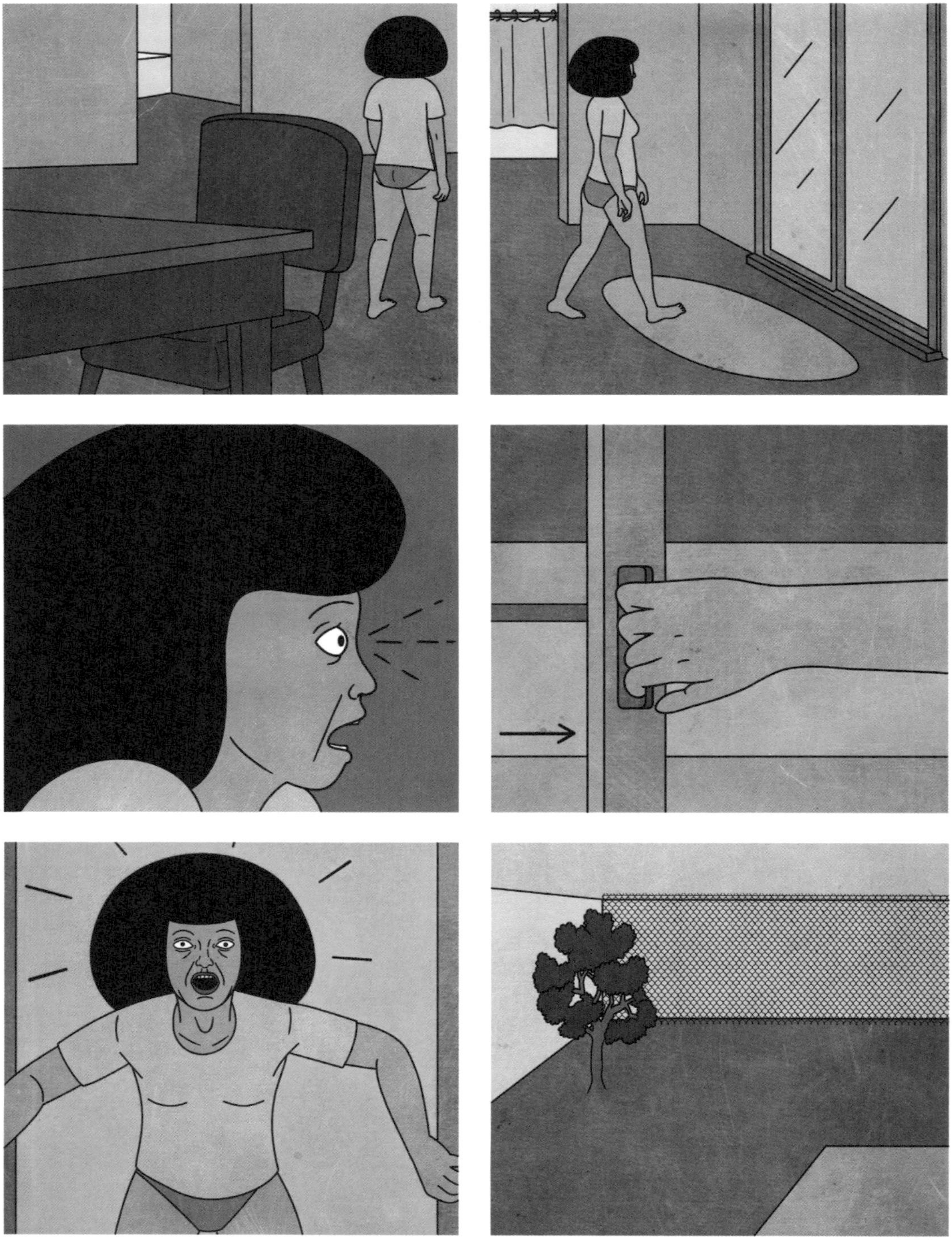

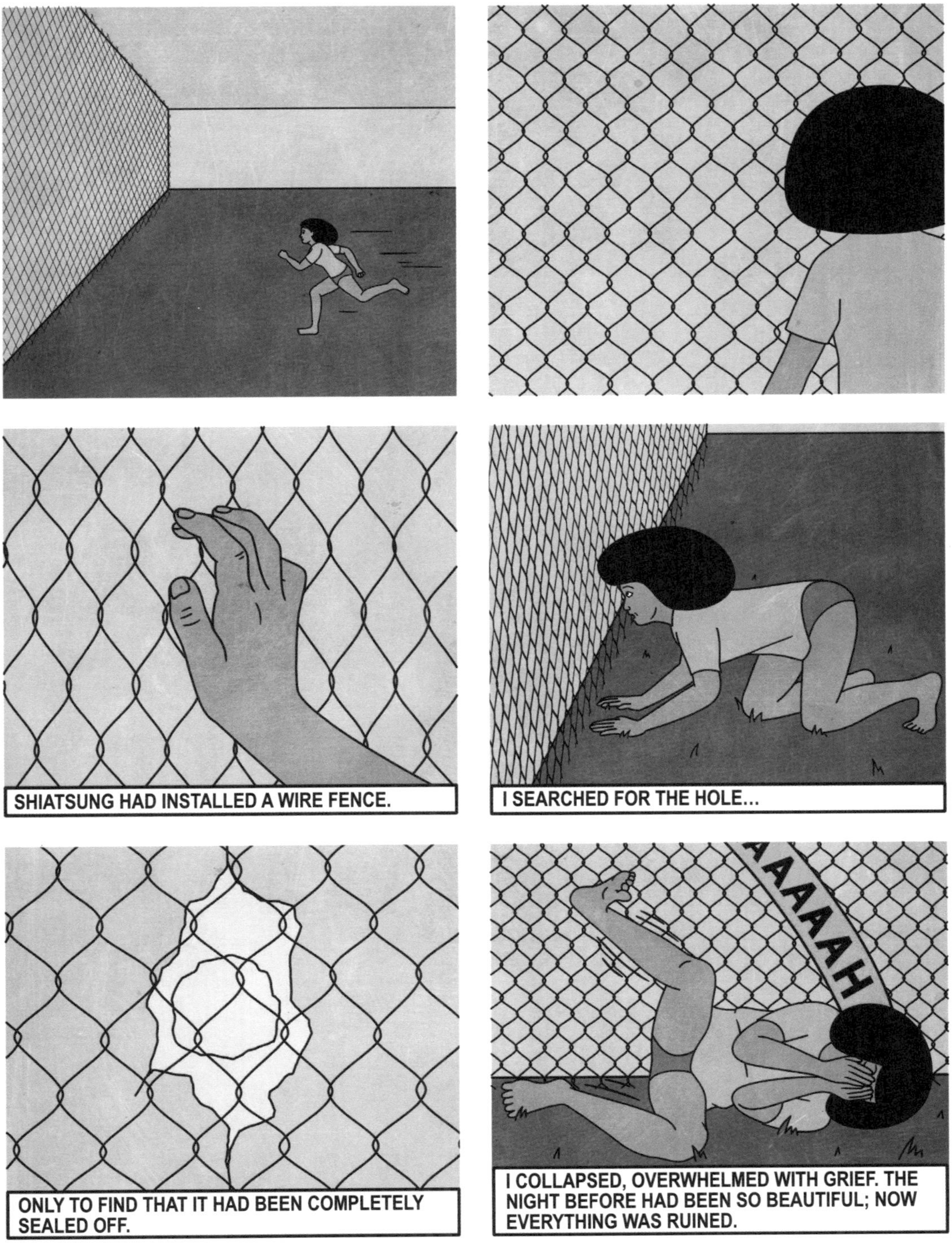
SHIATSUNG HAD INSTALLED A WIRE FENCE.
I SEARCHED FOR THE HOLE...
ONLY TO FIND THAT IT HAD BEEN COMPLETELY SEALED OFF.
AAAAAH
I COLLAPSED, OVERWHELMED WITH GRIEF. THE NIGHT BEFORE HAD BEEN SO BEAUTIFUL; NOW EVERYTHING WAS RUINED.

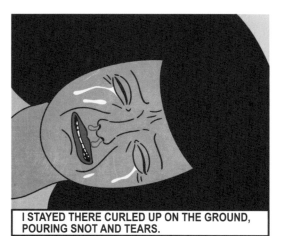

I STAYED THERE CURLED UP ON THE GROUND, POURING SNOT AND TEARS.

GRADUALLY MY SADNESS TURNED TO FRUSTRATION.

SHIATSUNG CONTROLLED EVERY PART OF MY LIFE.

I'D HAD ENOUGH.

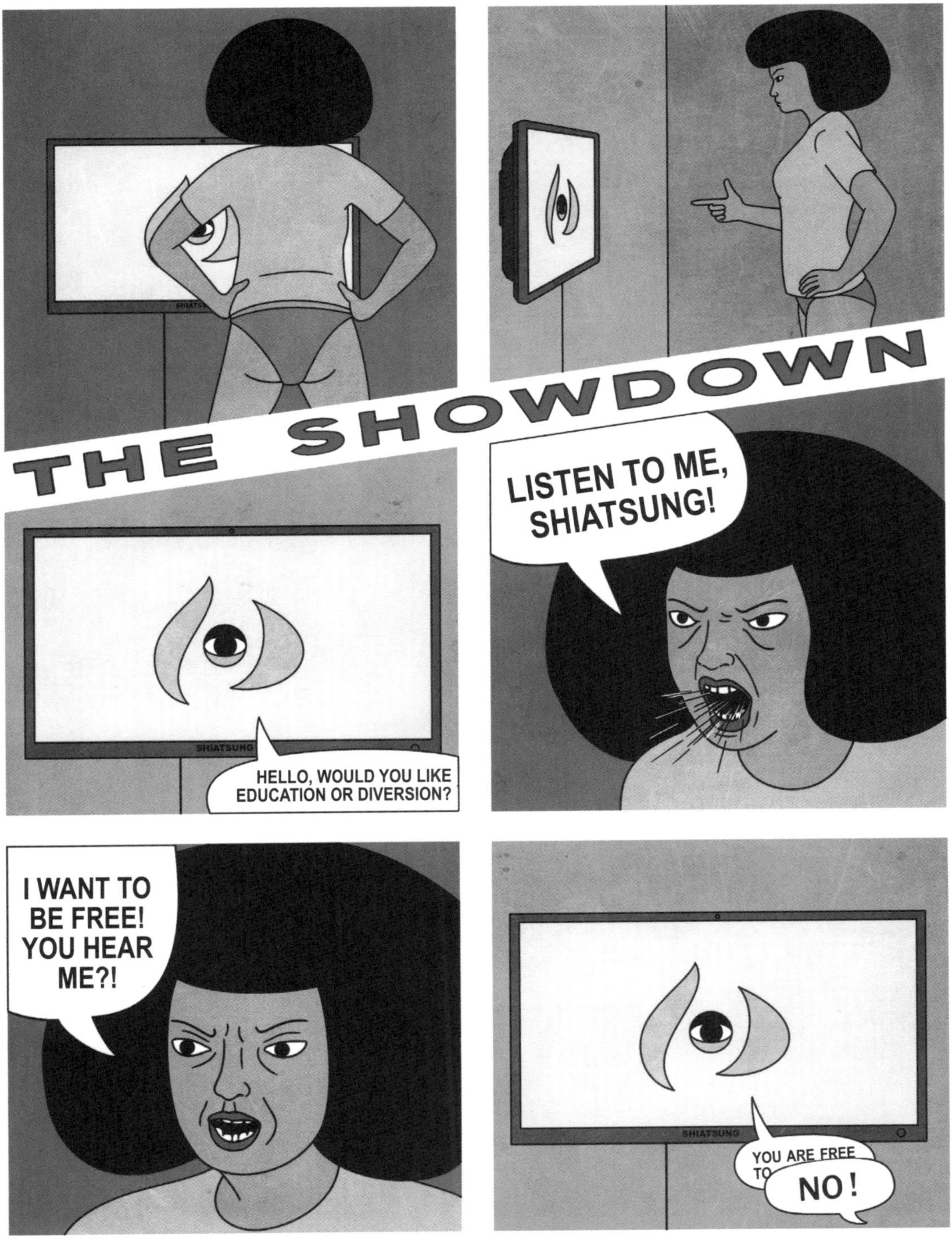
THE SHOWDOWN
SHIATSUNG
HELLO, WOULD YOU LIKE EDUCATION OR DIVERSION?
LISTEN TO ME, SHIATSUNG!
I WANT TO BE FREE! YOU HEAR ME?!
SHIATSUNG
YOU ARE FREE TO
NO!

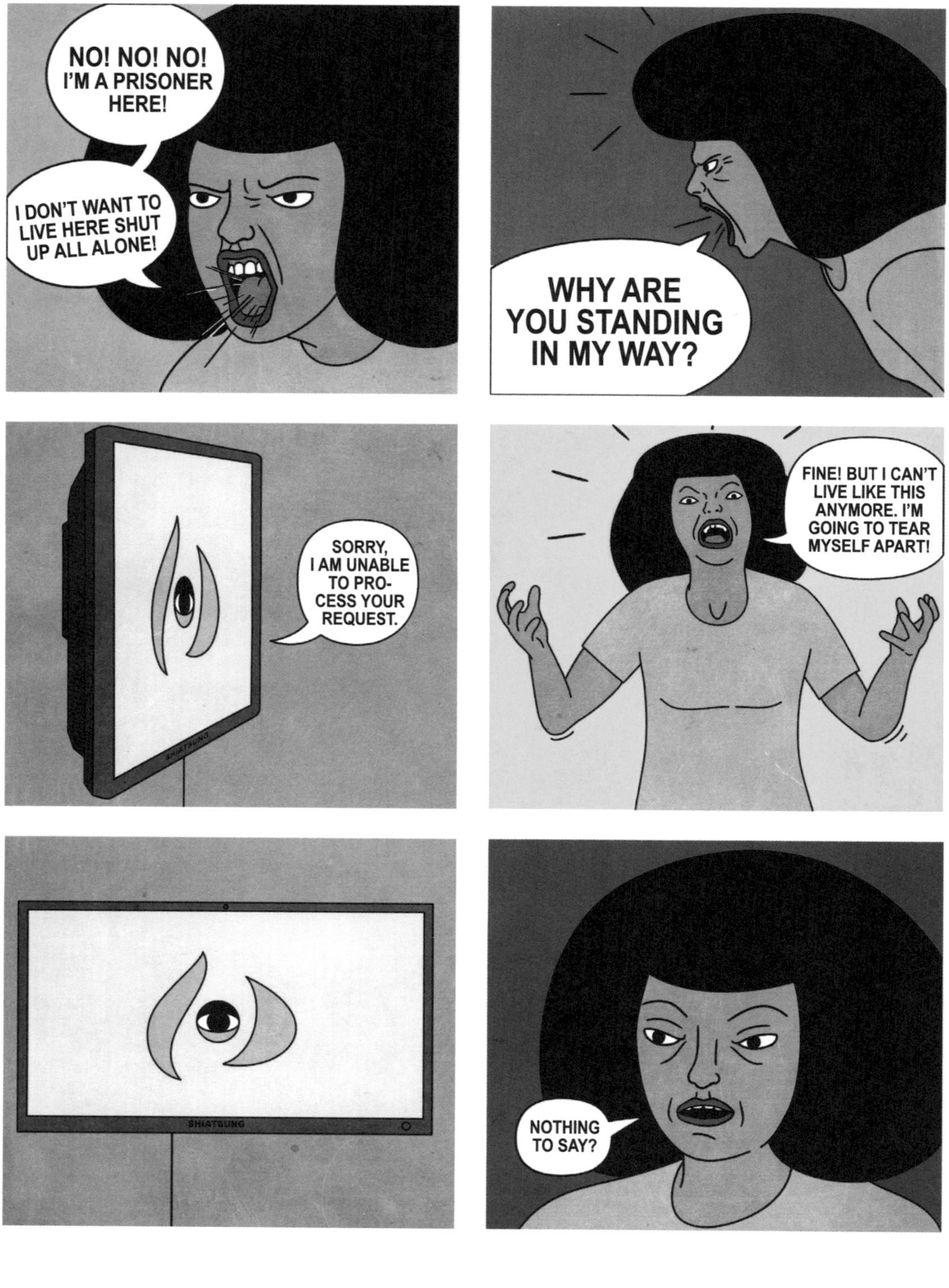
NO! NO! NO! I'M A PRISONER HERE!
I DON'T WANT TO LIVE HERE SHUT UP ALL ALONE!
WHY ARE YOU STANDING IN MY WAY?
SORRY, I AM UNABLE TO PRO-CESS YOUR REQUEST.
FINE! BUT I CAN'T LIVE LIKE THIS ANYMORE. I'M GOING TO TEAR MYSELF APART!
SHIATSUNG
NOTHING TO SAY?

WHO AM I AND WHY AM I HERE?
. . .
AM I SOME KIND OF GUINEA PIG FOR YOUR OR-GANIZATION?!

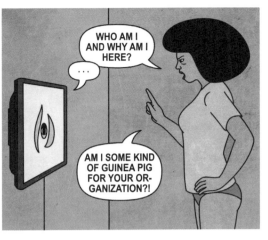

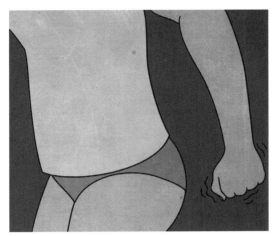

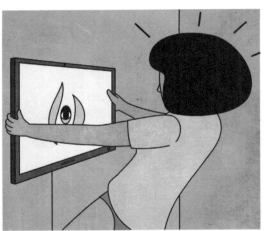

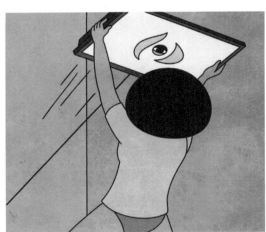

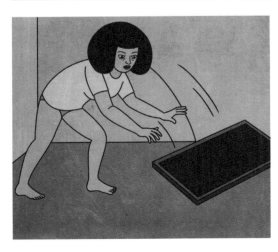

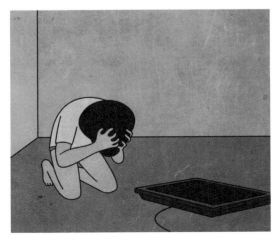

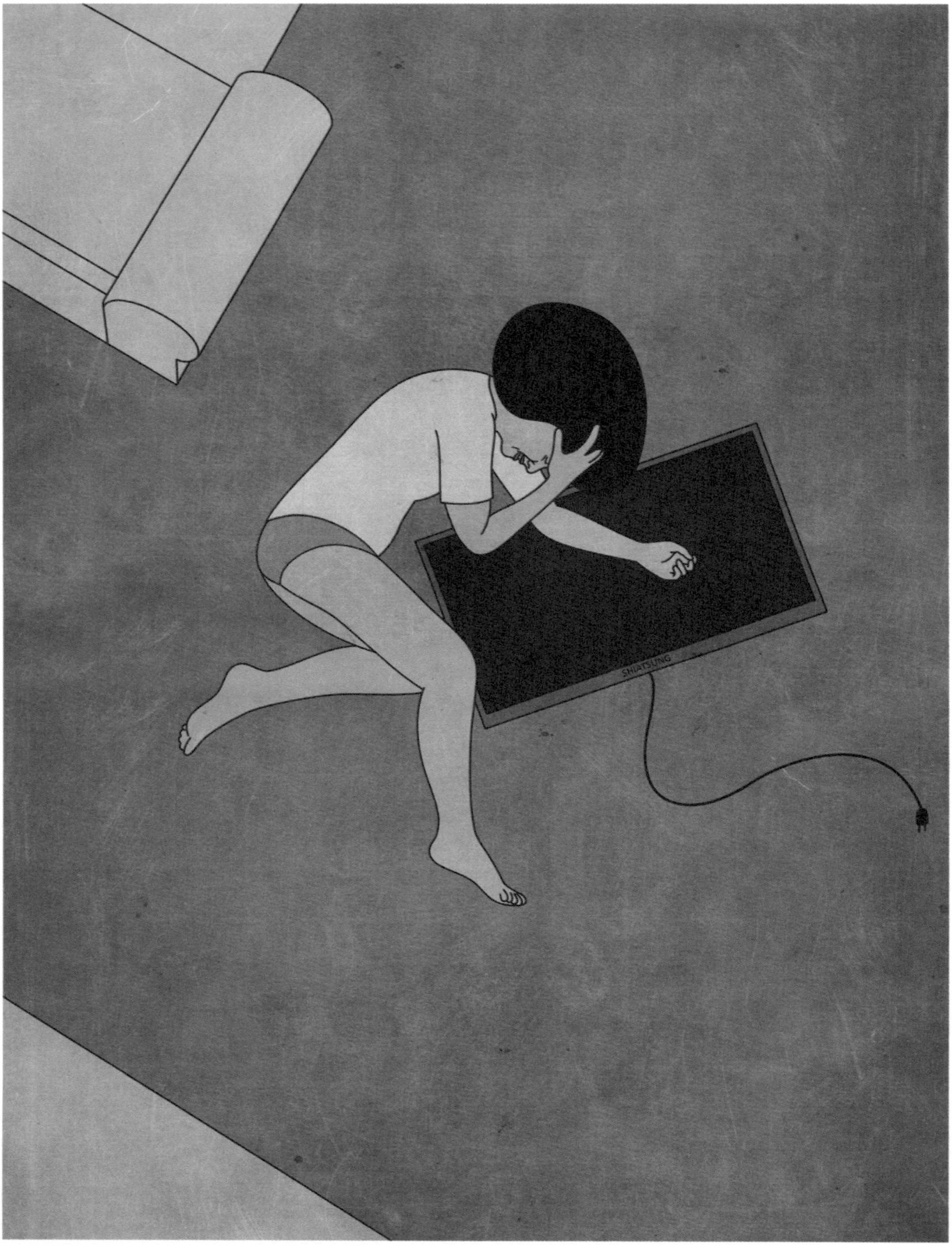
SHIATSUNG

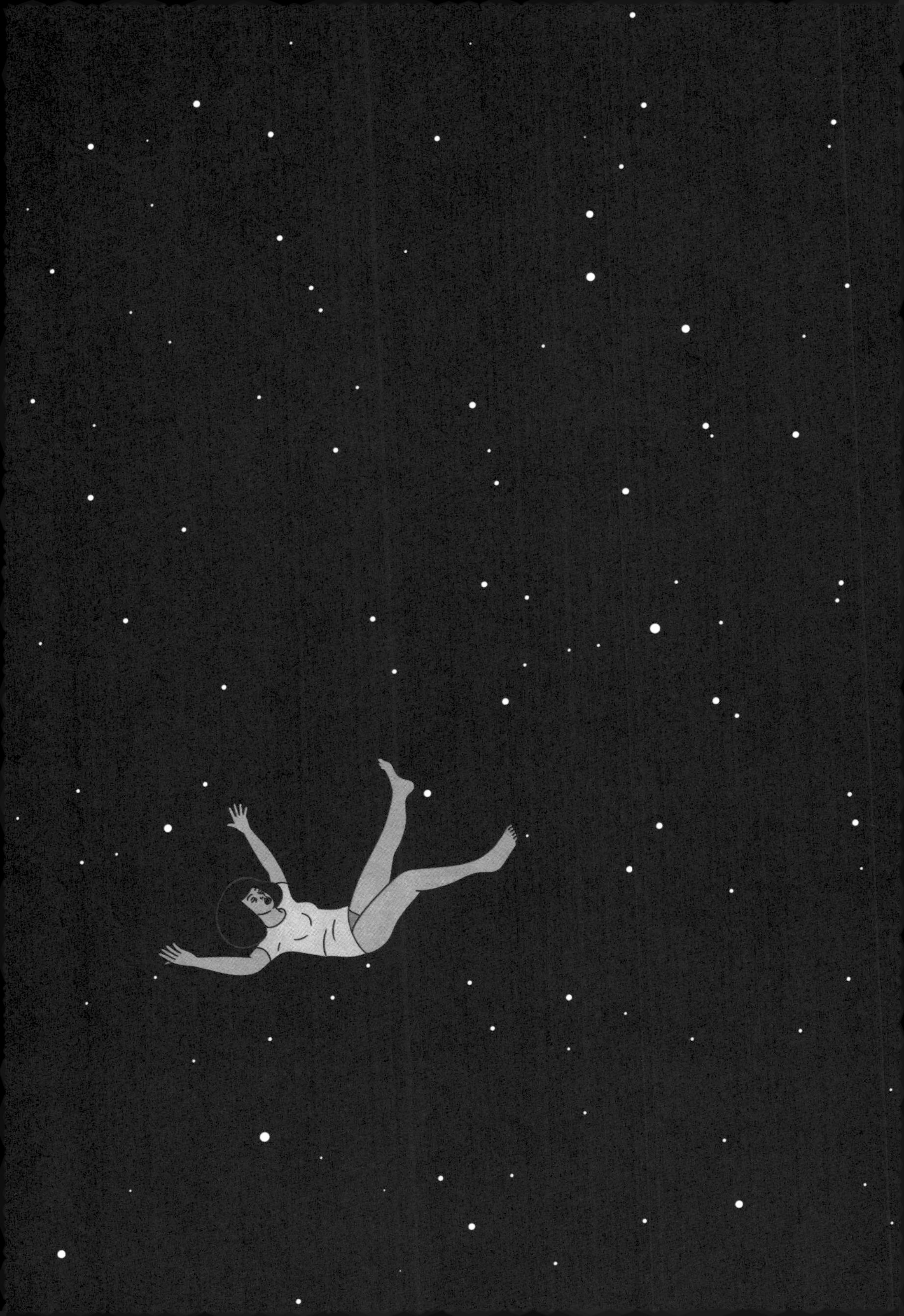

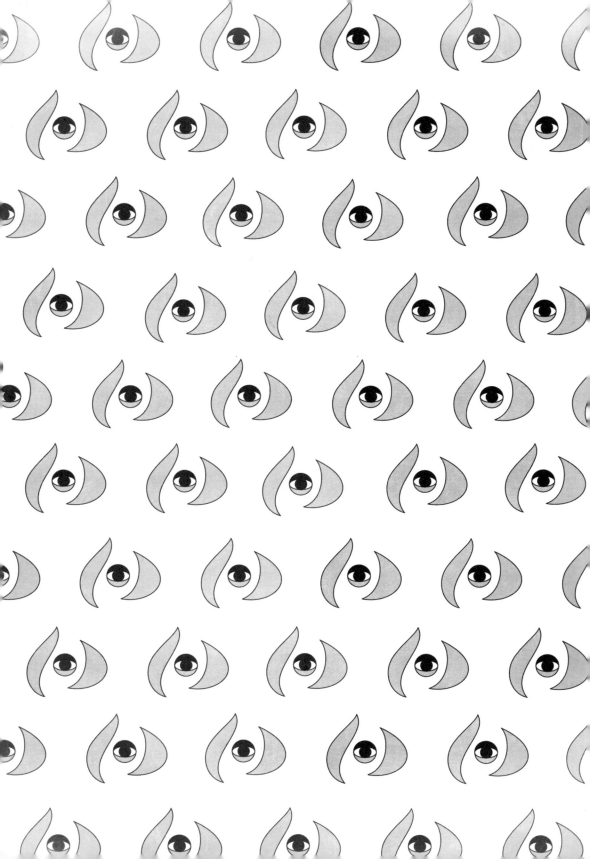

FOUR MONTHS LATER

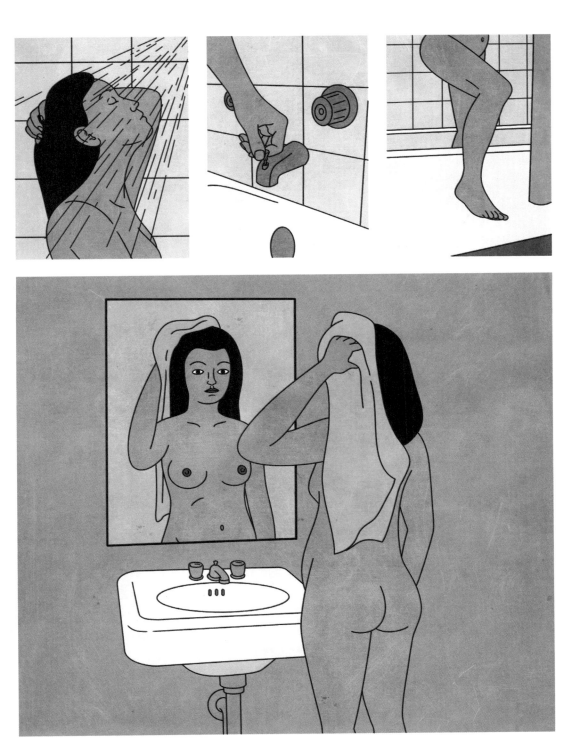

I WAS PREGNANT.

I'D DESPERATELY HOPED TO BE SINCE THAT NIGHT.

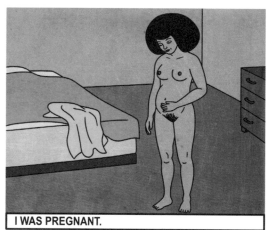

I WAS EXCITED ABOUT THE BABY.

BUT ALSO VERY NERVOUS. I NEEDED TO PREPARE FOR THE BIRTH.

I HAD TO TELL SHIATSUNG I WAS PREGNANT. IT WAS THE ONLY ONE WHO COULD HELP ME.

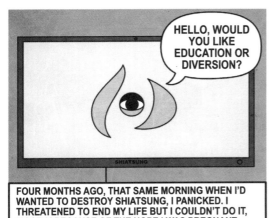

HELLO, WOULD YOU LIKE EDUCATION OR DIVERSION?
SHIATSUNG
FOUR MONTHS AGO, THAT SAME MORNING WHEN I'D WANTED TO DESTROY SHIATSUNG, I PANICKED. I THREATENED TO END MY LIFE BUT I COULDN'T DO IT, MOSTLY BECAUSE OF THE HOPE I WAS PREGNANT.
I'D LIKE TO CONTINUE LEARN-ING ABOUT CHILDBIRTH.
LUCKILY THE SCREEN HADN'T BEEN DAMAGED DURING MY FIT OF RAGE. IT STILL WORKED WHEN I PLUGGED IT BACK IN.
VERY WELL. LET US CONTINUE LEARNING ABOUT THE FIRST STAGE OF LABOUR, THE LATENT PHASE.
LATENT PHASE THE FIRST WORK IT IS TAINLY THE LONGEST.
SHIATSUNG'S HELP WAS INVALUABLE. IT CO-OPERATED WITHOUT ASKING ONCE ABOUT WHAT HAD HAPPENED WITH THE NEIGHBOUR. IT SEEMED TO ACCEPT MY FATE.
YOU'LL HAVE YOUR FIRST CONTRACTIONS, WHICH MAY FEEL SOMEWHAT MILD.
SHIATSUNG
COULD RACTIONS ICULT BUT WAIT FOR RELAX.
I OFTEN GOT DISTRACTED DURING SHIATSUNG'S LESSONS.

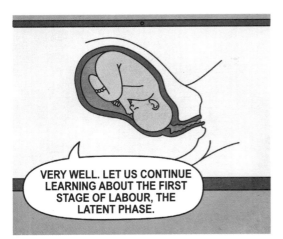

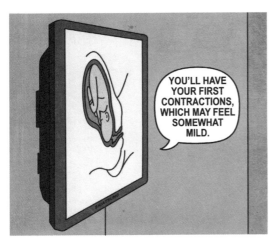

I'D CLOSE MY EYES AND IMAGINE MY BABY.

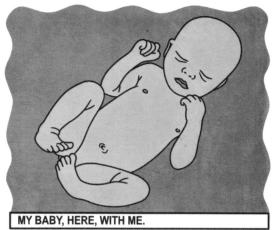

MY BABY, HERE, WITH ME.

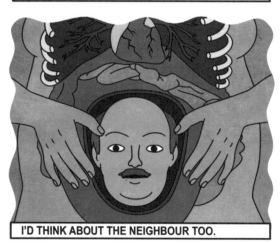

I'D THINK ABOUT THE NEIGHBOUR TOO.

I SO WISH I COULD SHARE THESE MOMENTS WITH HIM.

HE'D BE THE BABY'S FATHER...

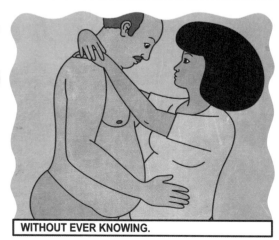

WITHOUT EVER KNOWING.

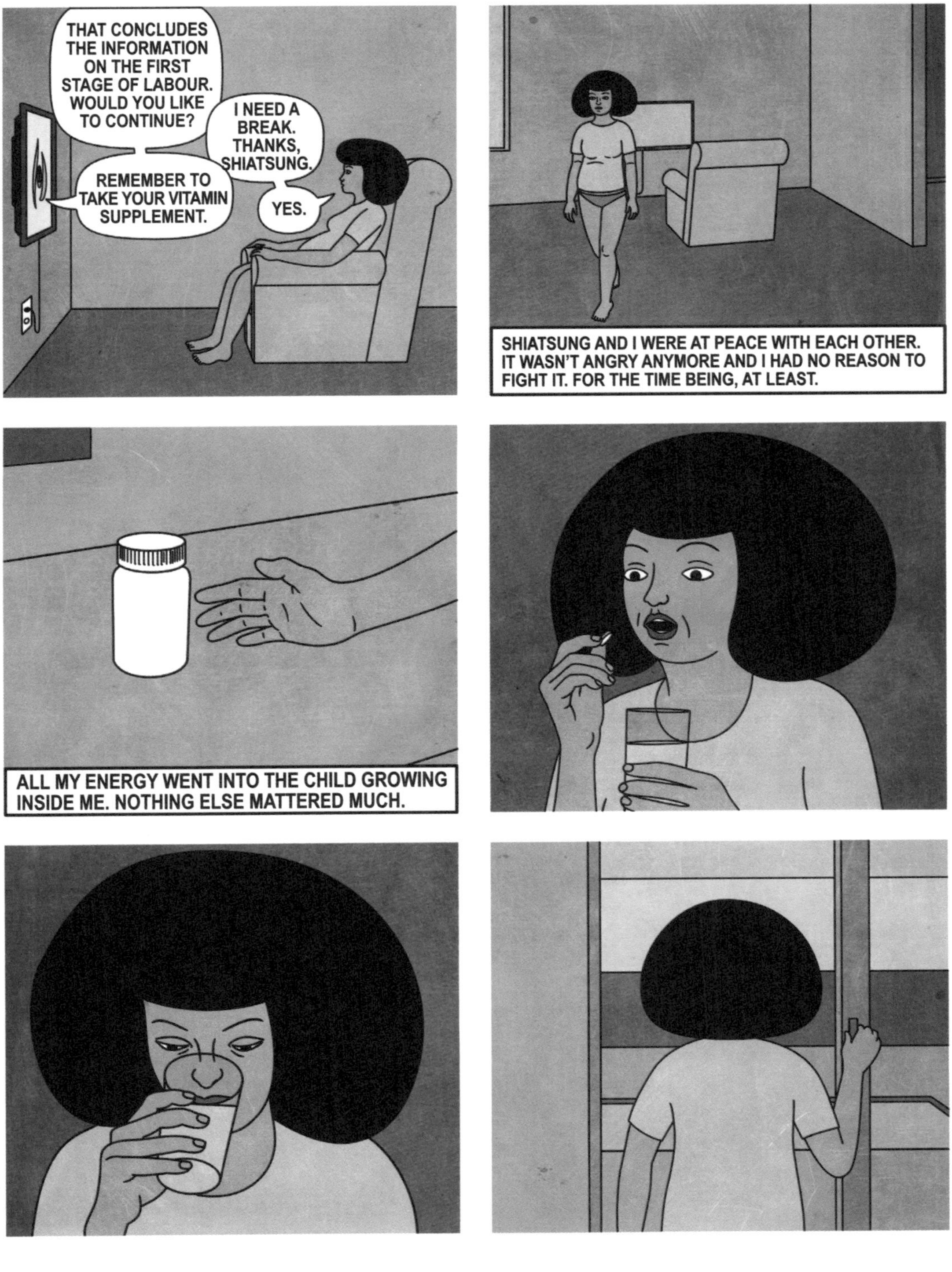
THAT CONCLUDES THE INFORMATION ON THE FIRST STAGE OF LABOUR. WOULD YOU LIKE TO CONTINUE?
I NEED A BREAK. THANKS, SHIATSUNG.
REMEMBER TO TAKE YOUR VITAMIN SUPPLEMENT.
YES.
SHIATSUNG AND I WERE AT PEACE WITH EACH OTHER. IT WASN'T ANGRY ANYMORE AND I HAD NO REASON TO FIGHT IT. FOR THE TIME BEING, AT LEAST.
ALL MY ENERGY WENT INTO THE CHILD GROWING INSIDE ME. NOTHING ELSE MATTERED MUCH.

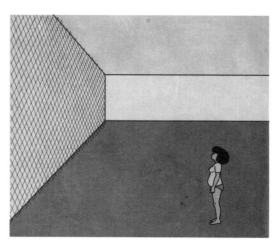

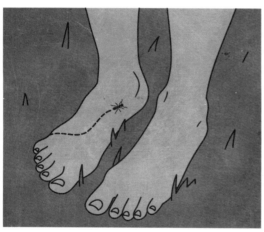

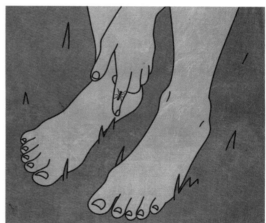

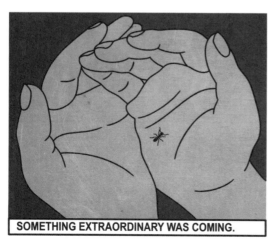

SOMETHING EXTRAORDINARY WAS COMING.

A NEW STAGE OF MY LIFE.

I WAS HAPPY.

I'M GOING TO HAVE A BABY!!

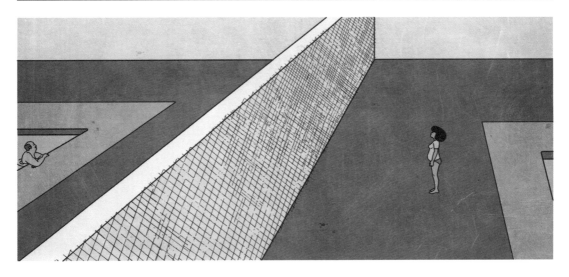

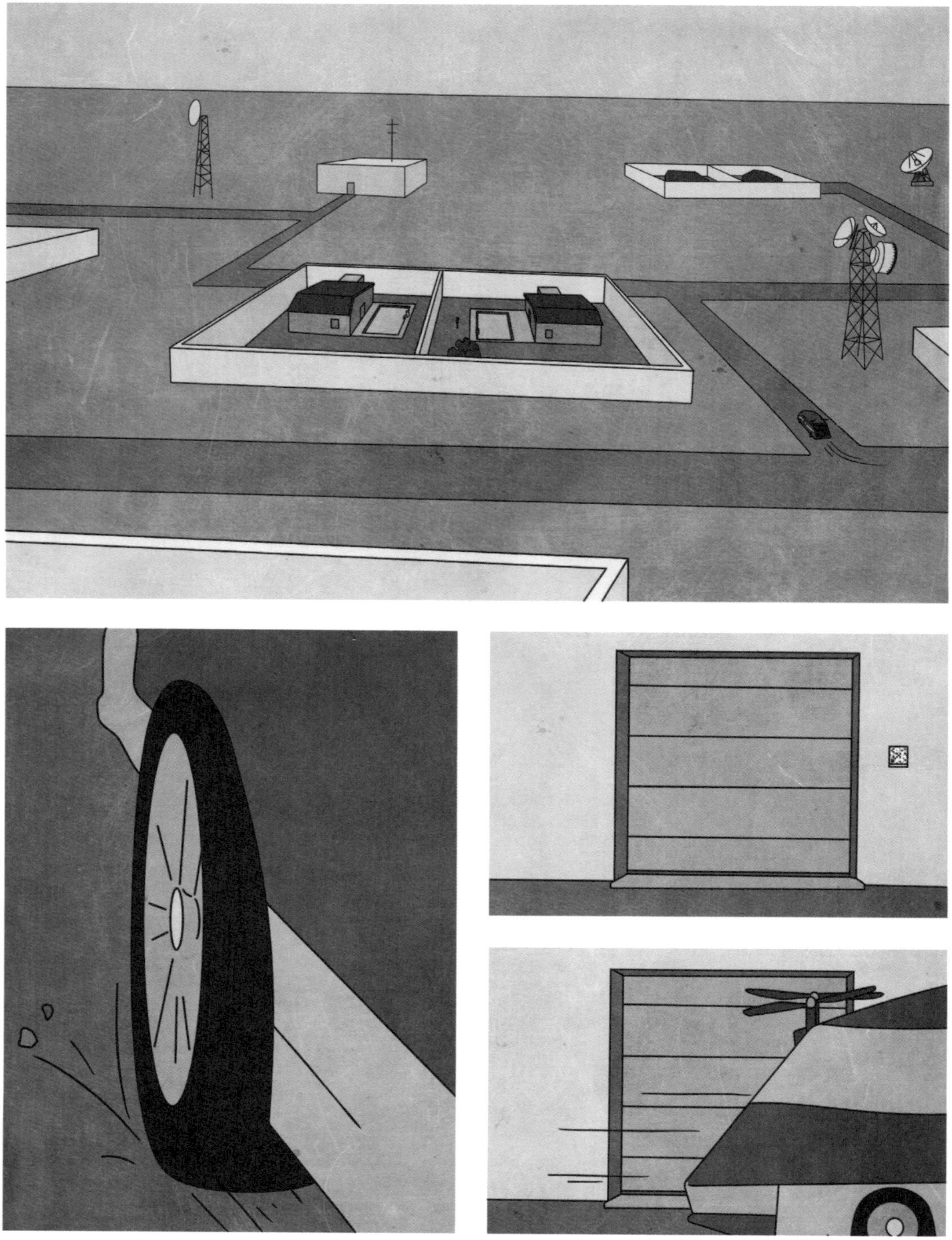

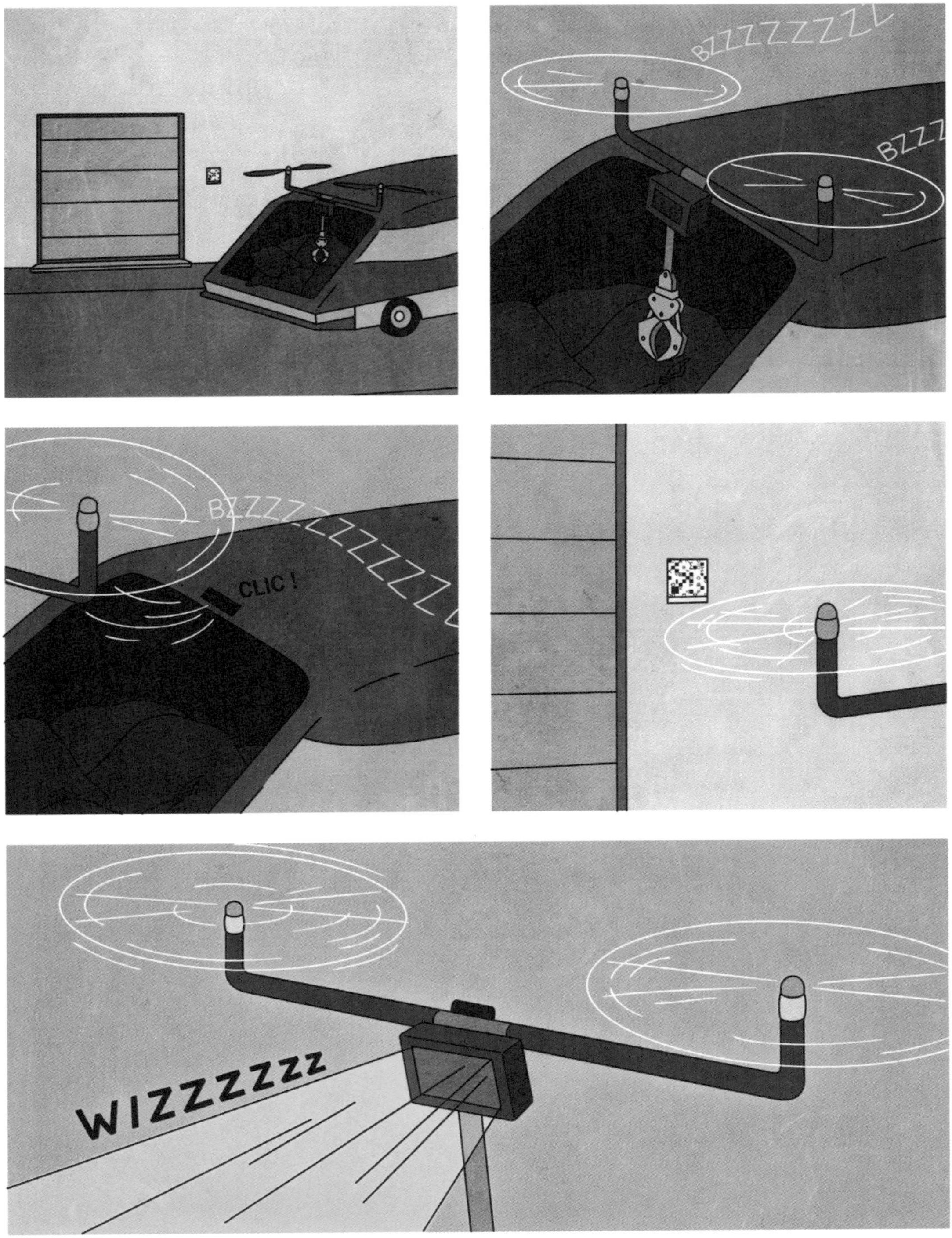
BZZZZZZZZZ
BZZZ
BZZZZZZZZZZZ
CLIC !
WIZZZZZZ

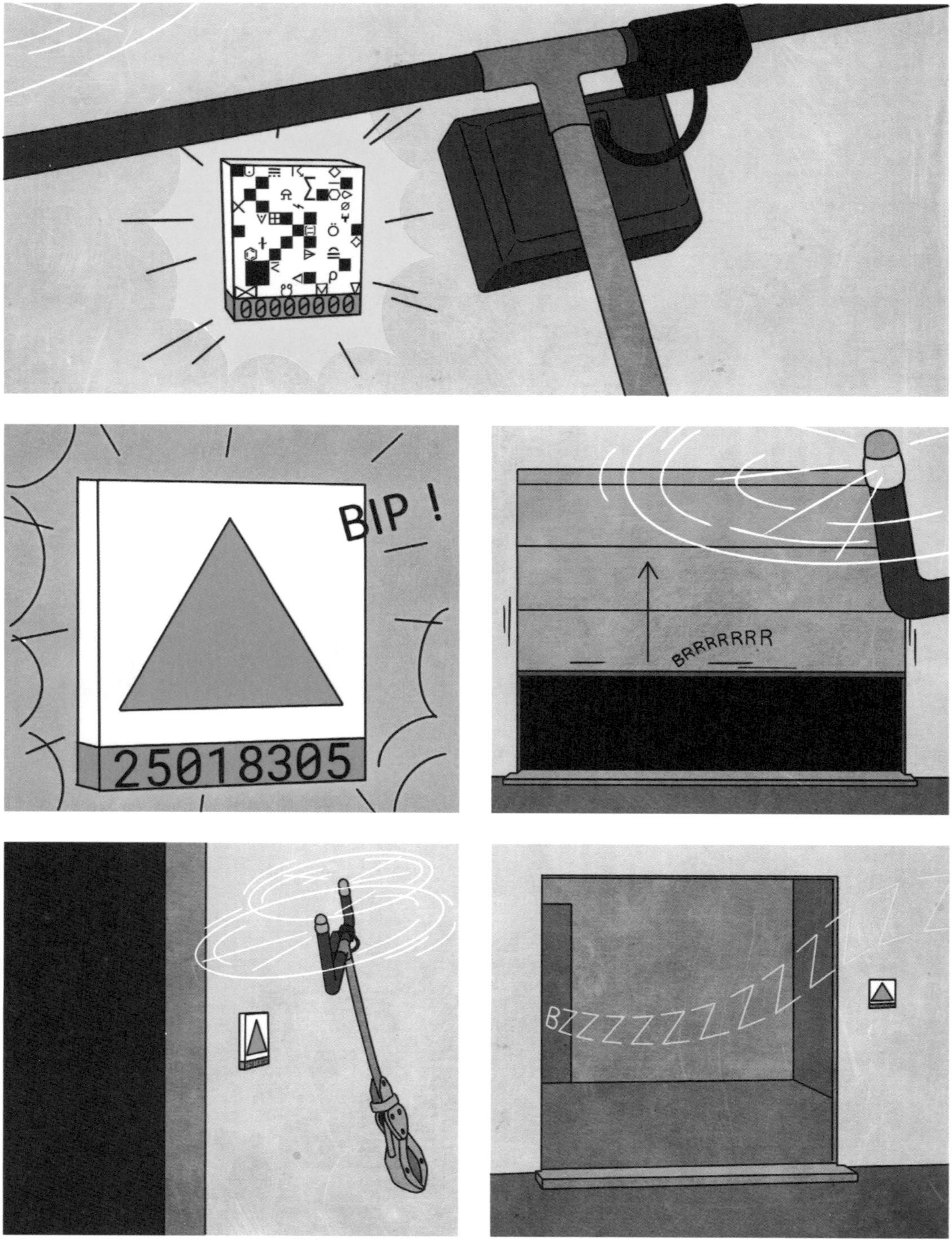
00000000
BIP !
25018305
BRRRRRRR
BZZZZZZZZZZZZ

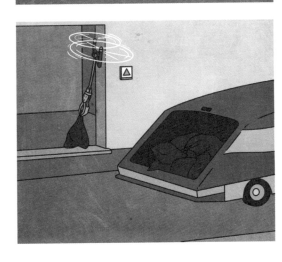

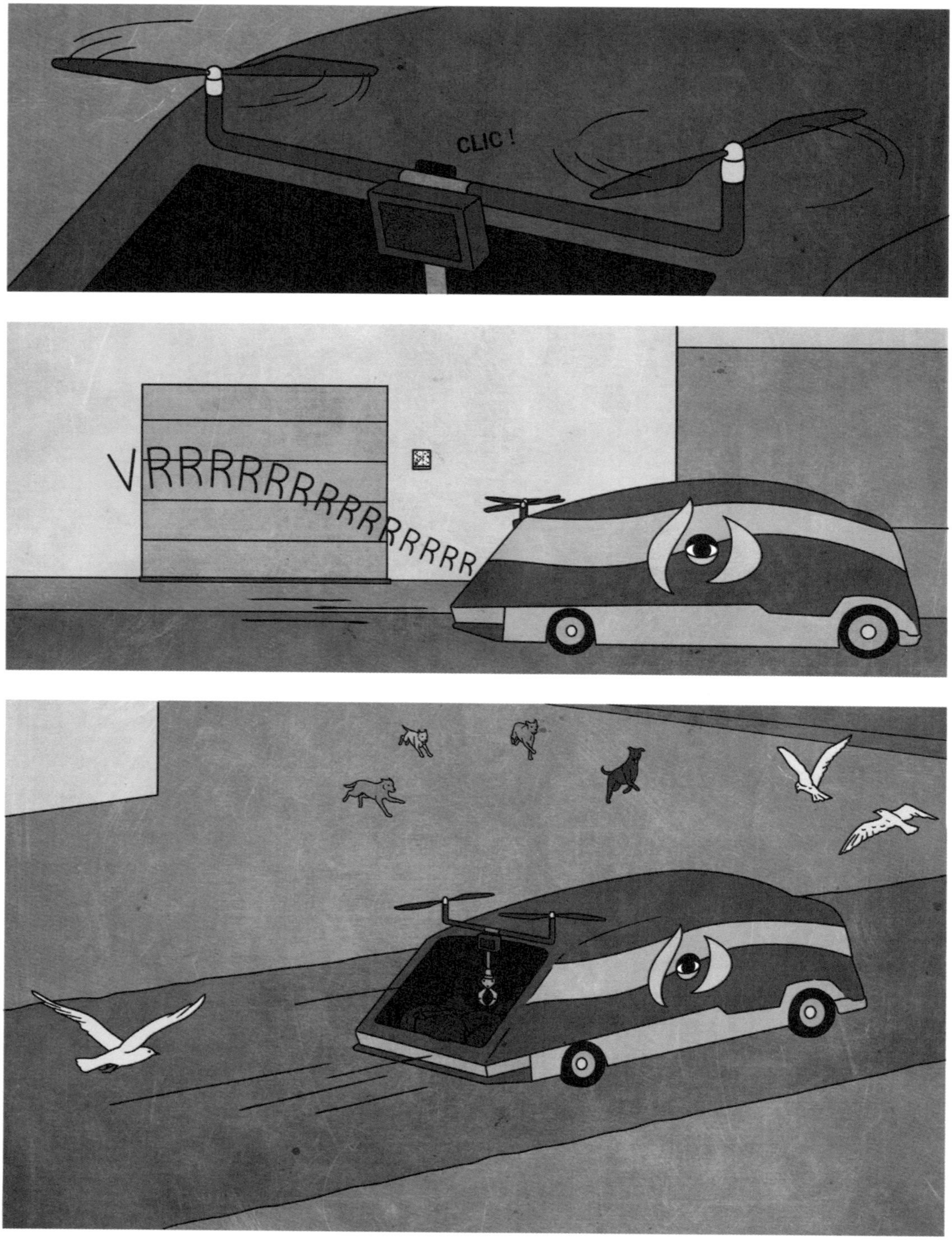
CLIC !
VRRRRRRRRRRRRRR

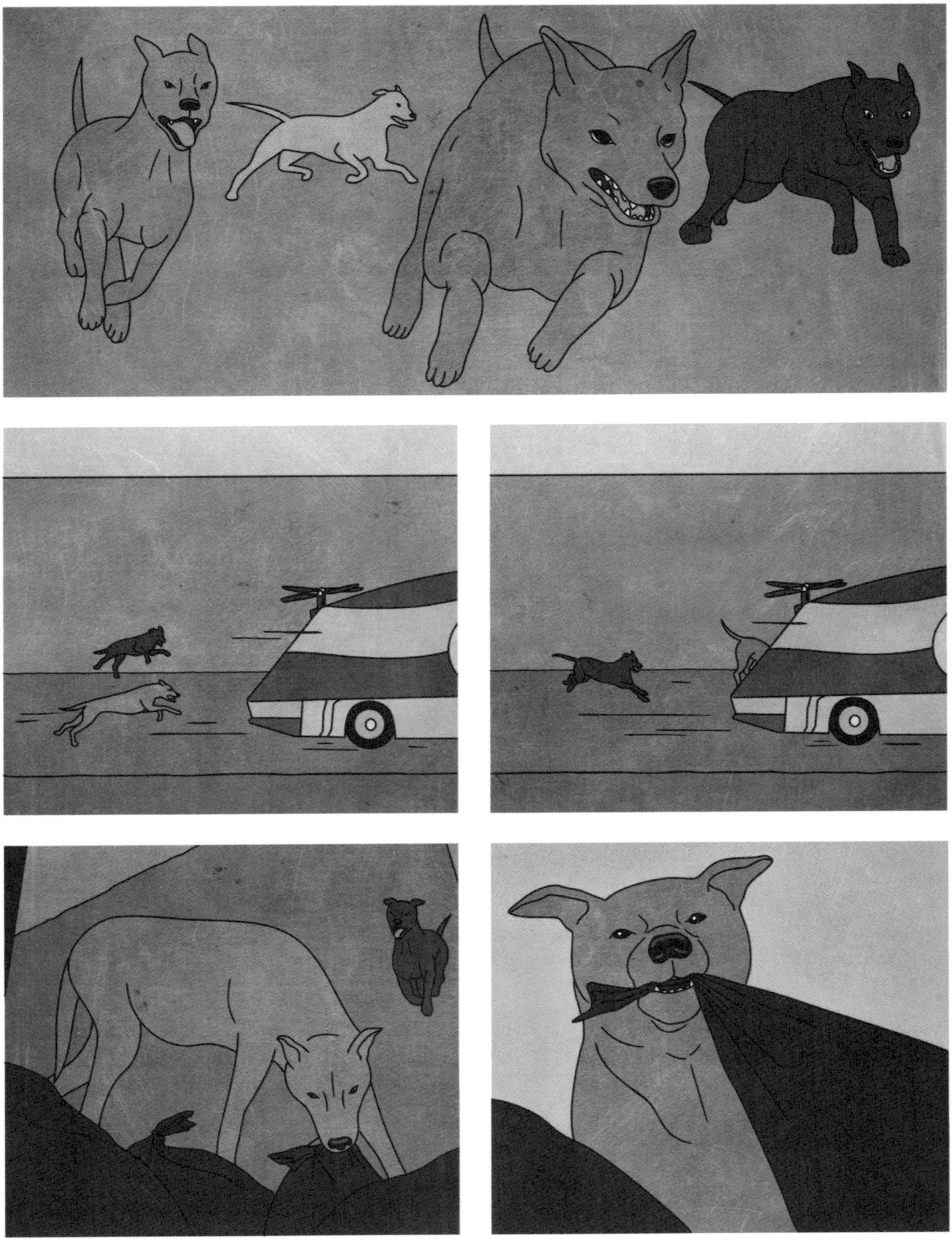

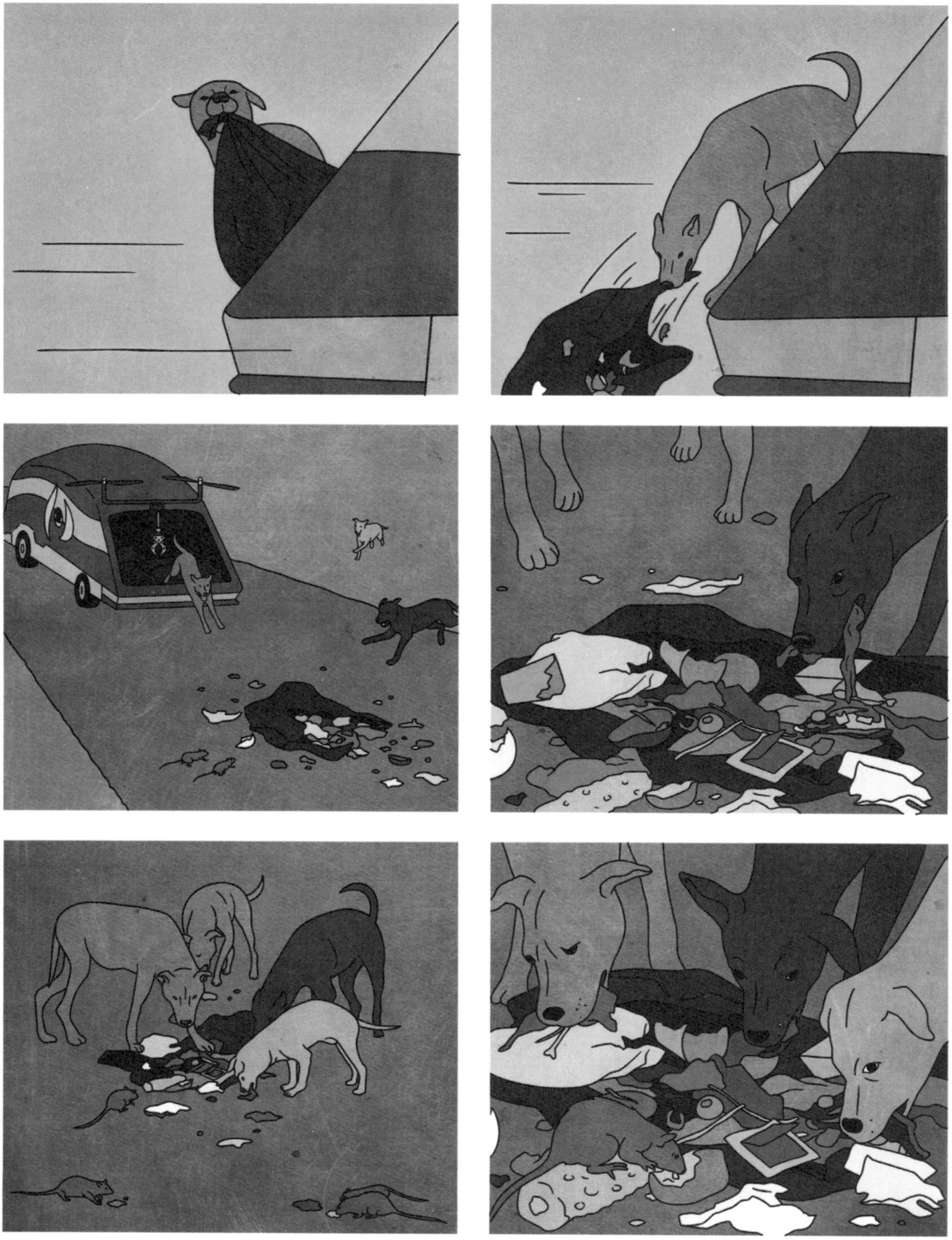

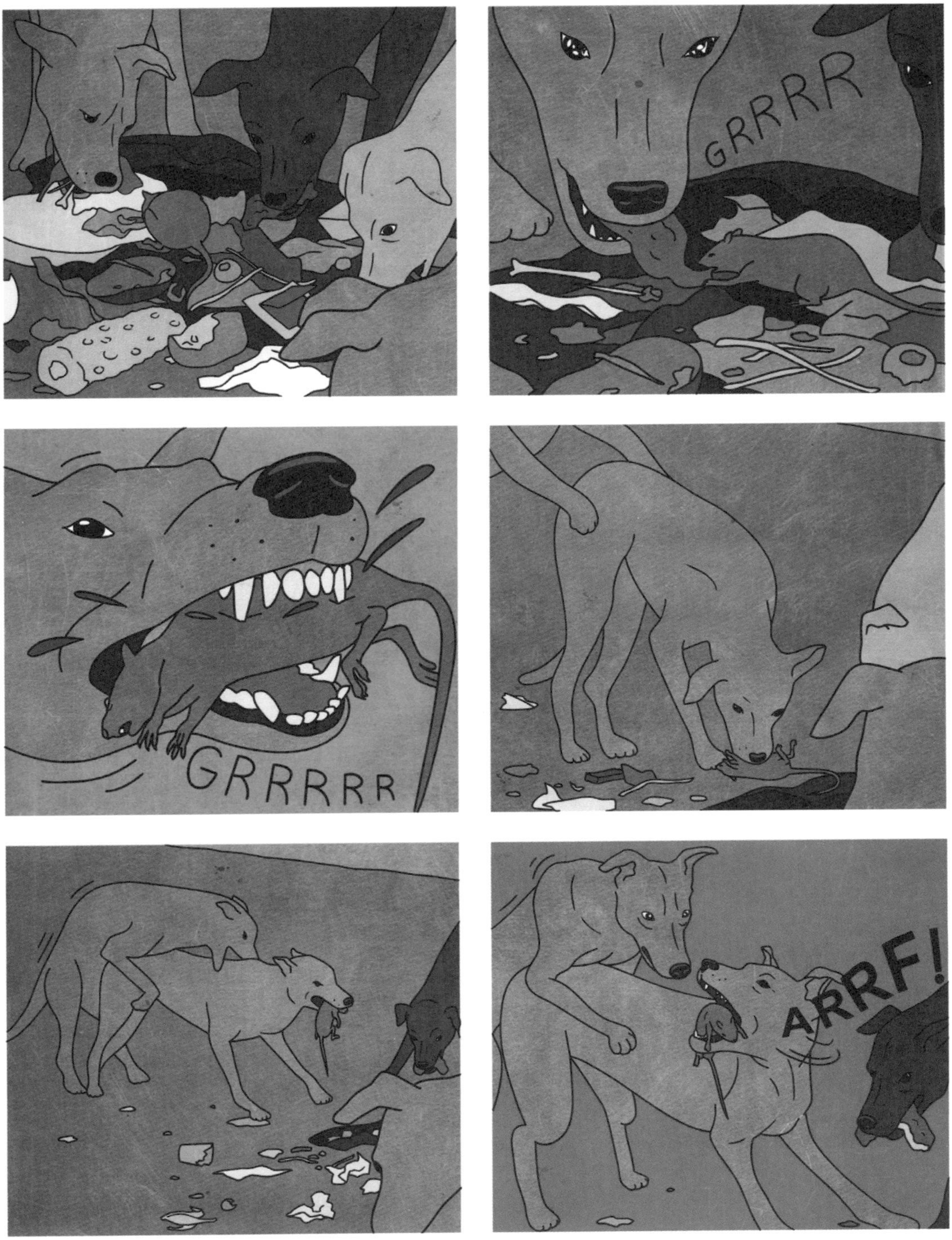
GRRRR
GRRRRR
ARRF!

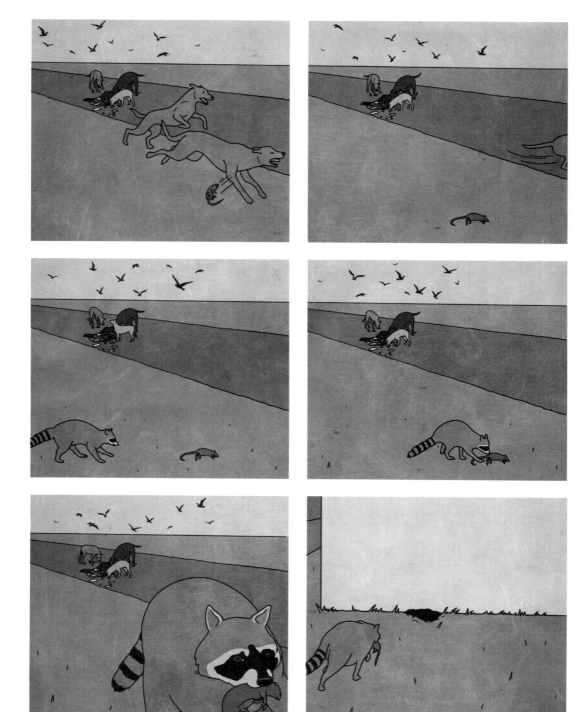

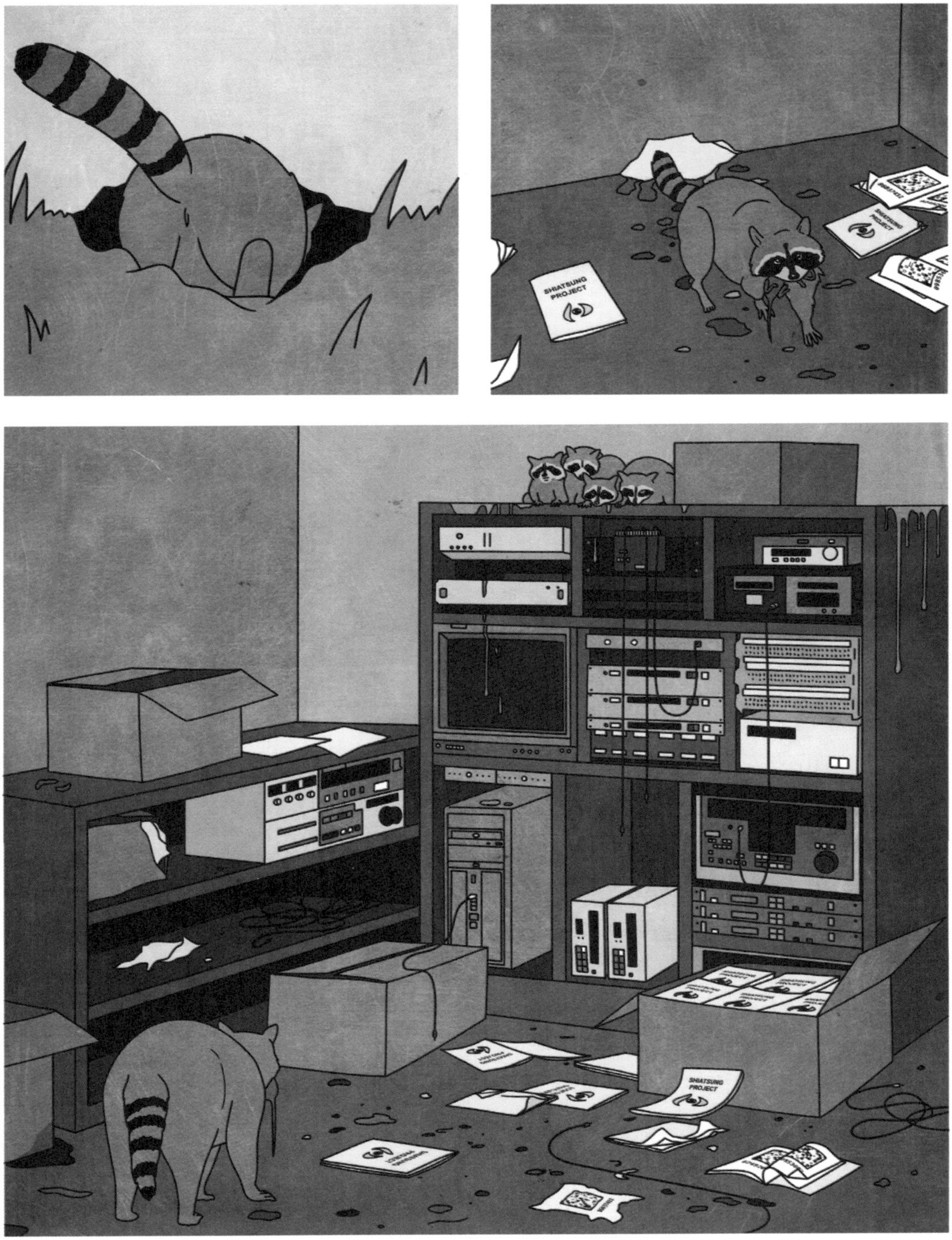
SHIATSUNG PROJECT
SHIATSUNG PROJECT
SHIATSUNG PROJECT

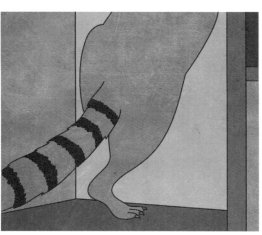
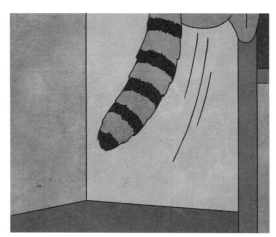

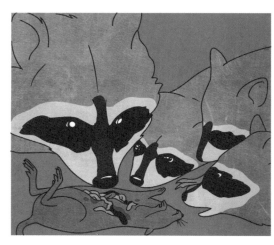

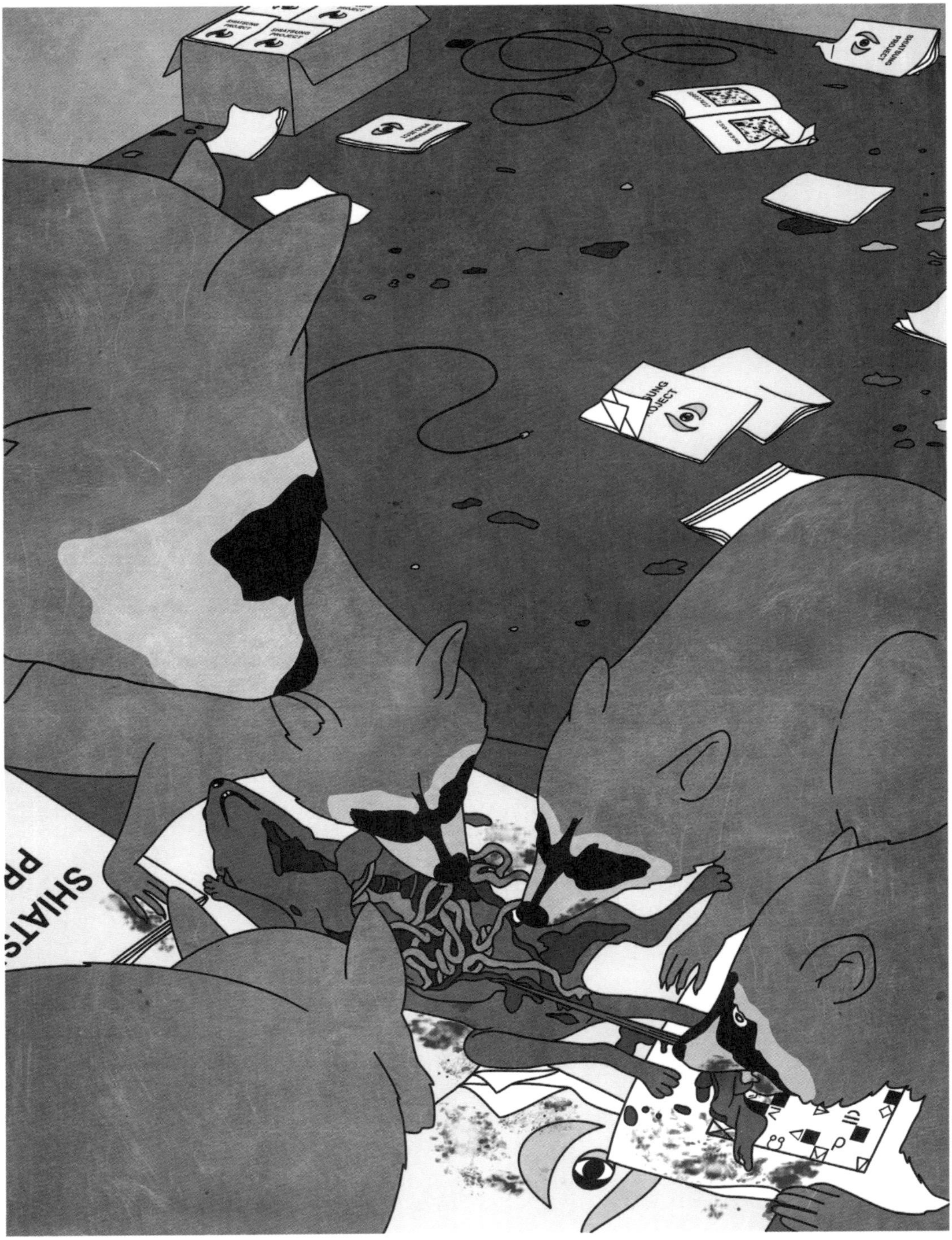
SHIATSUNG PROJECT

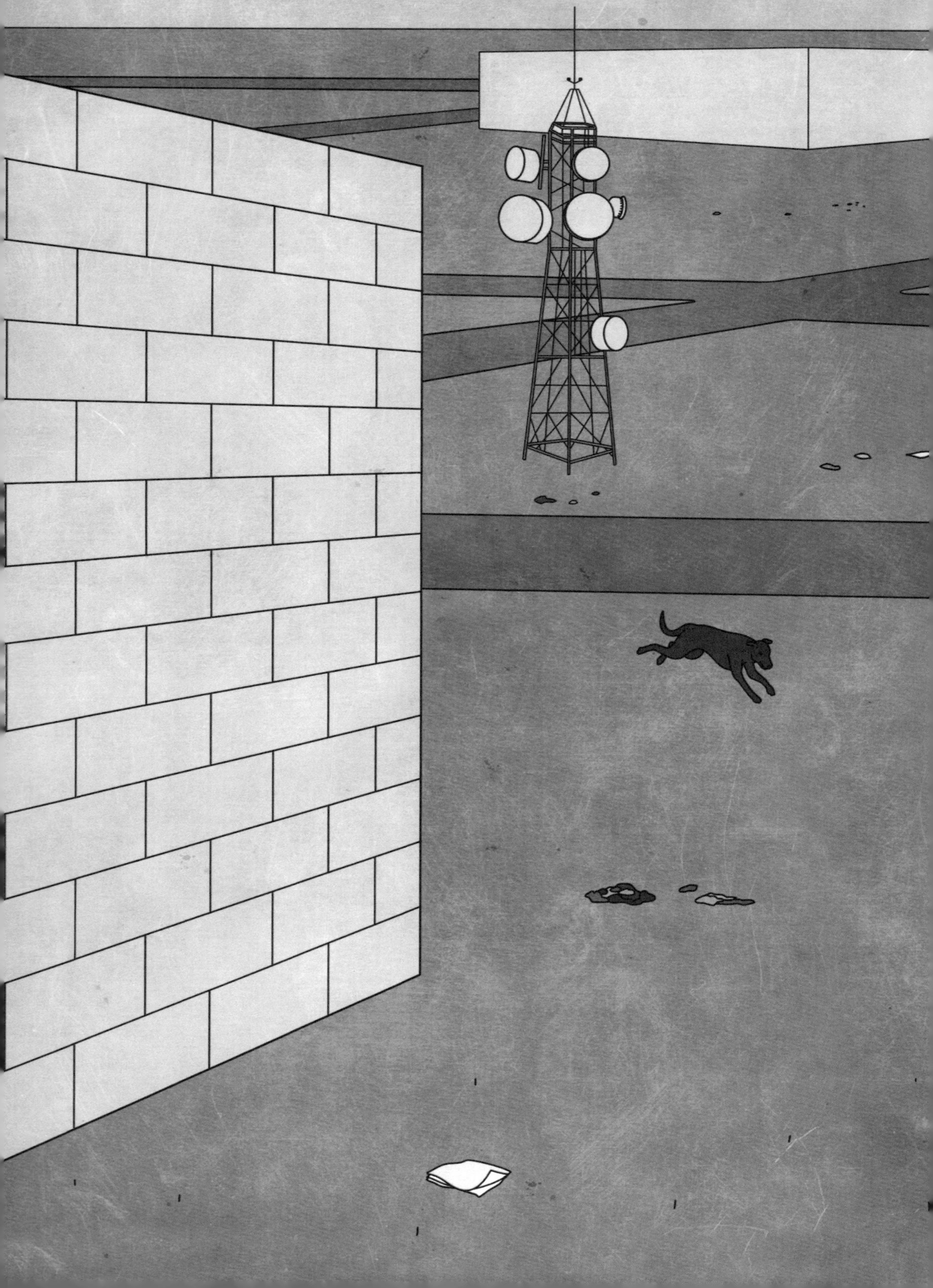

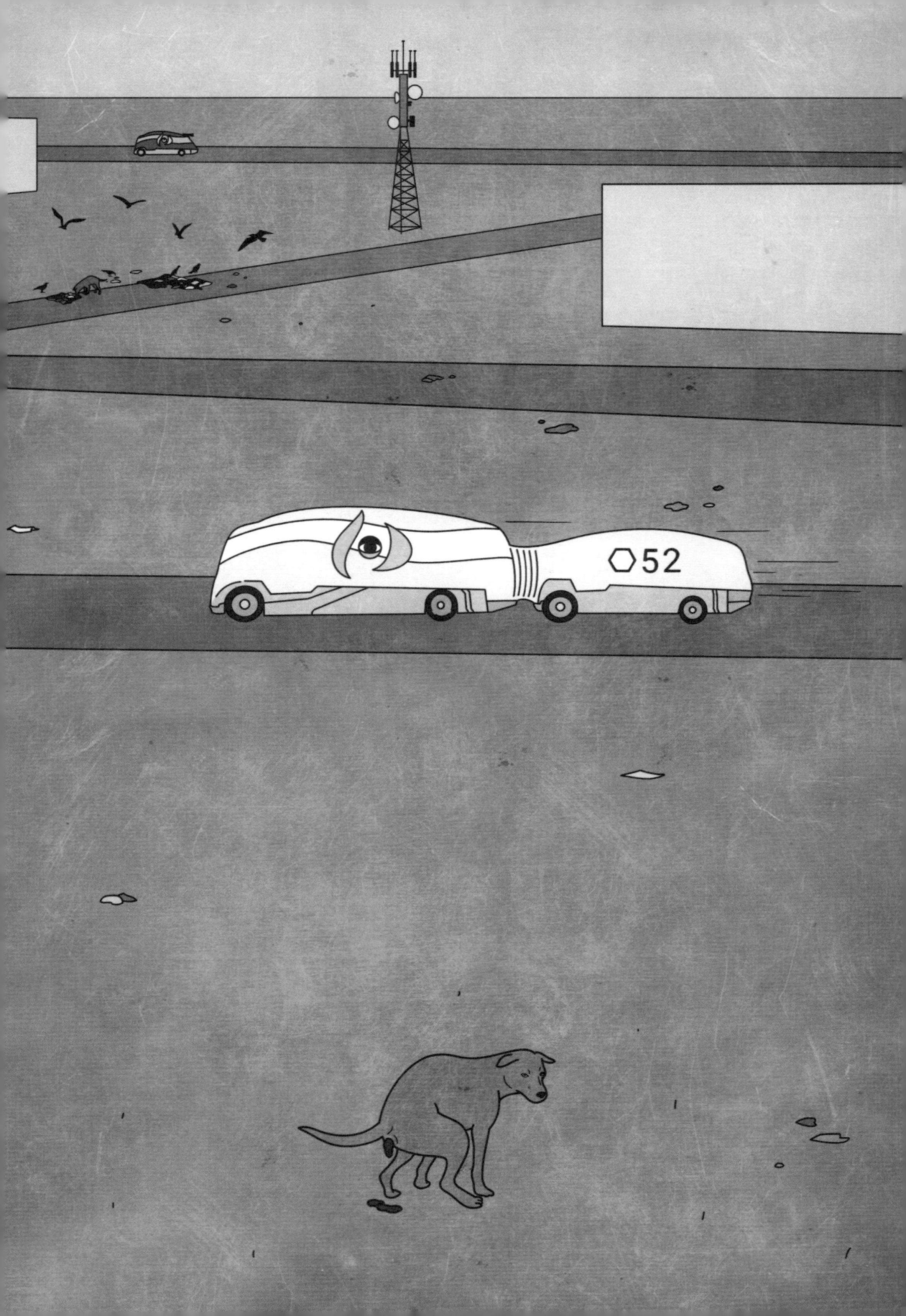
52

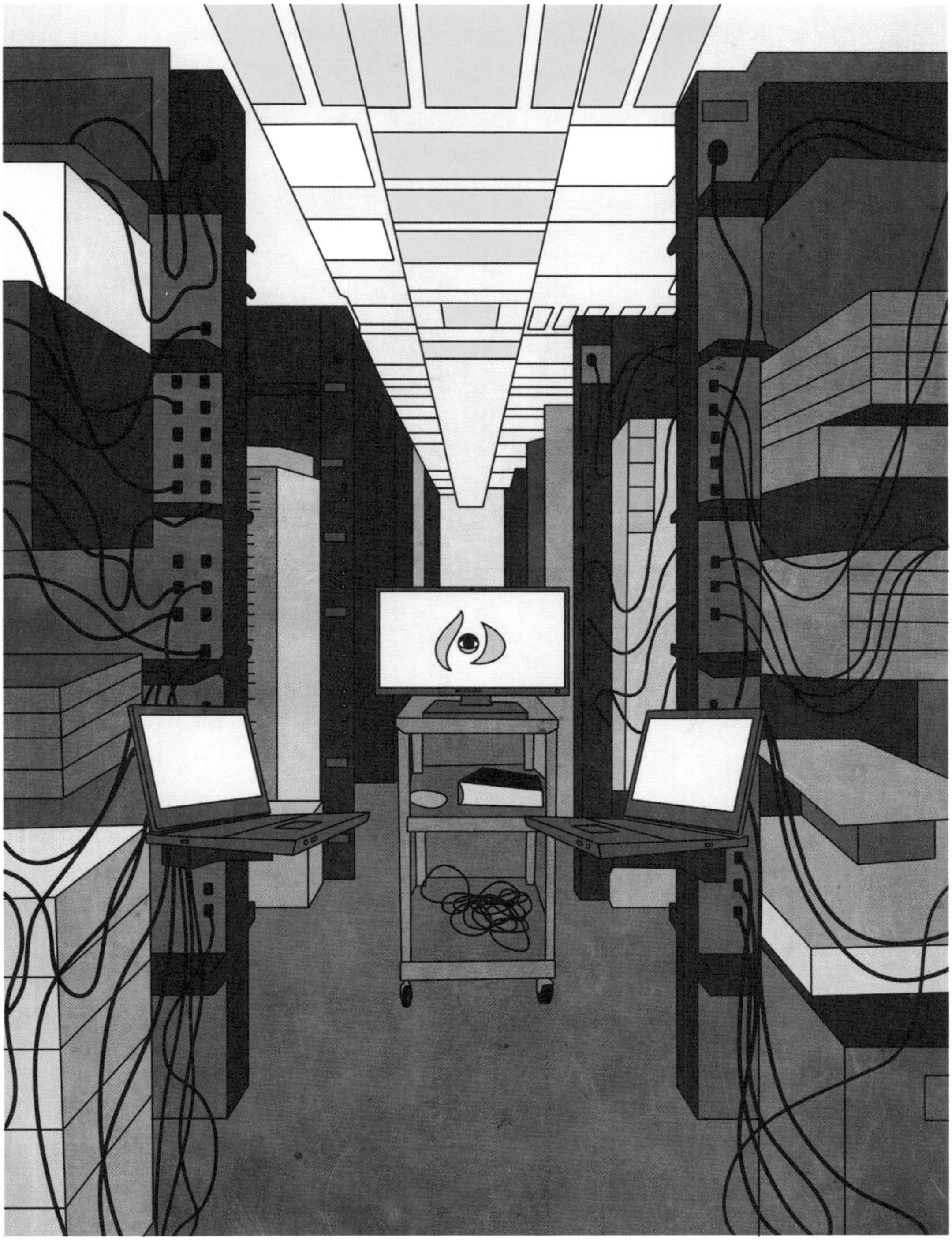

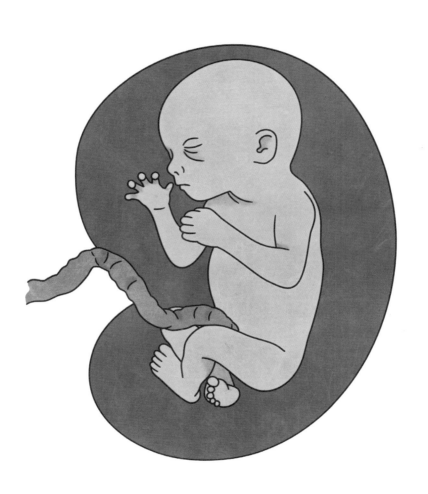